Raffaello! Raffaello!

RAFFAELLO CARBONI AT EUREKA, BEFORE AND BEYOND IT

Also by Desmond O'Grady

Fiction
A Long Way from Home
Deschooling Kevin Carew
Valid for All Countries
Dinny Going Down

Non-fiction
Eat from God's Hand
Caesar, Christ and Constantine
Correggio Jones and the Runaways
The Turned Card
Rome Reshaped
Beyond the Empire
A Word in Edgeways
Tuscan Places

Travel
The Sibyl, the Saint and the Shepherd

Drama
Marriage Gamblers

Raffaello! Raffaello!

RAFFAELLO CARBONI AT EUREKA, BEFORE AND BEYOND IT

DESMOND O'GRADY

ARCADIA

© Desmond O'Grady 2018

First edition published as *Raffaello! Raffaello!* by Hale & Iremonger, 1985; second edition published as *Stages of the Revolution* by Hardie Grant Books, 2004.

New edition published 2018 by ARCADIA
the general books imprint of
Australian Scholarly Publishing Pty Ltd
7 Lt Lothian St Nth, North Melbourne, Vic 3051
Tel: 03 9329 6963 / Fax: 03 9329 5452
enquiry@scholarly.info / www.scholarly.info

ISBN 978-1-925588-62-0

ALL RIGHTS RESERVED

Cover design: Wayne Saunders

Contents

Preface..*vii*
Introduction ....*x*

Naples 1868
In a nutshell..1

Urbino 1
Phosphorus—but peeved 4

Rome 1
Mr Foxy picks up a new scent..................................13
Cracking the cocoon..24

Rome 2
Civis Romanus sum...32

Go North, Young Man
Hanover...46
London 49

Australia: Great Works
No stopping place..55
Nuggets galore..61
Traps on all sides..70
The diggers' Charley 79
Scobie collides with a spade 86
Profound ditch of perdition 91
Sullen excitement...98
A mere cloak to cover a democratic revolution 112
Massacre Hill..125
Foreign anarchist becomes hero 138
Back to Ballarat 152
'With clean hands, I go out......................................157
Great Works' greatest work......................................164

v

Homeward Bound
Further lucky strikes 173

Urbino Once More
You can't go home again 177

Milan
Make war not love 182

Palermo
Living a novel 189
A perambulating Pasquin... 197

Turin
A captain first, then crowned a poet:
Soon the whole wide world must know it............................208

Naples
Tread lightly 215
Sciocchezze! Dummes Zeug! Nonsense!................................222

Rome 3
Lolly water laced with rum 229
The patriot's reward – *basta così*...238

Acknowledgments..245
Notes and sources 247
Bibliography...259
Index..261
About the Author 268

Preface

Raffaello Carboni was more perceptive than those who later saw the Eureka Stockade protestors simply as either heroes or villains. Carboni recognised their complexity. In *The Eureka Stockade* he showed that many of the miners, like himself, were small capitalists whose initial aim was to get rich and get out. They saw the land simply as a quarry.

In Carboni's case there was an interesting interlude when he spent time with the aborigines and saw the land in a new and attractive light. But for a long time the serious business was devastating the landscape to rip out its riches.

Moreover, initially he was contemptuous of protestors with republican aspirations and/or Chartist ideals. With the Mazzinian revolutionary outlook as his background, he had not been impressed by the gradualist Chartists he had observed in London.

But Carboni underwent a conversion. At a certain point he saw the struggle against misgovernment in Ballarat as in continuity with the Italian struggle against injustice.

The crucial moment for Carboni was when the protesting miners gathered and pledged solidarity to one another, saluting the Southern Cross flag invented for the occasion. Rapacious adventurers became mates in the name of universal values. They were no longer exploiters but avid for justice. This was before the Stockade battle.

For Carboni it was a replay of a scene which he had already experienced in Rome. His Italian experience had also taught him the importance not only of participation in seminal events but also of writing about them. That spurred him to write his book which is so lively and, at times, confusing that it seems merely a rushed record of events but it is also an interpretation.

Subsequently the emphasis has fallen on the Stockade battle which was far more dramatic, but also more ambiguous, than the solidarity meeting. Carboni acknowledged the Stockade battle's ambiguities which is more than some of our contemporaries are prepared to do.

The miners who wanted to protest against both the licence, a work-permit levy which taxed equally those who found gold and those who 'bottomed on mullock', and against the brutal manner in which the fees were collected, built a wooden enclosure or stockade where they could drill. It would not have been suitable for defence and became even less so after it was foolishly extended. Carboni criticised its extension.

The protesting miners and those in the Government Camp were frightened of each other. The attempts to mediate were wrecked by hardliners on the government side and hotheads among the miners. These hotheads rashly attacked troop reinforcements sent from Melbourne and later violently requisitioned in the zone near the Stockade.

Carboni deplored the disorganisation and excesses of some of the Stockaders. But he deplored likewise the pettiness of the government authorities and the mayhem of the troops after they had overrun the higgeldy-piggeldy Stockade in a clash in which 30-odd miners were killed.

Although Carboni documented the defects of the Stockade itself and some Stockaders who were drunken brawlers, he still celebrated its heroes. He dedicated his book to the Canadian Captain Ross and made it a tribute to the Irishman Peter Lalor who was elected leader of the Stockaders after Carboni, at least according to his account, declined this position.

Of course, in a period of unrestrained migration, Australia was enriched by newcomers of varied backgrounds, some of them from beyond the British isles. Carboni was one of these and he made a significant contribution. But what was Carboni's background? Giuseppe Garibaldi and Giuseppe Mazzini were crucial in his formation.

Mazzini has been called 'the Moses of Italian unity'. The nationalists succeeded in turfing the pope out of Rome to create a short-lived Republic. Garibaldi's troops, who were fresh from fighting in Latin America, were crucial to this success.

Garibaldi's dramatic presence as well as Mazzini's ideas made a lasting impression on Carboni who had to flee when the pope, with the support of French forces, re-established his rule in Rome.

Carboni went first to Germany, then England where he heard of the Australian gold finds. He sailed to Australia, no longer a political fugitive but a hopeful gold seeker. He arrived close to the time that Garibaldi spent a day on Three Hummocks island in Bass Strait while skippering a ship trading between South America and China.

The Garibaldi–Mazzini heritage was not just Italian or ethnic nationalism but a belief in the right of peoples to realisation of their aspirations and the need for heroes to inspire idealism.

Mazzini's idealistic nationalism contrasted with Karl Marx's emphasis on class struggle. For Mazzini, Marx's ideas were illiberal, intolerant and destined to produce dictatorships. During most of the 20th century it seemed that Marx was more influential and had been more long-sighted than Mazzini. And that those who emphasised the importance of nationalism, for instance within the Soviet Union, were anachronistic. But the perspective is different after the dissolution of the Soviet Union.

Carboni had sympathy for Socialism but, if true to Mazzini, would hardly have had any for Communism.

His Italian background helped him interpret what happened in Ballarat. Many like flambouyant Carboni for his theatrical qualities, his liveliness, his in-your-face manner of addressing his readers. But even some who relish his colourfulness see him as a lightweight if not a blowhard. In other words his lively qualities tend to obscure his political acuteness regarding an event which influenced the development of democracy in Victoria and Australia as a whole. Through Carboni, both Garibaldi and Mazzini had a part in this.

In their own country a successful revolution led quickly to widespread disillusion. Mazzini, who considered the new nation rotten with materialism and egotism, said it was a parody of the Italy he had wanted. Garibaldi, after reaching a compromise with the monarchy, left for the island of Caprera which reminded him of his Bass Straight island. And, after seeing many former companions clamber abroad the political gravy train, Carboni, who had kept in touch with Peter Lalor and his trial judge Mr Justice Barry, may have suffered nostalgia for the Australia he had left.

Introduction

For many years Australians called Raffaello Carboni, Carboni Raffaello, in much the same way as Italians call the comic strip character Gordon Flash. And like Flash Gordon, Carboni seemed to have disappeared over the horizon; Brian Fitzpatrick, introducing the 1947 edition of Carboni's *The Eureka Stockade,* said 'he is now as if he had never been.'

Obviously he 'had been' before arriving in Melbourne and most likely 'was' for some time after he left Australia. Who was Carboni and what became of him after he left Australia were mysteries worth a few idle thoughts when I was a student at the university of Melbourne. I did not go to Italy to solve the mysteries but when I arrived in Rome I looked into them. Or, rather, unwittingly slept in one of them.

For some days I lodged in a refuge for deadbeats, divided by plywood walls, because it cost only 200 lire (about 30 cents) a night. I shared it with, flatulent, incontinent, rowdy hobos. Incongruously, high in the side walls were niches with busts of several popes for this had been the atrium of the huge Santa Trinità dei Pellegrini (Holy Trinity) pilgrim complex consisting of a hostel, convalescent hospital and church. I was to discover that Carboni spent his first period in Rome at Santa Trinità. By chance I had lodged at the same place and subsequently did so much research, from Laverton to London, from Sicilian Bronte to Berlin that, when I sought Carboni's death certificate from the Rome Registry Office, and the clerk explained he could not provide it unless I was a relative, I said I was. By then, in a certain sense, it was true.

Our knowledge of Carboni remains spotty: there is much more documentation about Carboni in Ballarat and Palermo than, say, about his last years in Rome where his linguistic skills gained him employment, like James Joyce thirty-four years later, in an Italo-German bank. For the periods when next-to-nothing is known about Carboni's life, only the broader socio-political story can be told, but it is not irrelevant as he involved himself in it.

My narrative begins with an imaginative reconstruction of an episode which, according to a footnote to a Carboni play, occurred in Naples in 1868. Then it follows Carboni's life chronologically from his first years in Urbino. It is possible to recreate the context of these early years but there are only faint traces of Carboni before his arrival in Rome. Even the records of his Urbino school years were found not there but in the Roman archives of the Piarist religious order, which taught him. The most important Italian source, his plays, were waiting to speak for him at the Santa Cecilia Conservatorium of Music in central Rome. I had vainly sought his writings in libraries and rare book shops all over Italy without realising that the Conservatorium, which I passed frequently, had a library to which Carboni had given autographed copies of his self-published plays. I have used his plays for both their explicit and implicit autobiographical material. The introductions and interpolations, which recount the origins of his plays and rail against those who prevented their performance, are more engrossing than the dramatic texts themselves. Choice was possible in placing references to Carboni's writings for he claimed that even brief poems were written over a decade or more in three continents.

While selection and shaping of biographical material are inevitable, and inferences have been made, this biography is an interpretation of evidence rather than novelised history. Even the 'haze which did not conceal' the troops approaching the Eureka Stockade and the 'almost incessant rain' late in the month Carboni died are documented. I mention this to reassure readers as well as to fend off licence-hunting critics.

Researching the biography resembled prospecting. It threatened to become an obsessive quest in which the effort could far exceed the returns; one could follow a lead for months only to bottom on mullock, soil and rock without gold. There were distracting rumours of fabulous strikes by others. One worked in bad air due to exhalations not from buried vegetation but from dusty, yellowing papers. Much dross had to be washed away before even a speck of gold emerged.

Pursuing Carboni's 'far-flung' life was not solely a paper chase. In West Berlin I met Alfred von Seefeld, a courteous 78-year-old notary whose eponymous grandfather was Carboni's close friend during his time in Hanover. Von Seefeld supplied a letter Carboni had written to his grandfather from

Naples in 1867, and information about his forebear. I visited the Schmorl und von Seefeld bookshop, the oldest and largest in Hanover, where *The Eureka Stockade* was on sale in the 1860s. The bookshop still stands in the same site and is run by Martin Schmorl, a fifth-generation relative of von Seefeld's partner, Ernst-Viktor Schmorl.

Carboni's London address proved revealing. He lodged in the centre of the City, which had scarcely changed since reconstruction after the Great Fire. As he was surrounded by banks, it seems appropriate that he left from there to seek gold.

A trace of Carboni's Calcutta friend, Francois (Babu) Saint Yves, was found. The Municipal Library in Coriano, outside Rimini, yielded records of the teaching career of Carboni's brother, Antonio.

Among the discoveries made were that Carboni was naturalised in Melbourne, and also the correspondence between him and Governor Hotham and other officials about his compensation claim. Carboni's concluding comment in his accont of his time in Australia was:

> if the gentlemen editors of the Melbourne press ... would for once give a pull, a strong pull, and a pull together, to drag out of the Toorak small-beer jug, the correspondence on the above matter [the compensation claim] ... it would astonish the natives, teach what emigration is, and I believe the colony at large would be benefited by it.

Here the correspondence has been retrieved from the Toorak small-beer jug; may it still astonish the natives of whatever hue.

After the first version of my biography appeared, I found that, on his return to Italy, the former poacher Carboni became a gamekeeper. Moreover, some of his countrymen turned a cold eye on his antics and made withering assessments of his writings.

The documents unearthed have made it possible to smoke Carboni from the chimney of fantasy where he sometimes repaired. I am not referring to his whimsical advertisements for his plays, described as being written in Paris or among the 'whales of the Pacific' (readers could choose for themselves), but to lies such as some details he gave of his army career or in describing Goffredo Mameli praising his songs in Rome before Mameli reached the city. However, the lies are of little import. Carboni spent himself generously for goals which proved largely chimeric. Literature and Italian unity both disappointed him.

His Australian experience had a Bridge-of-San-Luis-Rey aspect because most of those involved had developed elsewhere – they just happened to be seeking gold together in Victoria. Indeed of the stockaders killed in the Eureka clash, Carboni lists only one native-born Australian. Most participants can be properly understood only if their earlier experiences are taken into account. Carboni had similar experiences to those in Eureka before his arrival, both accusations of sedition and knowledge of the importance of a collective pledge of solidarity which, rather than the fighting, for him was the high point of Eureka. This helped him frame events in Australia just as experience there enabled him to frame some of what he later saw in Italy. In other words, he applied Italian patterns to Australia and, in his writing after his return home, Australian patterns to Italian events. A player in decisive episodes of both nations, he helped bring them closer.

In Italy Carboni had learnt the importance of creating secular saints to forge a tradition. As well as attempting, in *The Eureka Stockade,* to rescue from oblivion his slaughtered comrades, he put Peter Lalor on a pedestal. His use of the first person makes him a protagonist but he presents others as heroes rather than himself.

On his return to Italy he went on celebrating heroes, this time those of the Risorgimento, when many of his companions had moved on to govern the new nation. His plays were ignored, partly because the revolution had won out and its limitations were revealed. This was in contrast with Victoria, where the goldfields protest had been crushed but there were immediate beneficial consequences, such as the establishment of the local miners' courts presided by their representatives. Eureka also spurred broader developments, such as wider suffrage, and, largely thanks to Carboni, became an influential legend.

Carboni ended as nobody's hero and a forgotten man. However his writings and his outrage at their neglect provided just enough gold to survive the wash of time.

Naples 1868

In a nutshell

From the corner of the suddenly darkened restaurant, Death was walking towards Raffaello Carboni with arms outstretched. The only light, a lantern, was beamed on the chalky, pâpier-maché skull. A woman screamed. Although he had drunk copiously, Carboni realised it was a mask but nevertheless felt his scalp tighten; it was not Death but someone who wanted his death. The outstretched hands beneath the mask had nearly grasped Carboni when he slashed with his heavy Bowie knife, ripping the mask from the wearer whom Carboni recognised before he fled into the tepid Neapolitan night. Waiters and Carboni's companions gave chase. Stocky Carboni's fright was such that the white speckling his red hair and full beard might have appeared at that moment. Trembling, he strained to extract his knife embedded in the table with the mask, still attached, upright like a grisly witness. He had nearly sliced the assailant's face in two.

It may have been this which made Carboni feel faint as diners demanded the gas for the lamps be turned on. Candles were lit. Two cooks, knives in hand, stood at the kitchen entrance, indifferent to the reek of burning oil. One companion patted vinegar on Carboni's temples, another called for cognac; disconcerted diners asked what had happened.

The cognac revived Carboni's pulse. Only an imbecile would play such a stupid Carnival joke, if it was a joke; yet some still claimed man was not descended from the apes! With former Garibaldian comrades-in-arms, Carboni had been arguing against locals who claimed they had been better off under the Bourbons. Carboni, as usual, had been the most passionate Garibaldian. There was something vehement in his very appearance; although short, he was robust with high forehead, straight nose and expressive eyes. At the moment, they were enlarged by fear.

One of those bested in the argument had donned a Carnival mask while another had turned off the gas lights and, in the sudden dark, had trained an oil lamp on his gruesome friend. Something more sinister than a Carnival joke? Walking death: he would have to check which lottery number corresponded and punt on it. It would take more than a papier-mâché mask to cow a man who had been in the '49, '59 and '60 campaigns. He had not had such a turn, though, since a shot from a murderous trooper on the Ballarat road had knocked off his floppy cabbage-tree hat.

Even the trattoria's name, del Fosso, had been a presage – 'the Ditch'! He had to play also the lottery number which corresponded to Ditch in the Neapolitan cabala book which matched words with numbers. His luck was probably in, if only he knew how to recognise it; certainly a change for the better was long overdue. Then it came to him – Ditch, fall in it: 50.

Too pat, like the devil in the old melodrama. He would not fall in even though he felt all his fifty years. His old wounds ached whenever he dragged his feet up and down the Prefecture stairs vainly seeking financial help to publish his plays. Death was dogging him like his debts. Although the fight to unite Italy was all but won, his own to forge a new drama was just beginning. He finished the cognac.

Those who had pursued the assailant returned one by one. He had escaped on the seafront crowded with families seeking a breath of fresh air. Carboni thanked the waiters, reflecting however that one of them must have allowed the gas to be lowered. Spies everywhere. Wasn't he betrayed right and left in Naples – by the ballerina Amina, by obtuse theatrical directors and even by the Prefect's secretary who would not receive him? After all, he was an outsider, a foreigner. He could not wait to return to Rome. In Turin those who now had leading positions in united Italy had crowned him Poet; his new plays would ensure that, in Rome, he was crowned at the Campidoglio. Neapolitans' idea of theatre did not go much beyond pâpier-mâché masks!

His companions were calling on him to toast Giuseppe Garibaldi with spumante. Carboni drank but his deep-set eyes glared at the other diners. He would rip away the death mask of old Italy. Looking at his companions, he thought of the enthusiasm of the youths who in 1860 had followed Garibaldi to Sicily. All that idealism could not be squandered. Once the tricolour was planted on the Campidoglio, a new spirit would sweep the nation; he would help forge it, for Rome was his city, even though he had fled it almost twenty years earlier in 1849.[1]

Urbino 1

Phosphorus – but peeved

Carboni was convinced he had a right to call himself a Roman because he had been participated in the defence of the Republic there in 1849. But he was born in Urbino about 8.30 p.m. on 14 December 1817, son of Biagio Carboni and Girolama Fioravanti of San Sergio parish, and was christened by a Father Bertoni that same day: Rafaele Domenico Crescentino.[1]

When Raffaello (to use the spelling Carboni later adopted) was born, his family lived in a steep street intersecting a broader thoroughfare where the Renaissance painter Raphael (to avoid confusion, the English form of the painter's name is used throughout) had grown up in his painter-father's spacious house. At his birth Raffaello's parents were both 30 and his brother Antonio was two. Biagio, who was literate,[2] had a shop which may have been an artisan's workshop. The house where Raffaello was born was level with the stockade-like, 14th-century Albornoz fortress across the gully which was named after a Spanish cardinal who had subjugated Urbino's anti-papal rulers. The fortress provided a splendid view of the brown stone of Urbino's walls and the browner roof tiles, the cathedral dome and the ducal palaces' two minaret-like towers. Urbino seemed a ship's prow sustained by the waves of hills which, as they rolled towards it, jostled and crossed. On the east, the waves gradually subsided towards the plain of the Adriatic Sea, thirty-five kilometres distant. On the other sides they tossed as far as the eye could see.

Urbino was a sentinel over via Flaminia, the road 450 metres below, which ran to Rome. Earthquakes and tremors were counterpart to the tumultuous landscape. Storms of startling violence broke over the hilltop ship city.

Livid clouds floated up and past it, the downpour occasionally overflowing the scuppers of its steep brick streets which, to prevent slipping, were ridged like gangplanks.

Biscuit-coloured brick was underfoot, on all sides. The streets were brick, the walls were brick. Carboni grew up in an intensely urban atmosphere, even though Urbino had only a few thousand inhabitants. Although the city was sharply distinct, it had an intimate relationship with the carefully husbanded countryside which gave wheat, olives and wine. Nature was a constant presence. Each Saturday, the marriage of rural and urban was celebrated at market: oxen bellowed and cowbells rang in the beaten earth square at the foot of the ducal palace. The countryside penetrated the city too in the fragrant wood fires, in the oil used for lamps, in the horse-drawn carriages, in the cock crows and donkey brays audible in the Renaissance square.

When Raffaello was two the family moved ten minutes walk away to San Bartolo parish which was dominated by the city's focal point, the ducal palace, Europe's first and perhaps finest. The 200-room edifice's decrepitude was a reminder that Urbino had come down in the world. Raffaello grew up in a town whose glories were in the past. The dukes of Montefeltro no longer inhabited the palace: the most illustrious, the Renaissance mercenary captain Federico, lay in San Bernardino church on a hill opposite the city; his presence could still be felt but Urbino was no longer a cultural capital. The transfer of Federico's great library to the Vatican in the mid-17th century seemed a symbol of the emptying out which had made the ducal palace a shell and Urbino a shadow of its former self.

With the election, in 1700, of one of the noble Urbino family Albani as Pope Clement XI, the city had a second period of splendour. Although unimaginative in his policies, the wealthy pope was a keen art collector who embellished his town with obelisks and works of art sent from Rome and, near the city centre, built a large palace. But after Clement's twenty-year pontificate, the city relapsed into lethargy, a forgotten outpost, an abandoned Renaissance jewel in a knot of the Apennines.

The town's somnolence was broken by Napoleon's invasion. It was only in June 1796, when the French general with an Italian name swept into Bologna, that an end to papal rule seemed possible. It was a shock as severe as the earthquake which, seven years before, had destroyed the dome of Urbino cathedral. The following year the French established a Roman Republic, but with the restoration of papal power in 1799 they left central Italy. French troops occupied the Marches region again in 1807. In 1814, as French forces withdrew in a vain attempt to stave off final defeat, Urbinites burnt Napoleon's portraits and the togas and caps of the judges who applied his law. By the following year it seemed as if the old order had been re-established once and for all throughout Italy. The Viennese emperor ruled again in Lombardy; the Veneto region was an Austrian province and there was an Austrian grand duke in Tuscany; and in Southern Italy the Bourbon royal family ruled once more.

Although it may be significant that, in one of his plays, Carboni was to give his mother's surname to a character who encouraged young rebels,[3] it is unlikely that Carboni's family favoured the French 'enemies of the Church'. Parish records show that Biagio and Girolama Carboni confessed and took communion regularly; Antonio was to become a priest, and Girolama's sister Veronica was a nun. But even those opposed to the French appreciated some of their innovations in civil law; moreover, their advent had aroused nationalism and a recognition that papal rule was not as immutable as Catholic dogma.

Carboni was born three years after the French withdrew; his elders' stories and impressions of that period would have been merely background to his boyhood. And he was probably anything but indignant about imprisonment of the Papal States' liberals in Urbino. But when he was 13, Urbino was part of the zone, from Ferrara to Spoleto, which revolted two days after Pope Gregory XVI's election. Austrian forces helped quell the revolt in which some papal soldiers had changed sides. The papal legate, 81-year-old Cardinal Giuseppe Albani, took drastic measures to re-establish order. Raffaello was old enough to participate in this drama which may have affected his later choices.

He was already a day student at the all-male College of Nobles. The presence of both Antonio and Raffaello at the College suggests that their father Biagio earned well or their mother, Girolama Fioravanti, was from a well-established family. There are some pointers in this sense: her sister Veronica became abbess of a Rimini convent, and a Girolamo Fioravanti,[4] perhaps a relative, was assistant tax collector in nearby Coriano where Antonio was later to teach.

The College of Nobles occupied a whole block. It was three storeys at the front but, because of the slope, six at the back. The massive edifice was impressive but severe. A small astronomic observatory was perched above the roof. From the courtyard a broad marble stairway led to the high-ceilinged, well-lit first-floor classrooms. A plaque at the head of the stairway proclaimed that the Piarist Fathers had returned to the College in 1827.

Cardinal Giovanni Francesco Albani had established the College in 1699, the year before he became Pope Clement XI. The Piarist Fathers, whose founder, the Spanish saint José Calasanz, had opened his first school in Rome in 1597, directed the College until 1808. Under Napoleon Bonaparte it became a State school. The Jesuits then ran it for twelve years. There had been friction between the Jesuit and Piarist Order. The Piarists, founded to run schools for the poor, had invaded the Society of Jesus' (Jesuits) domain by also establishing schools such as the College of Nobles. The rivalry between Piarists and Jesuits may have contributed to Carboni's later antipathy to members of the Society of Jesus. He began at the college shortly after the Piarists returned, replacing the Jesuits.

Although not confined to the aristocracy, the College of Nobles was an elite school. Compared to the several hundred day students, the boarders were an internal elite but the top dogs were the nobles. Carboni was neither a noble nor a boarder. Extant portraits show the nobles came from all over the Marches region and beyond: from Sinigallia, Fano, Cesena, Gubbio. Some were dandies with flowered waistcoats, ruffed silk shirts and bejewelled hands. As well as these trappings, many have the clifflike faces and haughty mien of those born to command, but others look sensitive. Carboni probably admired the nobles and became friendly with some. Later he quickly made the acquaintance of leading figures in several countries.

Among the famous graduates of Piarist schools are Haydn, Mozart, Schubert, Bruckner, Goya and Victor Hugo. It was claimed that the Piarists did not 'dry up their pupils' minds and hearts'. The students in Urbino were to learn 'liberal and knightly (dancing and fencing) arts'. After the three Rs, they were given a thorough grounding in Latin and 'to avoid monotony learnt the Old Testament'. As well as a daily Latin composition and study of Ovid, Cicero, Catullus, Virgil, Julius Caesar, Livy, Sallust, Horace and Tacitus, they read Dante, Petrarch and 'expurgated editions of dramatic poets' (that is, dramatists). They exercised in the two branches of rhetoric, eloquence and poetry, but also studied philosophy, mathematics, physics, botany and civil law.

The emphasis on Latin authors partly explains the hold Rome had on Urbinites' imagination. Moreover, historical memories were vivid. The Emperor Vespasian's inscription at the tunnel built during his reign through the nearby Furlo pass to Rome was still clearly legible in Carboni's time. Contemporary articles testify to interest in the battle in which the Carthaginian General Hasdrubal had been defeated and decapitated at the nearby Metaurus River. That was in 207 BC, but the image of the past was so powerful, and there was such stress on continuity, that it seemed yesterday. Time was elided and historical figures became contemporaries. All life could be seen as repetition or variation of classical exemplars.

On Thursday, 10 September 1829,[5] students of the College's Senior Grammar classes gave a public display of their learning for the end of the school year. Such 'speech nights', were a feature of Piarist education. Attended by parents and civic authorities, they sometimes included recitation of poems composed by the students. They were similar to the Piarist practice of historical commemorations (of figures such as the dukes of Montefeltro or the poet Torquato Tasso at the Urbino court) through narrative poems by various local authors, often clerics. The form of these 'academies' may have influenced Carboni's later theatrical writing, which could have drawn inspiration also from student plays, with both sung and spoken parts, which the Piarists arranged during Carnival.

On that Thursday which preceded the two-month school holidays, Carboni and his schoolmates in their customary dark flannel suits performed in the high-vaulted great hall which seated more than 200. The hall, light grey with white stucco moulding and discreet use of gold tint, was of the sober baroque design which Francesco Borromini had inaugurated with Rome's Propaganda Fide building. The statuary was another reminder of Rome: there were full-length coloured marble statues of the Urbinite Pope Clement XI and of another bishop. Even more significant were the busts in oval niches on the side walls, reminders of the world which was to be the subject of the students' performances. In the 18th century the Albani family had collected Roman statuary and there were casts of the Emperor Caracalla, three Roman generals and two female allegorical figures in the hall of college they had established.

Under the classical statues' severe gaze, students had to answer questions from the audience, such as 'which of Tacitus' twenty-five Lives did you analyse?', 'Explain the life of such-and-such a character in Tacitus from point A to point B'. A student could be stopped at any point of his account and another be asked to continue it.

It was a prolonged quiz. One student from the first group, which consisted of a boarder and nine-day students, was Raffaele (as spelt in the programme) Carboni. Another was Antonio. Eleven-year-old Raffaello may have rattled off answers to outshine his elder brother.

One group of questions concerned ancient Roman customs and military life while the audience could request any grammatical exploit, such as a disquisition, with illustrations, on gerunds. A barrage of questions concerned Militades, the Athenian general who made himself tyrant of the Thracian Chersonnese: 'Why does Tacitus call enemies of. Greeks and Romans "barbarians"? What was the tripod on which the priestess sat to make pronouncements? What does Tacitus mean by "Colonies"? What is Despotism? What is Democratic government? What does Anarchy mean?'

Style was important. Students were taught to shape their prose through essays on themes such as 'Meekness triumphs over Anger'; in Latin free verse, they composed addresses from Urbinites to the happily reigning pope Leo XII, a Salute to the Madonna or Some Considerations on Fashionable Young Men, an apt exercise in Urbino where Baldassare Castiglione had written *The Courtier* (*Il Cortigiano*), which established European criteria for gentlemen.

The education probably reinforced Carboni's self-confidence and polemical promptitude. Familiarity with Tacitus' mordant style, his psychological insight and historical grasp may have been a key formative influence. The other side of the coin, however, was that the rhetorical tradition tended to exclude the new, to suggest that only rearrangement of old material was possible and that raising the volume could hide lack of experience or feeling.

It was a dubious training for someone whose allegiance was to the arts. Carboni wanted to be a writer and found local inspiration. He was impressed by stories of the Sibyl of Pietrala which he called Peterlato, the first hill to the south-west overlooking the via Flaminia. And Carboni probably noted the floating quality the landscape assumed when hills emerged from fog as from a sea. Somewhere between Urbino and heaven, it was the suspended, dreamlike but precise landscape he saw also in the work of Raphael and other local painters, against which images of man achieved sharp definition: nature could be captured and transformed in art.

He learnt music, and apparently much more, from Luigi Vecchiotti who had studied music under a Franciscan friar Stanislao Mattei. Among other students of Mattei were Gioacchino Rossini and Gaetano Donizetti. In 1827 a farce by Vecchiotti, *Fidelity in danger – or Three enamoured of a widow*, was staged at Rome's Valle theatre. In the same year, he received his appointment as choirmaster at Urbino cathedral, for which he also composed music. During carnival 1831 his opera *Adelasia* was successfully presented at the Valle. Three years later he married Maria, the daughter of the socially prominent Urbinite Marquis Raimondo Antaldi.

Curly-haired Vecchiotti, a chain-smoker, had a patriarchal air but was humble enough to study mathematics and physics at the Piarist Fathers' College after his appointment, at the age of 23, as cathedral choirmaster. A fervent Catholic but also devoted to the Piedmontese royal house, he must have made a deep impression on Carboni, for, even when Carboni had not seen the musician for eighteen years, he was to remember him 'with gratitude'.[6]

If the rhetorical tradition of the College of Nobles could be a straitjacket, Vecchiotti was a liberator. He was such a talented teacher that Rossini sent pupils to him. Widely read, Vecchiotti encouraged the new and original, although warning not to confuse them with extravagance. He was conscious that 'uniform studies which instruct big numbers cut the wings of those who can fly higher'; that 'the true genius is an enemy of pedantic methods and has within himself the path to perfection'; and, again, 'the true genius is like phosphorus – touch him and he ignites'.

His following comment on opera seems to have influenced Carboni's later artistic aims: 'Opera will reach perfection when the composer will be both musician and poet ... and will know how to write singing poetry'.

Vecchiotti's musical ideas were ahead of his time. Against those who claimed that only certain instruments were appropriate for church music, Vecchiotti advocated the use of all. He said those who implied some instruments were more sacred than others wanted 'Egyptian-mummy music'. He championed democratic church music: 'all are equal in God's church', he argued,'... and the first to consider are not those who, enjoying all pleasures outside church, want to prevent all delight inside it'.

As Vecchiotti was so responsive to talent, he may have fostered a conviction in precocious Carboni that he was destined for eminence. Certainly he would have reinforced Carboni's dedication to the arts. Like Vecchiotti,

Carboni had stage ambitions, and at 19 began to write a play about his fellow townsman Raphael, who, through his art, had achieved world renown. He may have been prompted also by the opening of Raphael's tomb in Rome in 1833. (It was found that Raphael had an unusually large larynx; the 'divine' painter probably had a booming voice.)

At 19, the ebullient redhead was completing his university philosophy studies. He was only 16 when he began philosophy, which corresponded roughly to a contemporary arts faculty. The university, founded in 1506, was one of the few Urbino institutions which had survived from the ducal period. However it had fallen on hard times and had been closed by the French, then again in 1831. With faculties of theology, law, philosophy and medicine, it had reopened the year before Carboni began his course (1833).

Carboni studied logic, ethics, metaphysics, algebra, geometry and physics. Later he produced somewhat dubious documents to show he had excelled in ethics, algebra and geometry.[7] His last year as a student was 1836–37 but he missed one year (1834–35) altogether. It seems he did not graduate. Not for the last time, when about to achieve a goal he changed direction. But Antonio, who lacked Raffaello's panache, graduated in theology.

What derailed Raffaello? The scant evidence suggests he was under domestic pressure. In November 1837, his beloved mother Girolama had died. This may have deprived him of financial or psychological support, and perhaps both. Antonio was already living at the local seminary. Bad blood developed between Raffaello and his father, perhaps because of Geltrude Scogli, a servant Biagio was to marry. Years later Antonio reminded Raffaello that he left home 'very peeved'.[8]

If Raffaello was unhappy at home, Urbino could have seemed a refuge for mediocrity, a familiar prison, a marooned ship. What did it have to offer? In recent years there had been some building, including a new theatre, but the economy was parlous. Peasants and sulphur miners from nearby zones had begun to emigrate. There were limited opportunities for a putative genius.

Rome was another matter. In Rome, Raphael, his namesake, had found fame, fortune and love; there the musician Vecchiotti had won acclaim. Duke Federico's library and the Albani family's renowned villa were in Rome; it was the capital not only of the Papal States, but also of Catholicism. Moreover, Raffaello and Antonio shared a conviction that they descended from a family which included Roman proconsuls.[9] This may have been a family tradition but it was more likely invented by two brothers enamoured of Rome. It would also have given them a claim to a nobility superior to that of the College of Nobles toffs. The aspirations of Raffaello may have been ignited by them as well as by Vecchiotti. In Rome, a potential high flyer could take wing. Carboni acted on his prolonged classical indoctrination: impatient, peeved, he took the via Flaminia to Rome.

Rome 1

Mr Foxy picks up a new scent

The 21-year-old Urbinite was employed, in November 1839, as assistant sacristan by Rome's Archconfraternity for Pilgrims and Convalescents at Santa Trinità dei Pellegrini (Holy Trinity of the Pilgrims). The monthly salary was 1.45 scudi, which was boosted the following month to 1.50 scudi.[1] (A lawyer's clerk earned 12 scudi a month, but Carboni's board and lodging were provided at the Archconfraternity.)

Presumably Carboni's contact with the Archconfraternity was through its Primicero (Chancellor) Prince Filippo Albani, who shared an Urbino background and whose elder brother Giuseppe had been a powerful cardinal. Near Holy Trinity were other reminders of Urbino boyhood: the adjacent home for spinsters was named after an Urbino saint.

At Holy Trinity, Carboni was not training to be a priest. He had to assist its priests in liturgical ceremonies, maintain the church in all its gilt and marble splendour and carry out duties in the hostel-hospital. One of Rome's major institutions, the Archconfraternity was housed in a huge, trapezoidal complex occupying a whole block. It consisted of a late baroque church with a heavy 1723 facade by Francesco de Sanctis, who had a surer hand designing the Spanish Steps (the church's main pride was Guido Reni's 1625 painting of the Trinity); the adjoining pilgrim hostel; a convalescent hospital; and a large oratory, or meeting place for prayers or discussion. The thirty-metre long barrel-vaulted atrium was decorated with the busts of pontiffs (Urban, Benedicts, Clements and Innocents, many of them members of the Archconfraternity) who, during Easter Week, had washed pilgrims' feet at Holy Trinity.

On the two upper floors were 488 beds, most of which took two people. Nearly a thousand meals could be served at the same time in the ground-floor refectories. Two rooms accommodated a total of 110 people for foot-washing, a necessary salve because pilgrims were encouraged to walk the eleven kilometres circuit to Rome's four major basilicas daily for two weeks. Accommodation was free for various periods according to the distance pilgrims had travelled: the maximum stay of five days was reserved for Portuguese pilgrims. During the day pilgrims visited the basilicas; at night before eating they heard a sermon, said the rosary and their feet were washed and then dried with towels fragrant from aromatic herbs. There was also accommodation for 120 male and 60 female convalescents. Twenty staffed the institution.

In the mid-16th century Filippo Neri inspired a lay group to succour pilgrims who otherwise were at the mercy of those offering lodgings or thieves, who were sometimes one and the same. This was the origin of the Archconfraternity. The members of the group wore a red (to signify the charitable heart's ardour) habit with a hood for use in public to preserve anonymity while doing good. In 1555 the group was given the use of Holy Trinity church and attached buildings. Because of the special spiritual benefits available, the pilgrim influx was greatest in Holy Years, which occurred every quarter-century. In other years pilgrims came mainly at Easter. It was decided to fill beds during the slack periods by accommodating poor convalescents in what became Europe's first convalescent hospital. In 1562 Pius IV recognised the group as an Archconfraternity, which enabled it to have branch confraternities which were established in Naples and Massa Carrara in Tuscany.

When Carboni began walking the Archconfraternity's long corridors, it had passed its peak. Once it had housed more than 300,000 pilgrims annually; nobles and prelates had begged to obtain money and victuals for it or competed to serve at its tables. For the first time since Holy Years were inaugurated in 1300, none was celebrated in 1800 because Napoleon had deported the pope. In 1825 Leo XII had revived the practice, but with mediocre results: the French Revolution had taken its toll. The Holy Year tradition was broken; relations with many states were difficult. Not only did fewer pilgrims come, but between 1776 and 1832 there were no bequests for the Archconfraternity. Nevertheless it was a convenient pied-à-terre for Carboni while he explored Rome. Some foreigners found Rome merely an anachronism. However, for an Urbinite reared in love and awe of imperial Rome which had become the pope's city, the impression that time had stopped would add to Rome's charm. Carboni, who fancied himself to be a descendant of Roman proconsuls, was heir to the past which seemed preserved for him. Moreover, although quick to use the knife, Romans were cordial and ready to accept outsiders who were not made to feel strangers.

The city was as majestic as Carboni had been told, but also unassuming. It was a rustic metropolis. The distinction between nature and the urban still preserved in Urbino had broken down; vegetation was the imperial city's last invader. Huge trees grew in the Colosseum; there were haystacks near the city centre. Goats slept in the classical ruins which emerged from ten metres of garbage. Oxen grazed in the Forum; twice weekly a cattle market was held amid the still-inhabited remains of the Theatre of Marcellus, which was begun at the time of Julius Caesar; farm labourers were hired daily in the square before the Pantheon. The city was huge with silence as well as with time. At night, after Holy Trinity and other church bells ceased tolling, almost the only sounds were the clop of horses' hooves and the bleat of sheep and goats. Almost the only illumination came from tiny oil lamps before Madonna images on the walls in many streets. It was as tranquil as Urbino, more like the world's largest village than a capital city.

In fact, Rome lived within the vestiges of its past. Its 150,000 inhabitants, the same figure as 150 years earlier, occupied only a small part of the area within the walls built by the Emperor Aurelian when the population had topped a million. The occasional houses in the virtually uninhabited areas often nestled in the remains of Roman aqueducts, public baths or mansions. Among the vineyards, pastures and wasteland were isolated monasteries or churches, ponds and wells where frogs croaked and mosquitoes, which spread malaria in summer, bred. People lived mainly in the crooks of the curving, unbanked Tiber. The Holy Trinity complex was strategically placed in via dei Pettinari (Wool-combers' Street), leading to the Sisto bridge, which, since its construction for the Holy Year of 1475, had taken much pilgrim traffic. The Tiber flooded often, swirling yellow-brown 100 yards down the narrow streets to Holy Trinity, clotting its cellars with mud. At least the floodwaters shifted some of the garbage left by people who, because of the good climate and poor accommodation, lived largely in the streets. In the square before

Holy Trinity, as elsewhere, plaques threatened anyone dumping rubbish, rubble, straw, weeds or dead animals with huge fines by the 'Monsignor of the Roads', but dumping continued as if to confirm an ambassador's comment: 'In Rome everyone gives orders and nobody obeys them but things work well enough.' In this case, they worked well only for those with insensitive noses. Smells of rotting refuse, of sheep, goat and fowl droppings and human excrement mixed with those from open-air vendors frying broccoli, fish or, blessed relief, brewing coffee. In addition, the nauseating smell of tanneries weighed on the Holy Trinity zone.

Rome was smellier as well as more magnificent than Urbino. All the extremes were sharper, even though there were no topographical class distinctions and tradespeople occupied the lower floors of nobles' palaces. The city was an unpredictable melange of princely and plebeian, sacred and profane. Ostensibly the sacred was in control. In Rome Carboni may have been thankful for a brother who was a priest. Nobody could forget Rome was the papal city, a city ruled by priests. A high proportion of Romans lived from the Church or aspired to do so. Because ecclesiastical garb meant security, many who were not priests but were somehow linked to the administration wore a cassock and a tricorn hat with broad, rolled brim. Clericalism was a synonym for careerism which was embodied in the pontifical bureaucracy, the Roman Curia.

In the 18th century papal rule had been, if not permissive, indulgent. But the shock of a French-installed republic caused, from 1823, a belated reaction led by 'Zealots' who tried to impose religious practice and morality through decrees and police. 'Don't think' seemed to be the eleventh commandment. Paranoia soured paternalism in the period Carboni was working at Holy Trinity.

Pope Gregory XVI resided in the huge 16th-century Quirinale, a palace originally built by Sixtus V as his summer residence. Easter Week was one of the rare occasions when the pope returned, with his gossipy court, to the Vatican. Papal residence at the Quirinale was significant. Alternative residences, such as St John Lateran and the Vatican, had primarily religious connotations and were distant from the seat of civil power, the Campidoglio (Capitol). But the Quirinale was a palace rather than a residence attached to a church and, riding higher than the nearby Campidoglio, dominated the city centre. It symbolised the pope's temporal power more than his spiritual sway.

He presided over the city, leaving little autonomous space for civic authorities. Palaces of aristocratic families, such as the Rospigliosi and the Colonna, clustered near the papal court. As in other Roman palaces, in the papal court princes of the Church rubbed shoulders with retainers and the pope's relatives without any attention paid to difference of rank.

Gregory XVI, a Camoldese monk and scholar, enjoyed jokes such as dousing guests in the palace's formal gardens with sudden jets of water. This was in tune with the court's simple domestic life, but its official functions, in the Quirinale's sumptuous salons, followed strict protocol. In public, Gregory seemed austere although he had an eloquent nickname: Gregory Drink. Born in Belluno in north Italy, erudite Gregory pushed through law reforms and encouraged missionaries, but for many his pro-Austrian sympathies. were a sore point at a time of rising Italian nationalism.

Nationalism eventually claimed Carboni but initially he was probably more entranced by pageantry than politics. The Catholicism he had known in Urbino would hardly have prepared him for its scale in Rome. Funerals and penitential processions were almost as elaborate as in Spain. Ceremonies in the 400 or more churches were spectacle as well as liturgy, with the sacred drama culminating at Easter. The Sistine Chapel choir's castrated counter-tenors aroused curiosity as well as admiration. Each time cardinals were nominated, three public holidays were granted. The facade of the palace where the newly created cardinal resided was illuminated; in the street before the palace two orchestras played music by composers such as Donizetti and Rossini; inside, a prolonged, brilliant reception was held for the church's new prince. The occasion was matched only when all Rome gathered again at the cardinal's death, and his large red hat, with its pendant knotted tassels, lay at his feet before being hung behind his grave.

Carboni had time to enjoy Rome and its ceremonies, for the liturgical calendar which regulated the city's life provided frequent feast days. Indeed visitors had the impression that little work was done at any time. There were few workshops and the work rhythm was not dictated by clocks. Holy Trinity itself, like many buildings in the zone, testified to an institutional concern for the needy who had been the Church's responsibility since the fall of the Roman Empire. The small square in front of the church-hostel complex reached the back of a monumental Monte di Pietà building. This institution had been established two centuries earlier to combat usury by offering lower interest rates on loans than did Jewish money lenders. Beggars were treated indulgently. The unemployed could obtain free meals from scores of convents and monasteries. Pontifical institutes, cardinalate establishments, aristocratic households and parishes distributed money to the needy, sent lunches to the families of former servants, assisted pregnant women even if unwed, orphans and the aged.

Confraternities provided handouts in addition to spiritual assistance. In their districts they acquired popularity comparable to present-day football clubs: garish illustrations of the local confraternities' activities, such as visiting prisoners or, in the Holy Trinity's case, aiding pilgrims, surmounted collection boxes in restaurants and coffee bars. Even after the French had abolished many confraternities and sold their property, more than a hundred survived. Sometimes confraternity processions, colourful because of their members' gowns, ended in clashes with members of another confraternity.

Literature could be a way for the bright provincial to emerge. Carboni tried to learn languages and dramaturgy simultaneously by copying out the plays of Shakespeare and Goethe. He worked at a play, *La Santola* ('The goddaughter'), and may have drawn further inspiration for his incomplete play on Raphael by visiting the Urbinite's simple, cream, stone tomb in the nearby Pantheon. With a girlfriend called Angela, he seemed on the way to emulating the painter's amatory success.

A midsummer's dawn (24 June 1840) inspired a waltz and a poem 'Salute to the Madonna'.[2] It was assistant-sacristan style, conventional in form and feeling, proclaiming that all perfection was in the distant past. The classics were old and the old was classic. The longer dead the poet, the better. One could imitate but not invent; style meant obeying rhetorical rules, art was identified with artificiality. Cardinals, bishops and nobles attended Arcadian meetings in sylvan glades at which poets, who assumed names such as Polimeteo Metimeo and Filino Amatunteo and wore pastoral garb, read their odes, sonnets and epigrams in Latin and Italian. Academies controlled culture with the result, Giacomo Leopardi had complained, that poetry became neither fish nor fowl. Satiric verse was clandestine whether it was the caustic anonymous couplets left at night at Pasquino's statue near piazza Navona,[3] or the implacably anti-Gregory XVI sonnets of the respectable academician and papal employee Giuseppe Gioacchino Belli, which were published only after his death.

Rome was keeping the contemporary world, particularly any consequences of the French Revolution, at arm's length. Railways were considered with almost as much suspicion as certain books. 'Railways bring commerce,' Gregory XVI reputedly said, 'and commerce brings sin', by which he probably meant liberalism. Rome was sceptical of the new God Progress and of its prophet Science. As the sclerosis had theological sanction, Rome seemed a metaphysical city, visual proof of the Church's unchanging deposit of faith.

Carboni would hardly have found stimulus in the *Diario di Roma* newspaper's report of trial runs with threshing machines on farms near the city. There was little about local politics. Politics happened elsewhere: the *Diario* carried a report of a certain Daniel O'Connell warning that Ireland could never expect justice from England. Matters as distant as the moon. In his Archconfraternity in the capital of Catholicism, Carboni had woven a warm cocoon which protected him from contemporary energies and uncertainties. But he was reaching beyond Holy Trinity, for he had uncommon linguistic interests.

Each morning, a pair of Spanish Franciscan friars came to Holy Trinity from San Pietro in Montorio, on the Janiculum hill across the Tiber, to say Mass for Spanish-speaking pilgrims. Each morning, Carboni practised Spanish with them. One of the friars, tall, lean and nervous, suggested Carboni come to San Pietro in the afternoon to play bowls. At the end of Wool-combers' Street Carboni crossed the Sisto bridge, passed the house at the Settimiana Gate where Raphael is said to have courted the Fornarina (his model who worked for a fornaia or bakery), and climbed to San Pietro, which was built in 1481 for Ferdinand and Isabella of Spain. In its courtyard was a miniature church, the beautifully proportioned Tempietto built by the Urbinite Donato Bramante on the site where it was believed St Peter had been crucified.

The parapet before the church looked out to Frascati and Castelgandolfo in the hills twenty-five kilometres away. Below the parapet the Tiber flowed towards Ostia with, beyond it, the Knights of Malta priory on the Aventine hill, and farther still on the Appian Way, the imposing round mausoleum of Cecilia Metella. Opposite was the Quirinale where Gregory XVI resided, the Pantheon where Raphael lay and, on the far left, Castel Sant'Angelo where political prisoners languished. The long shoulder of the Janiculum hid St Peter's. The Apennines, visible beyond the city, were a reminder of Urbino to the north-east.

On entering the garden of San Pietro, Carboni found bowls was not the only game the Spanish friar had in mind. As Carboni put it, the friar, in his bell-shaped habit, did everything possible to make him note what could toll the bell. Carboni assumed his thick, burning red hair and his little golden moustache – the colours of a fox, he realised – had made him too attractive to the friar. With what he described as 'fox-like cunning',[4] pretending not to notice the friar's erection, Carboni left swiftly. He must have decided: better told than tolled.

It was a blow to his Spanish lessons but he was also learning German, English and French. For German he walked a hundred metres left of Holy Trinity to the 16th-century Spada palace. Here he took lessons from the Prussian custodian Ferdinand Cormann, whom he described as 'hearty, warm-hearted, nearly erudite and entirely a gentleman'.[5] A dog-lover with considerable biblical knowledge and a penchant for Latin tags, Carboni could have been attracted by a stucco medallion repeated across the palace's exuberantly decorated facade. The device of the original proprietor, Cardinal Girolamo Capodiferro, it showed a hunting dog seated before a column whose seeming thorns represented flames. It was the pillar of fire which guided the Hebrews out of Egyptian captivity and the attached motto 'Tempore Utroq[ue]' referred to the twelfth chapter of Exodus: 'And the Lord went on before to guide them on their journey; by day, in a pillar of cloud, by night, in a pillar of fire; he 'was their guide *at all times* (tempore utroque)'. The dog represented obedience, patience, faith and hope of reward. Carboni may have been short on patience and obedience but, through his life's journey, he was to have firm faith in the resurrection.

For English lessons he walked a few steps beyond Palazzo Spada and Palazzo Farnese to the English College. In the 16th century, during the reign of Alessandro Farnese *as* Pope Paul III, the zone had been redesigned to accommodate the dominant Farnese palace. Sangallo, Michelangelo, Vignola and Della Porta had worked on the palace, whose facade of varied classical orders was a harmonious anthology of Renaissance genius. But the piazza before it was a pungent example of Rome's combination of visual rapture and olfactory revulsion. It was a tip whose stench soared with the temperature.

Flies flourished. Passers-by could admire the palace for only as long as they held their noses.

Next to the Farnese was a 16th-century palace which had the name of Carboni's mother's family, Fioravanti, but he did not leave any reference to this. Fifty metres farther on was the English College which, like Holy Trinity, had been founded as a pilgrim hostel. That was in 1362 but, after the Reformation, in 1579, it had become a college to train English diocesan priests to work in England. The longest established overseas English institution, it was called 'Venerable'. Carboni's teacher was its vice-rector Monsignor Vincent Eyre, born near York in 1815, the eldest son of a papal count whose family produced many priests. Amiable Eyre, described by a friend as a 'theologian with a sense of humour', loved Roman rubrics. Carboni gave a glowing description of him as 'kindly, pious, direct, spontaneous and generous'.[6]

The evenings Carboni was on duty in the hostel and hospital, a young Jew, Maurizio Coen, came to keep him company while he paced the barrel-vaulted corridors. As Coen was learning French from a Parisian Monsignor, he and Carboni filled in the time practicing the language. Carboni met the Monsignor and was delighted by his Parisian accent; the Monsignor, for his part, loved Roman salads. Carboni, who had abundant oil and vinegar, took to inviting the monsignor to dinner in his room. The Parisian would then correct Carboni's translations.

The priest for whom Carboni served Mass usually spent from forty-five to seventy-five minutes confessing a plump, spruce young woman whose face was always hidden behind a blue veil. Carboni wondered what sins she could have committed to require hour-long confession, but the confessor hinted that, because of her angelic visions, she was close to sainthood.

Carboni was already irritated with the priest because he had insisted his confessional in the vestibule near the sacristy be cleaned on Carboni's hospital duty night. Carboni concluded the priest disapproved his perambulatory conversations with a Jew. Now, however, curiosity was added to irritation. Carboni wanted to see the penitent's face. Hidden, he observed her confession. Instead of the penitent being to the priest's left or right, they were face to face. The confession was more oral than aural. That evening additional bells may have tolled at Holy Trinity.

Two days later the priest told Carboni his penitent was to make a special penance that night in the locked church. As the priest had an appointment with the prior, he asked Carboni to accompany her to the confessional in the vestibule by the sacristy.

Carboni was alone with the young woman in the silent church where a single lamp brought out baroque gilt against depthless dark. He might have resisted the temptation if he had not seen her, two nights earlier, at confession. As they entered the vestibule, he lifted her veil and was seized by an uncontrollable desire to taste every part of her face, which seemed 'honied food for angels'. She threatened to scream but Carboni told her what he had seen two days earlier. It had the desired effect. As Carboni put it, without rehearsal 'we sang the duet: Adam and Eve in the earthly paradise'.[7]

He had not calculated, however, that when he fetched the priest, she would confess her still tingling sin. At the Vicariate, the priest accused Carboni of being an accomplice of the Parisian monsignor, whom he denounced as a French Republican secret agent. Both were arrested and Carboni's room at Holy Trinity was searched. In August's oppressive heat, he found himself in a flea-infested prison in Palazzo Madama, site of the governorate. At Monte Citorio police headquarters he underwent three interrogations for high treason against Gregory XVI and collusion with Parisian Republicans.

A woman had been his downfall; another was to save him. His girlfriend Angela, hearing of his arrest, rushed to Palazzo Altieri to intercede with Prince Albani. He read the report of Carboni's interrogation and ordered that the young Urbinite be brought to him.

Carboni arrived, handcuffed, accompanied by two pontifical police or, as he called them, 'guardian angels'.

'We're on velvet under this mild, paternal regime', Prince Albani shouted, 'but you, with your volcanic head, want to rebel against His Holiness Gregory XVI!'

Carboni convinced Albani that the only Republican he had ever heard of was the ancient Roman, Mucius Scevola. A lawyer, a certain Ricciotti, spoke in Carboni's favour. Changing tone, Albani asked 'Mr Foxy', as he called the redhead, if he knew why, in his prime, he was in prison. Probably Albani felt an Urbino lad from a solid family and, what was more, a College of Nobles' alumnus, would not mix with revolutionaries, but still Carboni's intellectual curiosity, his darting eyes, may have worried the Prince.

Carboni apologised for not resisting the plump penitent temptation.

Prince Albani understood the implication that priestly jealousy caused Carboni's arrest, but solemnly warned him such acts in a sacred place justified excommunication. Albani told the foxy fellow to return not to prison but to work humbly at the pilgrim hostel.

Cracking the cocoon

Mr Foxy had shown himself to be an impetuous young man with a capacity for getting into trouble. But his arrest was not merely an episode which ended fortunately: the accusation of being a conspirator helped make him one. It also spurred him to break his cocoon of conventional Catholicism, which was intellectually claustrophobic because all political aspirations, all contact with the new were excluded.

The unwarranted, anonymous accusation and perhaps police ministrations may have made him realise that the Regola district, where Holy Trinity was located, was a hot-bed of anti-papal conspirators. Many initiations into the seditious Carbonari movement took place in the hostelries of Regola, which was a zone of hovels and tanneries as well as of magnificent palaces. The hostelries in vicolo dei Vaccinari were considered the sect's headquarters; it was estimated 200 Carbonari lived in Regola.[8] There also, almost a decade before Carboni's arrest, the first Roman group of the Giovine Italia (Young Italy) movement inspired by Giuseppe Mazzini had been formed. Giovine Italia shared the Carbonari movement's aim of uniting Italy against the foreign and reactionary forces which had largely ruled it since the 1814–15 Restoration. But the two groups differed over methods. A major difference was that Giovine Italia made public its programme, which was to foment insurrections as a prelude to a democratic republic. The Roman Giovine Italia branch aimed particularly to undermine the Austrian-linked papacy. Its location in Regola indicated changing attitudes: this was one of Rome's traditionally pro-papal quarters, but now workers, and not only intellectuals, joined conspiratorial groups.

If Carboni did not notice the Regola conspirators by himself, they would have come to his attention through two young Giovine Italia members, Mattia Montecchi and Giovanni Battista Cattabeni, who sought him after his release from the republican charge. Like Carboni, Montecchi and Cattabeni had grown up in the Marches region. Compact Cattabeni was the son of a prominent lawyer. Montecchi's family claimed to be that of Veronese nobles whose

Romeo inspired Shakespeare and who were mentioned by Dante in the sixth canto of *Il Purgatorio*. However, Mattia Montecchi was to say, 'my family's nobility dates from my period in papal prisons.'[9]

Aged only 17, on his father's death Mattia became responsible for his younger brother and six sisters. They were living in via delle Muratte between the central Corso and the Trevi fountain. As their father had been a director of police in Bologna as well as governor of a small town, they had a monthly pension of 17 scudi. Mattia's sister Elena, a poet, gained another 20 scudi by teaching English and French in the noble Borghese household and privately; Mattia gained perhaps half as much as a lawyer's clerk while, by night-study, completing a law degree.

When a cholera epidemic isolated Rome in 1837 and caused economic difficulties, conspirators planned an insurrection, but their plot to storm Castel Sant'Angelo prison was uncovered. Although Montecchi was a suspect, he was not imprisoned. As Carboni's experience suggests, it was a period of plots and rumours of plots, of police paranoia and anonymous denunciations. Romans sensed Gregory XVI's flaccid government could not last.

In his play *Buffi e Buffoni* ('Comics and Clowns', which was the epithet Garibaldi was to hurl at retreating French forces) Carboni showed himself, Montecchi, Cattabeni and university students playing in the Colosseum.[10] For many years bull fights had been banned from Rome; the game Carboni described consisted of attempts to lasso players who took the bull's part.

While it was in course, a procession arrived for Mass, which was celebrated at the Colosseum. A priest and Swiss guards who accompanied the procession were suspicious of the bull game, as well they might have been, for even under their scrutiny, the players passed messages. For instance, Cattabeni told a trussed 'bull': 'The slave who wants to end his pains / Has first of all to break his chains'.

Another procession arrived of senior girls from the socially exclusive Sacred Heart convent, including Petronilla, described by Carboni as Montecchi's cousin. She drew Montecchi away from the guard's scrutiny to give him a scarf in the red, white and green Italian colours: patriotic chic?

Cattabeni handed Carboni a green-covered booklet, saying:

> Here's the word of the prophet of the Giovine Italia movement: rise, for God's sake, Roman youth; Italy calls you to the

battlefield; get rid of the foreigner. From London, Giuseppe Mazzini greets patriots and tells them to be ready …

Heady ideas for young Carboni, who, until recently, had linked republicanism solely with Mucius Scevola. Through Montecchi and Cattabeni, he discovered that Rome was not only rife with spies, but also with those who preached liberty. Why should there be censorship, fear of books, fear of ideas? Why should Rome be governed by priests who, among other things, made financial and sexual scandals even more scandalous? Why should election of Christ's vicar also be choice of an absolute monarch? And why did the pope-sovereign always have one foot in the grave? Gregory XVI was 76 but seemed almost 176 years old. Carboni was to call him a 'warty, rubicund, big-nosed friar'.[11] Now he could fully sympathise with the revolt in Urbino and elsewhere which had broken out, when he was 13, immediately after Gregory's election. Gregory's agent in suppressing that revolt had been Cardinal Giuseppe Albani, brother of the chancellor of Holy Trinity.

'Not bad but always afraid' had been the French novelist Stendhal's assessment of Gregory,[12] while Pellegrino Rossi, who was to be Minister of the Interior for Gregory's successor, described him as 'timid but at the same time irascible, determined to run all the Church's affairs by himself'.[13]

In contrast, Giuseppe Mazzini represented enthusiasm, the march of history, messianic patriotism. 'Believe the impossible' was his credo. As the Austrians in north Italy and the papacy also had smothered legitimate aspirations, Mazzini was infusing patriotism with religious overtones. A nation, he preached, was a spiritual entity. He aimed to fortify national identity while eschewing narrow nationalism. He promised resurrection as well as insurrection, if only intellectuals melded thought and action: 'Intellect', he wrote, 'is the treasure, the sacred deposit confided to the thinker by God, in order that he may distribute it among those of his brother men who are unable to reach it alone'. Carboni was seared by what he called Mazzini's 'scalds or stains' prose,[14] which was a stimulating contrast to the Roman academic literary tradition. One could educate through action but also build a nation by writing: literature was not solely a means of emerging, but a patriotic mission. It constructed the future; academicians merely embalmed the past. Intellectual and moral convictions, social and historical awareness, political passion would shape a new literature in opposition to retrospective classicism.

Mazzini made Progress, Duty, Liberty, Equality, Humanity sound like banner headline news. He addressed a society so static that one had to evoke revolution to bring about any change, but it was doubtful if any changes could satisfy the expectations evoked by that incendiary word. He preached meritocracy not aristocracy (not even that of the 'high clergy', for a simple parish system sufficed), education for all, citizens' rights. He advocated collaboration between social classes rather than conflict.

Carboni joined Mazzini's Giovine Italia movement. In the name of God and Italy, he would have sworn to consecrate himself wholly and forever to constitute, with other members, the one, independent, free, republican nation of Italy. Among the oaths was that of not belonging to other associations. But the secret society did not mention high society where the alumnus of the Urbino College of Nobles had a toe on the threshold. Through the Archconfraternity,[15] he came to the attention of Prince Alessandro Torlonia, the richest Roman, who had bought Villa Albani from Cardinal Albani. Once again, as on his arrival in Rome, Carboni showed a talent for winning the benevolence of the well-placed. The prevalence of patronage meant that anyone who wanted to become someone needed to know a noble. Towards the end of 1841, the subversive switched from sacristan to bank clerk; Torlonia, who appreciated the young Urbinite's linguistic talent, employed him as letter-copier. The secret society–high society contrast was not as sharp as it sounds. Perhaps because of a small middle class, many leaders of Italy's nationalist movement came from society's upper echelons. The contrast lay, rather, between Carboni's new ideals and his new employment – Torlonia was the banker of the Holy See. Carboni's employment by Torlonia after his arrest probably fostered the illusion that if he got into scraps, not only would he be bailed out, but his last state would be better than his first.

The Torlonia family, French in origin, had been settled in Rome for less than a century. Soon after their arrival, on the Corso near San Carlo church they had opened a silk fabrics shop, but also traded in grain and other goods. Giovanni Torlonia, the Furstenberg family's agent at the Holy See, opened a bank, supplied cannons to Napoleon and bought noble titles. Stendhal described Giovanni as

> a little old man with a worried look wearing a white waistcoat which is too long ... [there is] a kind of naivety in his limitless respect for money.[16]

The balls at Palazzo Torlonia in piazza Venezia, Stendahl claimed, were better planned than those of most European sovereigns, and grander than any given by Napoleon. They combined comfort with elegance; there were always enough people, Stendhal noted, but never a crush.

Stendhal reported Giovanni's comments on his sons at a ball in December 1827. Giovanni Torlonia said the elder son Marino was

> a simpleton, I'm afraid; he likes paintings the arts, statues; I'll leave him three million and two duchies. But the other one [Alessandro] is quite different – he's a man; he knows the price of money so I'll leave my banking establishment to him, he'll enlarge it, extend it and some day you'll see him richer, not than this or that prince, but than all Roman princes together; and if he develops half his father's shrewdness, he'll make his son pope.

Giovanni, who died three months after the ball Stendhal attended, had accurately forecast Alessandro's financial future. Giovanni used to tell how, pretending to be his own servant, he beat down merchants' prices; Alessandro, instead, wallowed in conspicuous consumption. Many tales celebrated the fabulous wealth of the thin-legged, thick-nosed Alessandro. In 1840 he was asked to contribute to the restoration of the Jesuit Gesù church in central Rome, burial place of the Order's founder, Ignatius Loyola. He funded the whole project thus becoming responsible for its plethora of yellow marble. He also acquired the nearby Argentina theatre, built the neo-classical Villa Torlonia and bought Villa Albani.

After exploring Catholic Rome and political Rome, Carboni caught up with the social set once he entered the Torlonia bank. Some prayed in St Peter's, some plotted in hostelries; others frequented theatres, sparkling receptions, masked balls, took coffee at the Caffè Greco and promenaded on the Pincio hill. Although in summer, because of malaria, visitors avoided Rome and inhabitants who could afford it fled to the hills, it was the winter capital of the European aristocracy. It was a refuge for deposed royalty and most of Napoleon's family. It was the climax of the Grand Tour at a time when travellers stayed months to get to know the city. Many foreign artists and writers, such as Goethe, Walter Scott, Keats and Byron (who was spied on for suspected links with Carbonari subversives) had lived in the piazza di Spagna area, which was called the 'English ghetto' (*'er ghetto de l'Inglesi*), as all foreigners were considered English. Rome's ten-day carnival also attracted many visitors.

Like a Renaissance prince, Alessandro Torlonia had spent thousands of scudi in decorating the family palace in piazza Venezia. But Renaissance artists were not on hand (however, Canova's Hercules was among the statues). Stendhal had been in ecstasy at the palace but, after changes, another French writer Paul Desmaris found the 'Italian Rothschild's' showplace in bad taste: simplicity among Roman nobles was on the way out. Desmaris wrote:

> The main courtyard is paved with coloured marble; a gallery surrounded by columns of pure Carrara encloses it on all sides. On the right are bank offices, opposite are apartments for parties and receptions. It is impossible to describe the gold, marble, paintings, costly furniture and bad taste which fills these rooms; unable to make it beautiful, they made it rich.[17]

At the Torlonia palace, receptions were given for up to 2,000 guests, at which cardinals mixed with aristocrats from all Europe. Operas were sometimes performed during these receptions which concluded towards dawn with a sit-down meal. The receptions were reputedly financed by profits from excessive exchange rates. But at least the bank invited clients to its entertainments. Many were English, as it served most English visitors, including Shelley some years earlier (Romans called the English *milordi pelabili clienti*, 'easily fleeced my Lords'). Perhaps one of them was a shapely blonde Londoner, with melting brown eyes and fine teeth, Jane Sarah Holbech. If so, Carboni was to see her again more than a decade later.

The Young Fox from Urbino, the ex-sacristan and subversive, Raffaello Carboni attended some Palazzo Torlonia receptions, perhaps as a linguistic go-between. Working in this setting, he seems to have dreamt of marrying into the Roman nobility. In his play *La Santola*, which has scenes set in a thinly disguised Torlonia palace, Concetta, the illegitimate daughter of a Roman duke, falls in love with the Carboni figure, Pastorello. To foil their marriage, the Roman prince courting Concetta reveals that she and Carboni-Pastorello are brother and sister! The bastards, which is the word Carboni uses, carry out a suicide pact on their mother's tomb.

It suggests that Carboni imagined himself the illegitimate son of a Roman noble. He was not the first or last talented young man from a provincial family who concluded he was a cuckoo in the nest. The play implies his mother deserved a Roman duke rather than Biagio; that Carboni, if he did not want to bed a sister, wanted to bed a noble's daughter; and, moreover, that he could not marry the woman he wanted – indeed, she was fatal.

Desirable women might have been more accessible if Carboni were noble. He already fantasised that he was a descendant of the ancient Roman consul 'de Carbonari Carbonis' (possibly Carbo), but such claims were more plausible the further he was from Rome. Artistic success, as Raphael had shown, could also improve one's chances, but work on his plays and poems was slow. A third way to improve his rating was through gold. The gilt in the Torlonia ballroom dazzled; the females, described as the prettiest women of Rome and London, were all forty-eight-carat. Carboni had caught the seductive scent of sterling and scudi; he was only a junior clerk on the lowest rung but he was on the right ladder, particularly as Giuseppe Spada was keen to give him a hand-up.

Spada had curled, abundant hair, drooping eyelids and narrow nose in a long, chalky face. Born in Rome in 1796, he had entered the bank under Giovanni Torlonia before he was 15. In 1823 he became a teller. He had an exceptional work capacity. For years on returning home from the bank, he studied English, French, Spanish, classical Greek, physics, mathematics and archaeology until 2 a.m. A musical enthusiast, he became secretary of the Philharmonic Academy and, after his marriage in 1828, often had home musical evenings with his friend Gioacchino Rossini. (A relative, Massimo, was to be a key figure in the controversial Vatican Bank, IOR, until the 1980s.)

As Spada dealt with the bank's foreign clients, Carboni's linguistic talent was obviously useful. In turn, the assistant for foreign correspondence, as Carboni became, was grateful for Spada's paternal advice, which, he considered, transformed him from a sacristan to a man and a gentleman.[18] But there are no roses without thorns – it was the title of a poem Carboni wrote, in May 1842, at the Temple of Vesta in Tivoli outside Rome, and he was to experience its truth the following year. Police broke into his room and took him once more to the Palazzo Madama prison. The young Fox must have left another trail. The motive, he was convinced, was his attempt to unmask a hypocritical prelate, but he was accused of writing Carbonari proclamations. This seems unlikely as the Giovine Italia Movement was in competition with the Carbonari, but even his name was against him – *Carbonari* (charcoal burners because some of the first subversives had this occupation) derived from *carbone* (coal), of which the plural is *carboni*. Carboni claimed that what the police found in his room were simply translations, for study purposes, from English and German. However his protestations that he knew nothing of politics were disingenuous given his Montecchi–Cattabeni links and his previous interrogation, although its record had probably been withdrawn at Albani's request.

Carboni was convinced he was a victim of the Jesuits. Since Pius VIII, in 1814, had re-established the Jesuits, who had been suppressed during the previous forty-one years, they had become the Church's main defence against liberalism. In 1843 there were 4,000 Jesuits worldwide with 649 in the Roman province, of whom a dozen were consultants in influential curial offices. The Jesuit headquarters was at the Gesù church near Palazzo Venezia. For those like Carboni who accused the Jesuits of inspiring the Holy See's opposition to Italian nationalism, 'Jesuit' was a synonym for 'underhand, mealy-mouthed, hypocritical, sinister, crafty, devious, ambiguous, machiavellian'.

Once again, as in 1840, Carboni had an influential friend who could be embarrassed by his misadventures: Giuseppe Spada. The Torlonia bank, which served the Holy See, could hardly have its assistant foreign clerk condemned as a subversive. Spada helped Carboni get away to Paris. Carboni was grateful, although realising Spada may have acted because he (Carboni), 'the pupil, was no longer learning from his master'.[19] In other words, it was better for all concerned if he were out of the way. He must have left Rome feeling he had unfinished business there; he had intended to make his mark, but had merely burnt his fingers.

Rome 2

Civis Romanus sum

Carboni probably returned to Rome in the second half of 1846 shortly after the newly-elected Pius IX had declared an amnesty for political prisoners. There is little record of Carboni's Parisian sojourn under Louis-Philippe's constitutional monarchy. Paris, with a population approaching a million, vigorous intellectual life and industrialisation (omnibuses had functioned for over a decade, and the first railway had been laid in 1840), must have impressed Carboni, who would have appreciated that priests did not govern.

The monarchy conceded a subsidy to political refugees, of whom Poles and Italians were the most numerous. In 1840, the Italians had formed a general committee representing all political tendencies. Carboni may have been in contact with it but he left reference only to conceiving, 'among the ducks of the Luxembourg Gardens', the comic opera *Il Sartore di Parigi* ('The Parisian tailor').

Carboni claimed to have heard Pius IX, from the Quirinale balcony, proclaim, 'Strangers go home ...'[1] Pius did not pronounce the phrase, but many interpreted a 'God bless Italy' speech of February 1848 as if a strong hint to the Austrians, who occupied much of north Italy, to repatriate.

Giovanni Maria Mastai Ferretti, the future Pius IX, had been a schoolmate in Sinigallia of Andrea Cattabeni, father of Carboni's friend Giovanni Battista. After becoming pope he asked Andrea, a lawyer who advocated greater civic rights, to live in Rome as one of his advisers. It promised well, confirming the liberal reputation of the youngest pope (aged 54) in centuries. In the Curia of his predecessor, many had criticized the future pope, saying 'in the Mastai Feretti household, even the cats are liberals.'

As a young man Giovanni Maria Mastai Ferretti had suffered epilepsy, been a horseman, a billiards-player and smoked 'like Vesuvius'. As pope he continued to play billiards, to smoke, to write verse riddles and he retained a sweet tooth. Before becoming a priest he had had a series of girlfriends, including a princess and an actress, as well as a close relationship with a married woman, Countess Giacinta Marchetti Milzetti. On the day he was made bishop, 3 June 1827, he had become an associate of the Holy Trinity Archconfraternity and was to be the last pope to wash pilgrims' feet there. Some criticised him as incurably Italian, but this punster with an affectionate, festive manner seemed certain to be more popular than the monkish Gregory XVI.

Within a month of his election in June 1846, Pius declared an amnesty for political prisoners. On release, one of them shouted *'Viva la libertà'*; Pius IX congratulated him and when word of this spread *'Viva Pio Nono'* (Pius IX) became a popular expression. Huge crowds cheered him at the Quirinale. People detached horses from his carriage and drew it themselves. Some Jews converted. Angelo Brunetti, a 46-year-old corpulent carter known as Ciceruacchio, took eleven barrels of wine to piazza del Popolo. He offered free drinks in honour of Pius IX, then burnt the barrels. It reflected Pius's popularity but also suggests why Ciceruacchio, eloquent though ignorant, won a big following.

In February 1847, Andrea Cattabeni arranged a meeting between Pius IX and the Piedmontese politician Massimo d'Azeglio who had written scathingly of Gregory XVI's repression. Members of Roman political clubs, particularly the Circolo Popolare, believed radical changes imminent. Although in June the Council of Ministers was established in disappointingly restrictive terms, the first anniversary of Pius IX's election was celebrated enthusiastically. University students carried the escutcheon of the pope's family, the Mastai, with its red, white and blue changed to the Italian colours red, white and green.

Some advisers feared reform of papal government, which the pope had initiated, would be as risky as restoring a fragile antique – the result could be a handful of dust. The curialists, the papal administration which was still largely that of Gregory, had good reasons to distrust popular support for Pius IX. If reforms did not satisfy the demonstrators, they could quickly change their tune. In fact, by July, although still shouting 'Long live Pius IX', they added 'death to the priests'. A mob attacked the Austrian embassy at Palazzo Venezia during a lunch attended by cardinals. Austria was the nationalists' *bête noire*.

Pius IX said Mass at the Jesuit St Ignatius church. The crowd trying to enter was brutally repulsed by Swiss guards. Vehement protests forced the guards to withdraw. Next morning, a doggerel attack on Pius IX circulated:

> *My dear liberals*
> *Here's cud – chew on it:*
> *Pius IX's a Jesuit!*

At one time, in fact, Pius had considered becoming a Jesuit; word of this may have increased resentment over the incident of the previous day. The only thing more damaging for Pius than association with the Jesuits, opponents of Italian nationalism, was protection by the German-speaking Swiss guards.

Pius's popularity soared again, however, when he protested against the Austrian General Radetzky occupying Ferrara. Pius was defending the Papal States which included Ferrara, but it was taken as a defence of Italy against the Austrians. There were demands that he lead the national unity movement. From Uruguay, Giuseppe Garibaldi wrote offering his services.

The pope maintained popularity by creating the Civic Guard. This horrified many curialists: it meant arming some who, under Gregory XVI, had been considered subversive. The day after the Guard's establishment, the Secretary of State Cardinal Pasquale Gizzi resigned in protest.

To shouts of 'Long live Italy' a torch-lit procession accompanied a plaster Pius IX statue along the Corso from piazza Venezia to piazza del Popolo. On 15 October Pius established, under a cardinal-president, a State Council whose twenty-four members would be nominated by regional and municipal councils. Shortly afterwards, Cardinal Gabriele Ferretti, who had replaced Gizzi as Secretary of State, likewise offered his resignation but was persuaded to remain.

The reforms worried the reactionaries without satisfying the radicals. Civil groups were granted only a token authority because, in the last analysis, the Secretariat of State still called the tune. Pius IX now seemed too much pope to be prince and too much prince to be pope. And the political clubs which inspired demonstrators wanted neither prince nor pope. Pius's popularity declined rapidly, for he had not lived up to expectations as a nationalist leader.

On the first days of 1848, hearing the rumour that he was afraid to be seen in the city, Pius IX drove out without guards. On other occasions, even the most violent had knelt for his blessing. This time, however, about 300 led by the wine carter Ciceruacchio followed his carriage shouting menacingly, 'Death to the Jesuits and the governor [of Rome]'. It was a change from the first eighteen months of Pius's reign but, even then, many who knelt for his blessing, convinced he had the evil eye which brought misfortune, had secretly made propitiatory gestures.

On 10 February, from the Quirinale balcony, Pius delivered his 'God bless Italy' speech. He spoke in a religious rather than political context. After condemning violence and pointing out that the Papal States' 3 million inhabitants had the support of 200 million Catholics worldwide, he said 'God bless Italy and conserve for it the most precious gift of all, the Faith'.

Ciceruacchio and others seized on 'God bless Italy', ignoring the remainder of the phrase; they rekindled wild enthusiasm for Pius IX as potential leader of an Italian federation. It seems that the popularity pleased emotive Pius, who was always inclined to see Providence at work. However it was not clear whether he was pulling the populace with him or being pushed. He was not politically shrewd enough for a difficult situation which was rapidly becoming more complex. Some said that Pius's heart was greater than his head, others that he had the best heart in the worst era. Although in 2000 he was to be declared a saint, in 1848 prudence was not conspicuous among his virtues.

In Paris on 24 February, Louis-Philippe abdicated. A scene in *Buffi* e *Buffoni* shows Carboni and friends celebrating Louis-Philippe's fall and the establishment of a French Republic. The celebration took place at the Falcone trattoria, in piazza Sant'Eustachio near the Pantheon, which was frequented by artists and writers. One of them was occasionally seen bent so low over his rice, which he spooned up with such speed and intentness, that strands of his blonde hair fell in it. He was Nikolai Gogol, who was writing *Dead Souls*. He disapproved of Pius IX's reformism but approved the Falcone's broiled lamb 'as good as that of the Caucasus'[2] and its cherry pie which was liable to make the 'most consummate gastronome salivate for three days running'. After his meal, Gogol would sometimes decry the greediness of neighbours just beginning theirs, then repeat their order.

Carboni's companions at the Falcone were excited because they were to be joined by a bevy of patriotic Sacred Heart convent girls, including Montecchi's cousin Petronilla. They arrived, but the celebration attracted the attention both of Swiss guards, who commented on it in sausagey Italian (*Ja, ja*

Tagliani star pano), and, according to Carboni, of Jesuit spies who were seeking a foxy, red-haired subversive. Carboni fled and his tracks were covered by his friends and Falcone waiters.

Presumably prompted by the demise of Louis-Philippe, on 19 March Pius IX introduced a statute welcomed even by Masonic Lodges. The successful Viennese revolt against Metternich that month inspired nationalist uprisings throughout north Italy where liberal and even Jewish patriots rallied to Pius IX's name.

On 25 March, under spring sunshine, the Colosseum was packed with a colourful, enthusiastic crowd: there were people wearing traditional costumes, soldiers in uniform, seminarians in the distinctive garb of their different colleges, and members of the religious orders, such as Capuchins and Dominicans, in their distinctive robes. Banners flew. Even a hostile observer, the Frenchman Alphonse Balleydier, acknowledged it was a 'sublime spectacle' worthy of a theatre.

Sermons were given in the amphitheatre twice weekly but this was political theatre, even if the main performer was a priest, Father Alessandro Gavazzi, devoted to the cause of Italian unity but in bad standing with the Church. Tall Gavazzi, of the Bamabite religious Order, wore a black mantle and a black habit emblazoned with a red, white and green cross. He threw his mantle about to effect and underlined his oratory by tossing his lank, black mane. It was said he was 'too eloquent not to be verbose' as he incited the audience to. fulfil their patriotic duty by a crusade against Austrians 'a hundred times more barbarous than the Muslims.' Saying that Christ had made the cross a pedestal of liberty, he called on Romans to 'break the chains of slavery'.

It was similar to the invitation to liberty that Carboni and his Giovine Italia comrades had exchanged at the Colosseum. If Carboni was not at the Colosseum when Gavazzi harangued the crowd, he surely would have heard of it. There were other speakers, including priests and two generals, before Gavazzi returned to the podium and called on the pope to bless the anti-Austrian crusade as he had blessed Italy. At this point Ciceruacchio appeared with Luigi, his 17-year-old son, whom he offered for the cause of national unification. It made a strong impact. Gavazzi's oratory built to a crescendo as he pledged before the cross, 'a symbol of liberty', that the crusaders would not return to Rome until the last of the barbarians (meaning Austrians) had been expelled. The crowd rose as one man. Holding their right hands outstretched towards the cross which stood in the middle of the Colosseum, they repeated, after Gavazzi, the vow to spend themselves for Italian liberty. It was a solemn pledge of solidarity.

Then they all marched uphill to the Quirinale palace for Pius IX's blessing, but he sent out a message that, as representative of a God of peace, he could not bless torches which could set Europe on fire. After negotiations, he eventually agreed to receive five representatives and blessed their banners on condition the troops remained defensive without crossing into Austrian territory. But this proviso was not broadcast.

The volunteers left Rome to fight against the Austrians in what they considered a holy war. Like crusaders, their flags and uniforms flaunted the cross. Mattia Montecchi was secretary to General Andrea Ferrari, commander of one of the two divisions, and Giovanni Battista Cattabeni had been one of the first to enrol. It was said that Pius IX himself had been a soldier but, in fact, for health reasons he had obtained exemption from military service. Even Mazzini advised his followers to support the pope's army, and King Carlo Alberto was co-operative. It seemed Pius could be the warrior-king who would unite Italy.

However, on 29 April Pius IX came out publicly against the war of independence being fought in his name. He was pope also of the Austrians. Soldiers who considered themselves his crusaders found they were denounced as rebels. Especially among the 9,000 troops of the two divisions of volunteers defending Vicenza, confusion and disillusionment were acute. Eventually the disgruntled first Legion returned to Rome from Vicenza singing 'we'll shit in Pius IX's tiara'.[3] In central Rome a right-wing priest-journalist was killed. Pius IX sought Swiss reinforcements. In the Pantheon at some time that year the ex-assistant at Holy Trinity, Raffaello Carboni, began a poem which, among other things, recommended excision of the cancer of the papacy.

The Minister for the Interior, Terenzio Mamiani, resigned when Pius IX replied evasively to his request to arm and ally with other Italian states against Austria. To replace him in a position which was virtually that of prime minister, Pius chose a Tuscan who lodged at the Hotel d'Inghilterra, Pellegrino Rossi, an aristocrat, jurist and economist who became a Swiss citizen, university lecturer and deputy before becoming French and moving into the top echelon of society there. France made him its ambassador to the Holy See. With the fall of Louis-Philippe, he was without a job until Pius made his offer. Rossi proposed a vigorous programme of reforms but the clergy were diffident, as he was a layman who wanted restrictions on their control of ecclesiastical property. The plebs were also diffident because he was a noble. All opposed his plan to increase taxes.

When, at 1 p.m. on 15 November, Rossi entered the Cancelleria building to expound his governmental programme, soldiers who had returned from Vicenza surrounded him and he was struck down by an assassin's knife. Ciceruacchio's son Luigi was thought to have been the killer. The Bostonian Margaret Fuller, a friend of Ralph Waldo Emerson who was reporting for the *New York Tribune,* found 'horrible justice' in the assassination.

Next day, the populace clashed with Swiss guards at the Quirinale, where the shouts were no longer *'Viva il papa'* but *'Viva la Repubblica'.* The cannon called 'San Pietro', which Alessandro Torlonia had donated to the Civic Guard, was rolled up from nearby piazza Pilotta to threaten the Quirinale entrance. Torlonia opened his stables and let the populace use his horses. During this demonstration, a church historian, Monsignor Giovanni Battista Palma, was shot dead as he stood near the pope at a Quirinale window. Pius IX had sought Palma's collaboration only a few months earlier and now blamed himself for his friend's death. The Consulta Palace opposite was occupied by soldiers returned from Vicenza who sought Cardinal Luigi Lambruschini, leader of the curial conservatives. Lambruschini survived by hiding in a haystack of the papal stables.

Two days later, Pius IX replaced the Swiss guards at the Quirinale with the Civic Guard and militarised police. On the 23rd, Circolo Popolare representatives freed Holy Office prisoners and prostitutes from St Michele prison. The following night, dressed simply as a priest, Pius IX fled south to Gaeta to place himself under the protection of King Ferdinand of Naples. Some months later he was to vest there as Benedictines two Australian Aboriginal teenagers, Francis Xavier Conaci and John Dirimera, who had been brought from New Norcia, Western Australia, by the Spanish Benedictine Rosendo Salvado to study in Italy.

It was a decade since Carboni's arrival in the pope's city when his eyes were still turned admiringly to the past. Rome had seemed not only unchanging but unchangeable, and the pope eternal. Now the pope had fled while Carboni was of the winning party. The past was paralysis; the current of history was moving again; the future was being invented daily. Its lineaments, however, were obscure.

At dawn on 9 February, the Constituent Assembly proclaimed that a Roman Republic replaced the pope's temporal power. The Assembly's executive committee was Carlo Armelline, Aurelio Salicetti and Carboni's friend Mattia Montecchi; their headquarters was at the Quirinale. Goffredo Mameli, a young Genoese poet, summoned Giuseppe Mazzini from London with a terse telegram: 'Rome Republic. Come.' As he entered Rome through Porta del Popolo on 5 March, Mazzini felt 'an electric shock … a spring of new life'. The Assembly gave him a triumphal reception: two weeks later Montecchi stepped down and Mazzini took his place as triumvir while Aurelio Saffi replaced Salicetti.

Carboni and other Giovine Italia members must have been satisfied to see their mentor virtually ruling Rome. The Republic introduced enlightened legislation including universal suffrage, which was practiced however only by males, abolition of the death penalty and freedom for all religions. But some Romans considered the Republic as a carnival, the brief period in which the normal order is reversed, chaos conquers the cosmos, the profane prevails over the sacred, the clown replaces the king. In fact, the Republic was not to last much longer than a carnival, just over five months. Carboni wrote later that the Roman Republic was badly handled, although without specifying the mistakes.[4] From a small room in the Quirinale, Mazzini showed moderation, declaring there were to be no attacks on wealth. But there were grave financial problems, pro-Republican and pro-papal violence, and threats of intervention by Austria, France, Spain and Naples.

The Catholic powers were competing to rescue the pope, and news arrived that in north Italy the Austrian Field Marshal Julius Jakob von Haynau was repressing insurgents. It was only a matter of time before the young Republic would be attacked. For the inevitable battle, the man who was to become, for Carboni, an even greater hero than Mazzini was at hand – Giuseppe Garibaldi, who had the allure of his successful South American guerrilla campaigns. His troops were stationed at Rieti but Garibaldi, elected as deputy, returned in February for the Assembly. He was carried into the assembly hall as his arthritic pains were excruciating.

Carboni's political education was proceeding apace. On 16 April the French Republic, which had been welcomed by Carboni, Montecchi and Cattabeni, decided to send troops to aid Pius IX. Louis Napoleon, despite being a former member of the Carbonari, wanted to appease French Catholics and precede Austria. Nine days later, 10,000 French troops under General Nicholas Oudinot landed at Civitavecchia.

The French were convinced that *'les Italiens ne se battent pas'* ('Italians won't fight'), but Mazzini was determined to baptise the Republic through the shedding of its defenders' blood; on the bloodstained rock of Rome he would build his nation. The city seemed ill-prepared to resist the French until Garibaldi's legionnaires arrived from Rieti, marching down the Corso barelegged, unkempt and sunburnt behind the bronze-bearded hero of Montevideo on a white horse. They lodged at San Silvestro convent after chasing away its nuns; Garibaldi's white horse was stabled at Villa Torlonia. Two days later Luciano Manara arrived at the head of 600 Lombard *bersaglieri* who had participated in a Milan uprising against the Austrians. One of them, an aristocrat, was a school friend of Carboni.[5] At Civitavecchia the *bersaglieri* had fallen into French hands, but were released on condition they remained neutral until 4 May, by which time the French expected to occupy Rome.

Manara wrote:

> The first impression most of us experienced on entering Rome was that of indefinable melancholy. Our own sad experience had rendered us only too alive to the first symptoms of dissolution in a government or in a city, and in Rome we recognised with grief the very same aspect which Milan had presented during the latter few months of its liberty. We seemed to observe the same overweening regard to trivial matters, whilst those of vital importance were neglected. There was the same superabundance of flags, of cockades, of party badges, the same clanking of swords along the streets, and those various and varied officer's uniforms, no two alike, but all fitter for a stage than for military service; epaulettes thrown, as it were, by chance on the shoulders of individuals whose very faces seemed to declare their unfitness to wear them; whilst, in addition, the applause of an unwarlike population, echoing from the windows and coffee-houses, seemed to indicate only too clearly we had arrived just in time for the last scene of some absurd comedy ... this array of warriors in glittering helmets,

with double-barrelled guns and belts armed with daggers, reconciled us but little to the scanty numbers of real, well-drilled soldiers.[6]

Manara and his men, depressed by the comic opera scenes, were amazed at the transformation when, that evening, drums announced the French forces descending the via Aurelia:

> ... in all the streets of the Porta Angelica and Porta Cavalleggeri neighbourhood were bivouacked small but admirable line regiments, two magnificent carabineer battalions, with four or five parks of field artillery; two cavalry regiments were stationed in Piazza Navona; numerous bodies of volunteers kept watch on the walls; and the whole National Guard were in perfect order at their respective quarters. Then, as might be expected, the fantastic costumes were forgotten and everyone who wore the national colours grasped the weapon which was to defend him. We passed the night in St Peter's great square enchanted with the spectacle ...

The 9,000 troops who had pleasantly surprised Manara gave an unpleasant surprise to the French when they attacked the city's massive but untested 17th-century walls.

In *Buffi e Buffoni*, Carboni included a scene near Porta San Pancrazio on the Janiculum that day as Garibaldi, Goffredo Mameli, Ciceruacchio and others prepared troops to repulse the French. Carboni gave himself an unheroic role: in the nearby *Casa dei Quattro Venti* (House of the Four Winds), he was teaching Mameli's ode 'Fratelli d'Italia' to the same Sacred Heart girls who had come to the Falcone trattoria the night he fled. The eight girls were preparing to work as an ambulance corps. In fact, during the French assault, women carried away fallen defenders; the Republic's health services were directed by Mazzini's close collaborator, a Milanese surgeon Agostino Bertani.

Mattia Montecchi observed the French advance from St Peter's dome. Oudinot, who probably studied Letarouilly's 'Plan topographique de Rome Moderne', decided to enter the city through Porta Pertosa. The advance guards had as their reference a Vatican tower above Porta Pertosa. In clammy heat, at 11.30 a.m., the scouts neared a turn in the road only 100 yards from Porta Pertosa. Two cannons on the walls opened fire. The French, who had ten cannons in all, unlimbered one to respond, but saw, with dismay, that Porta Pertosa did not exist. Although still shown on Letarouilly's map, for years it had been walled up.

At his observation post on St Peter's dome, Montecchi could not imagine the French intended to enter Rome through a non-existent gate. From the dome at 12.45 p.m. he sent a telegram to the Triumvirate at the Quirinale:

> It seems to be a feint to tire out our forces. The most attacked bastion is the last one where our troops removed two shells. I do not know where they have put them. The enemy's cannons are set-up there. A few French have withdrawn from Villa Pamphili and are moving from the other side. Nothing new. Some scouts should be sent out from Porta Pertosa. If I'm not needed here, I'm coming down in a few minutes.[7]

While continuing to fire at Vatican ramparts from behind cover, the French sent other troops north and south along the walls. Oudinot had been wrongly informed that supporters were strong enough to open Porta Angelica near Castel Sant'Angelo. To reach it, the troops had to follow the Vatican walls northwards, exposing themselves to fire from defenders; a French surgeon said the slaughter was worse than anything in the African campaigns. The main force went south towards Porta Cavalleggeri, which entailed descending a steep hill through vineyards under fire from the walls and batteries on the bastions. As the walls curved into Porta Cavalleggeri, as well as it being in a valley, the French were fully exposed on either side of the gate.

Garibaldi, who had watched the Pertusa and Cavalleggeri assaults, now took the offensive. His troops had to cross narrow via Aurelia Antica where they met about 1,000 French infantry advancing to protect the main force. Carboni's university battalion friends, crying 'Death to Pius IX' and 'Death to the French-Croats', (the formerly admired French were now identified with Austria's hated Croatian troops) bore the brunt of the first attack on via Aurelia and in Villa Doria Pamphili. Garibaldi's Legion (the 'Montevideo Tigers') and the Roman Legion backed them in a fierce, man-to-man clash. Andrea Aguyar, a black giant of African origin who had been Garibaldi's attendant since the guerrilla leader had freed him from slavery in Uruguay, captured some French with a lasso. The French captured a Barnabite Order priest, Father Ugo Bassi, who was both a Garibaldian chaplain and soldier. By 5 p.m., after almost six hours fighting, the French were put to flight, with 500 killed and wounded against 200 Roman victims. When the tide turned against the French column, the Republicans sallied forth from Porta Cavalleggeri also and, to avoid being trapped, Oudinot retreated. Mazzini restrained Garibaldi who wanted to chase the French into the sea.

The French had mistakenly imagined that occupying Rome would be little more than a tourist jaunt. The Romans made it a tourist jaunt for the 365 French prisoners; they freed them and took them to admire the Colosseum and St Peter's, which were illuminated to celebrate victory. (The French troops had been told they would be defending the Roman Republic against Austrians and Neapolitan Bourbons.) Carts went from street to street to the cry of 'Bandages for the wounded'. Holy Trinity, across the Tiber from the Janiculum, had been requisitioned as a military hospital.

In battles at Palestrina and Velletri, Garibaldi then drove back Neapolitan forces which had reached the hills overlooking Rome. In the same days, Austrian forces occupied Bologna and the Marches. The French signed an armistice with the Roman Republic and Ferdinand de Lesseps, the future builder of the Suez Canal, negotiated a treaty which was ready on 31 May. However, for Louis Napoleon the honour of French arms was now at stake. Oudinot requested reinforcements and refused to sign the armistice. He announced he would resume hostilities on 4 June but, with 20,000 reinforcements, launched a surprise attack on the 3rd. The Romans sang a parody of the Marseillaise: *'Allons enfants de sacristie / le jour de honte est arrivé'* ('Come on, children of the sacristy / the day of shame has arrived'). Dogged defence on the Janiculum held the French at bay for a whole month until further resistance was impossible.

Badly wounded in the knee during the 4 June battle for Villa Corsini, the poet Goffredo Mameli had been taken to Holy Trinity hospital, where he lay near a wounded Genoese friend who was likewise close to Garibaldi, Nino Bixio. Agostino Bertani, head of the Republican medical services, amputated Mameli's leg, but a month later he died of gangrene.

Carboni, whose commanding officer was Luigi Salviati, would have been a useful interpreter for the many foreigners fighting for the Republic; he later mentioned a Captain Forbes among the Republican forces.[8] Carboni claimed that while acting as interpreter, under the orders of Montecchi transmitted by Cattabeni, he was lamed by French bullets and also suffered hand and forehead wounds. Until the end of his life he was troubled intermittently by his left leg. He was to write a poem allegedly inspired by standing above a fallen French soldier.[9]

At 6 p.m. on 2 August, with the French about to enter the city, Garibaldi assembled his men in St Peter's Square. He had refused the offer of a United States passport. After promising forced marches, hunger, thirst, battles and death, he left the city by the Lateran gate, followed by his pregnant wife Anita in soldier's garb, Ciceruacchio with his two sons, Father Bassi, Ignacio Bueno, a Brazilian who carried Garibaldi when the pain of his rheumatoid arthritis became unbearable, and 4,000 troops.

Other Republicans scattered in all directions. The Bourbon and papal coats-of-arms, which had been removed to avoid destruction by the Republicans, appeared once again on the Farnese Palace facade. It was no city for a Garibaldian who had already been arrested twice by pontifical police. On 29 August, at the height of summer, Carboni had recovered sufficiently to leave Rome.[10] He knew France and French but could not return there; not only had the French attacked the Roman Republic, but Parisian left-wingers who protested against this had been imprisoned. He would go instead to Germany.

He was 31 when he slipped out of the city that had become his only just before he had to leave. Although his participation in the Republic's defence had won him the right to consider himself Roman, he had not left his mark on Rome as had Raphael. Rather, the city had left its imprint on him. Although his brother was a priest, in Rome Carboni had become vehemently anti-clerical. Rome had meant the peace of Holy Trinity before his troubles began, his education by Spada, the excitement of the ideas of Montecchi and Cattabeni. Rome was the Falcone trattoria, his girlfriend Angela, amiable Monsignor Vincent Eyre at the English College, early morning mist on the Tiber, the first sight of red-shirted Garibaldi, Sacred Heart girls, flickering lamps in the night streets, the bull game, Torlonia receptions … he had become a man in the city whose architecture and memories measured mens' grandeur and transience.

He even owed knowledge of the language which would open Germany to him to the Palazzo Spada's custodian Ferdinand Cormann. As he travelled north, perhaps he thought of the hunting dog device on the Palazzo Spada facade which referred to the Lord as a pillar of fire guiding the Hebrews. He was their guide at all times. He had comforted a wandering people, He could comfort Carboni. In his fashion, Carboni was loyal to his faith and always to the city he was leaving.

Go North, Young Man

Hanover

Carboni visited several German cities, including Frankfurt, where he qualified as a teacher of Italian,[1] Berlin, and Dresden, where he saw performances of Goethe's *Faust*,[2] from which, in Rome, he had absorbed both German and dramaturgy. Finally, he settled in Hanover, becoming a close friend of Alfred von Seefeld and Edward Wedekind, a local judge. He also had a woman friend Anna.[3]

Fair-haired, blue-eyed von Seefeld, whose heavy brows and strong nose made his bony face pensive, had begun to study the book trade in preparation for a shop he was to open. Born in Berlin in 1825, von Seefeld had grown up in Hanover, but left secondary school before completing his studies. At 19 he already knew some Italian: he wrote in Italian the title page of what was to be a five-act play, *The Parasite – The art of making a fortune*, but proceeded no further. Von Seefeld later wrote travel books about Spain and Crete. He no doubt practised his Italian with Carboni, with whom he had other interests in common. Carboni may not have shared von Seefeld's enthusiasm for gymnastics, but both were apprentice playwrights, both appreciated the arts and opposed repression. Von Seefeld had collected pamphlets by Berlin and Hanoverian revolutionaries of 1849, and in that year participated in pro-free assembly and pro-free press demonstrations outside Elector Ernst Augustus's fortress-like residence.[4]

Hanover, with a population of 50,000, was the capital of largely agricultural Lower Saxony. The Market Church and a defence tower indicated the importance the town had acquired by the early 14th century. Outward-sloping facades of three- or four-storey edifices, in which painted beams formed a bold pattern against white, constituted a distinctive domestic architecture from the 16th century. Solid burghers added some 19th-century commercial Gothic, but the military imprint was strongest of all, with the barracks of the Royal Guard and the Jaeger Regiment, the Military and General Staff Academies, War Ministry, Armoury, Cadet College, Military Hospital and, soaring proudly, a Waterloo Column commemorating Hanoverian troops' participation in that battle. Like Duke Federico's Urbino, Hanover was famed as a source of mercenary soldiers.

From 1714, when Hanover's Elector George Louis acceded to the British throne as George I, until 1837, Hanover had been run as an aristocratic-military princedom. In 1837, with Victoria's coronation, the personal union between the two kingdoms ceased. As the Hanoverian law of succession precluded women, the kingdom of Hanover went to George III's fifth son, Ernst August. He had abolished the renewed constitution of 1833 as if convinced that the alliance with Great Britain should have saved Hanover from the French Revolution's pernicious ideas. But the chain reaction from the February 1848 Parisian revolt, and the protests in which von Seefeld participated, had forced the virtually absolute ruler to concede reforms and another constitution.

Hanover's rulers had long been coarse, dull and occasionally brutal. Their outlook, the aristocratic privileges, the military spirit and old customs could not be swept aside by a mere constitution. Early in 1850, when Carboni was in Hanover, there was tension between the new law and old attitudes. The opposition to beak-nosed, balding, white-whiskered Ernst August was tinged with anti-English spirit. In what had been, for 113 years, virtually an overseas province of Great Britain, British influence was widely evident and sometimes resented. The British Continental Gas Company had the street-lighting contract; other English firms were active; inhabitants of the Workers' Colony, presumably skilled people brought in to set up industries, rejoiced in names such as Addison, Barker, Hollingsworth, Nightingale and Young.

The tendency to criticise England distinguished Hanoverian liberals from their Italian counterparts who knew England as a refuge for exiles, a potential ally against both France and the papacy, and home of a legal system which they considered a model of fair play. Carboni must have sympathised fully, however, with the Hanoverians' struggle against an aging despot (Ernst August was 79 in 1850) and the movement to merge Hanover into a larger nation-state. Here again, as in Italy, the enemy was Austria.

In Hanover, Carboni resumed work on a poem he had begun a decade earlier when first influenced or, in his own phrase, 'scalded and stained' by Mazzini's message. Its title announced its theme: 'Nowadays there is no love'.[5] It lamented that, as all are intent on their own interests, the rich, even if Turks, are revered while Christ can call in vain for help. Evidently indignant at Austrian repression in Poland, Carboni wrote: 'Poland is strangled! ... why rave? / For the dead, you dig a grave ...'

Poland could be equated with Italy, Italy with Poland. The demand for independence and liberty was one; in more subdued terms, the same fight was being fought by von Seefeld and others in Hanover. But it was not going well for, after success in 1848, the liberal cause suffered severe setbacks. By 1850 many radicals and liberals had abandoned politics, and some emigrated. Little could be contributed by those, like Carboni, who were almost without means. Making ends meet was a constant struggle. Carboni may have found employment in Bruchhausen, outside Hanover, for it was there he obtained a good conduct clearance dated 7 June 1850, before setting out, through Hamburg, for London.[6] His poem 'Nowadays there is no love' criticised those intent on their own interests, whereas Carboni simply sought to survive by leaving for the land ruled by Victoria, who had been a member of the Hanover royal house. In other words, he was not a rich Turk but a poor Christian.

London

After the Roman Republic fell, many Republicans immediately sought refuge in London, which for decades had sheltered European political exiles. Whigs had opened Holland House and Lansdowne House to the exiles and thrown parties and receptions for them. Some exiled priests aroused interest as Inquisition victims, became Anglicans and, as a form of initiation, married. But as the allure of exiles had diminished by the time Carboni arrived, the competition for sympathy, attention and employment was intense.

Carboni had improved his German in Hanover, polished his French in Paris years earlier, and Monsignor Vincent Eyre, who was now a chaplain in Chelsea, had given him in Rome a good grounding in English. On 21 June 1851, Carboni qualified at the highest level in Italian, French and English and at the second level in Spanish and German at the College of Preceptors in Bloomsbury Square.[7]

One of Carboni's examiners was Antonio Panizzi, who had taught at London University before becoming the British Museum's assistant librarian; he was to establish its Reading Room. Even though under death sentence for his Carbonari activities in Modena, Panizzi had won acceptance by the English establishment. However, he was unlikely to give a leg-up to the red-haired polyglot, for he had to defend himself from envious English convinced they would be more suitable in the British Museum, and beat off compatriots who might slow his social rise. An Italian exile described Panizzi as irritated by 'the swarm of impostors and frauds who claimed to be Italian and political exiles.'[8]

Carboni lived at 4 Castle Court in a warren of lanes off Cornhill. It was in the centre of the City, the square mile bounded by former Roman walls on the north bank of the Thames where financial services and trading companies were concentrated. Other Castle Court inhabitants were a boot-maker, a shellfishmonger, a notary and two brokers.[9] The ground floor of Carboni's four-storey lodging house was occupied by Simpson's Tavern, whose oak panelling and half-glass facade dated from the mid-18th century. Almost directly opposite was the George and Vulture Tavern. It may have been in one of these pubs that Carboni imbibed 'acid disguised as French wine'.[10] Within a few yards of Simpson's was a cosy 17th-century coffee house where Carboni could compare the local brew with the coffee of Rome.

Carboni's Castle Court environs had the intimacy of Roman streets, but London, with 1.5 million inhabitants, was by far the most populous and extensive European city. The Euston, Waterloo and Paddington railway stations had initiated a transport system which progressively reduced the central city population while increasing that of the suburbs.

Although commerce thrived in the City, as translator and sworn interpreter, Carboni had to range far and wide to make a living. He complained he had to 'take off my hat half a dozen times, and walk from east to west before I could earn one pound'.[11]

While interpreter at the new Pentonville prison, Carboni brushed against the tragedy of deportation when the least infringement of the law could mean transportation to the world's end, Australia. With its 540 separate cells and eighteen-month periods of solitary confinement, Pentonville was a model for similar prisons. It attracted the interest of Italian exiles, such as Carboni's future boss, Antonio Mordini, who visited it in June 1851. In Pentonville, Carboni assisted a gentlemanly young German who, he claimed, had been duped by a Jew at the Deutsche. National Kaffeehaus near Leicester Square and then, because penniless, had resorted to stealing. The German's distraught mother and sister came from Berlin to bid him farewell as he was being banished to Australia.[12]

In 1850 a spell of sickness had forced Carboni to pawn his mother's pearl ring with Jews in Bishopsgate.[13] A few days later he saw a headline 'Disastrous Fire'. Rushing to the prostitute-thronged streets of Bishopsgate, he found only charred remains of the pawnbroker's. Carboni's conviction that the owners had arranged the fire to collect insurance sharpened his distrust of Jews.

Carboni complained he was rarely invited into English homes. He was familiar with Previtali's hostelry and other locales where Italian exiles gathered. He had a good friend in Count Carlo Arrivabene, who had taken part in a Milanese anti-Austrian uprising. Arrivabene survived by giving Italian lessons, but later taught at London University and became a journalist. Nurtured on Mazzinian revolutionary ideals, Carboni had little sympathy with London Chartist campaigns for universal suffrage. However he would have appreciated the large turn-outs to support European freedom-fighters, such as the Hungarian Louis Kossuth, and the anti-Austrian demonstrations that took place when, in 1850, Field Marshal Haynau visited the city. Haynau's draconian measures in Hungary were notorious, but Carboni would have known him better as 'the hyena of Brescia,' who had brutally suppressed an 1848 uprising there.

Unlike Mattia Montecchi who, after a period in Switzerland, reached London with Mazzini in mid-1850, Carboni was not absorbed by political activity. Thomas Carlyle's wife had found a house in Chelsea where 'Pippo' Mazzini, also known as 'Uncle', Montecchi and other exiles lodged. Mazzini, in a series of articles for the *People's Journal,* trenchantly criticised communism as illiberal, intolerant and destined to produce dictatorships. He planned insurrections, but prospects for Italian nationalism were bleak. Carboni's new hero Garibaldi was in New York, about to set off for Callao, Peru, whence he would take a guano cargo to China. Pius IX was once more happily reigning in Rome; moreover, he nominated Thomas Wiseman cardinal and, amid protests that he was parcelling up England for Catholic bishops, re-established the English Catholic hierarchy.

Little by little the struggle for Italian unity must have seemed a fading ideal, whereas the battle for money was a daily necessity. Wealth was flaunted on all sides, but Carboni lacked the key to it.

There was a sense of excitement for Carboni, as for 'Pippo' Mazzini and other Italian. exiles, in a new palace, not ducal as in Urbino but Crystal, described as 'an arch of lucid glass' more splendid than anything Kubla Khan decreed.[14] It had been built in only seven months from October 1850 (at a cost of £79,800) for the First Universal Exhibition of the 'Works of Art and Industry of all the Nations of the World'. The Crystal Palace, which occupied sixteen acres in Hyde Park, was not deserted as the Urbino palace of Carboni's boyhood, but full, as one observer wrote, of a 'myriad wonderful things'. It housed 13,937 exhibits.

Six hundred choirboys intoned Handel's *Hallelujah Chorus* when, on 1 May 1851 in the presence of 25,000 invited guests with another 400,000 people outside, Queen Victoria opened the Exhibition. As the royal procession was being formed, a sumptuously garbed Chinaman appeared from nowhere and prostrated himself before the Queen. Victoria smiled cautiously, for the prostrate Chinaman was an inscrutable mystery – imperial ambassador, rich merchant or ... ? To use the *Gentleman's Magazine* description of Victoria, the 'delicious creature' ordered a place be found for the Chinaman with the diplomatic corps. Later it was discovered he was merely a publicity-seeker with the unlikely name of He Sing. Each day, for a shilling a head, He Sing showed people over his junk moored in the Thames.

The episode probably struck a chord with Carboni, for his 'Voltairean bile' had been stirred by an incident involving a Chinese junk in the Thames. Puritans, Methodists and Presbyterians, Carboni wrote, had come to London in the name of the Israelite God Jehovah to protest against adoration of idols in a pagoda on the junk. But the idols, Carboni noted, had been made in Birmingham and Chinese money had been accepted for them.[15] Scornful of what he considered was the protectors' hypocrisy, but also intrigued by the exotic idols, Carboni began planning a stage farce.

There was an element of religion and hypocrisy also in the Great Exhibition, which he attended.[16] Two days after the opening, Victoria wrote to her uncle Leopold calling it 'the greatest day in our history ... Many cried, and all felt troubled and impressed with devotional feelings'. Here the productive process, represented in some cases by machines disguised as gothic churches or Egyptian temples, seemed as gratuitous as a work of art. The Crystal Palace was the world's biggest monstrance.

This new place of worship drew six million pilgrims although open little more than five months. Farm hands in smocks incredulously inspected the American McCormick reaper. Cranes, hydraulic presses, locomotives, telegraphic equipment competed with curiosities such as a stuffed elephant, a doctor's walking stick with an inbuilt enema, a chair chiselled in a block of English coal, and an air-conditioned hat. They inspired wonder and provided instruction for 'manufacturers and artisans of all classes'. Initially entrance cost five shillings, but subsequently for four days a week this was reduced to a shilling (the organisers cleared £180,000 profit). The Exhibition was closed on Sundays: competition with other religions could not be too blatant.

What was worshipped at the Crystal Palace? Progress: England and its machines promised perpetual progress. 'Endless progression, ever increasing in rapidity ... is the destined lot of the human race', forecast *The Economist*. But the dark satanic mills were not manufacturing sweetness and light. Blacking factories exploited children; prostitutes cried from street to street; some hospitals were slaughterhouses.

The transparent temple celebrated Britain's pre-eminence in the industrial age, even though the Irish and others did not always appreciate the boon of Pax Britannica. In his 'May Day Ode' written for the Exhibition opening, W.M. Thackeray aptly described the engines displayed as 'trophies of her [Britain's] bloodless war'. In the long peace since Waterloo, by winning trade and industrial wars, Britain had become the world's wealthiest nation. Although internationalism was exalted and half the exhibitors were foreign, because of its prominent role the British Empire was celebrated at the Crystal Palace.

The Gospel preached at the Crystal Palace temple reflected the mystique of merchandising, exalting a universal brotherhood in which free trade would know no boundaries. It was a glowing tribute to globalisation. The solemn rendering to God of what was Caesar's by affirming that His were the ideas, His the materials, His the product, converted the exhibits into cargo which had descended from on high. The Crystal Palace exhibition, as commentators repeated, was 'magic'. The sleight-in-hand was the message that there could be brass without muck.

Carboni might have asked if God was an Englishman. Perhaps he suspected, as he was later to write in a different context, that although Rome had been given the keys of the kingdom, 'Great Britain changed the padlocks'.[17] 'Whatever you do, make money',[18] he wrote, was a lesson he learnt in England, but it was surely in the Torlonia bank primer. Eking out a precarious living as a linguistic middleman, he must have sought the code to the cargo. A hint was provided by the exhibition at the Crystal Palace of minute gold specimens from Australia, but it was only in October 1851 that news reached London of a gold strike at Ophir, New South Wales.

Carboni set a scene of his play *La Santola* in the Crystal Palace in 1851, with the organ 'Alexandre' playing as the crowd sings *God Save the Queen*. The Carboni-figure Pastorello is invited by an Italian prince, whose daughter he wants to marry, to leave London to earn enough money to support a princess. The prince offers the reluctant Pastorello a berth to unspecified goldfields, any old goldfield in either California or Australia where 'gold nuggets are fished in those streams like stones in the gutters of Grenelles' and, again, 'at every fourth step you stumble on gold nuggets'.

Early in 1852 London heard of fabulous finds in Ballarat and Bendigo. What had been founded as a prison was built on gold! There was a new topic for conversation at Carboni's coffee bar, at Simpson's Tavern and the George and Vulture Tavern. The news excited the banking houses around Castle Court; within a year a *Mining Gazette* was being published there and in adjacent Birchin Lane the Austral Mining Company was established.

Carboni tore an illustration of Golden Point, Ballarat, from the *Illustrated London News*; gold galore! That was where he was headed. But so were tens of thousands. The Victorian gold finds recalled those of California a few years earlier which had enabled many to make their fortunes. It seemed that half London was marching to the rhythm of the Virginia cradles, a contraption for washing soil from gold, at 16,000 miles distance. Clerks, shop assistants, artisans, frustrated Chartists bought mattocks and spades and begged shipbrokers to provide them with a passage, any passage, on a ship bound for Australia. Somehow Carboni found one on the *Prince Albert* in the second half of 1852. Urbino was shaped like a ship but this was Carboni's first long sea voyage: he would spend months on a journey in which some perished. But gold lust transformed men. Carboni was a new man already; no longer a political exile, but an avid migrant.

Australia: Great Works

No stopping place

Hobson's Bay, the innermost reaches of Port Phillip, was packed with clippers when Carboni arrived late in 1852, about the same time as Garibaldi, returning from Canton to Callao, stopped at Three Hummock Island in Bass Strait between Melbourne and Tasmania. Each day for much of the year, several clippers had dropped anchor off Melbourne after a voyage of fifteen weeks or more from Europe. The first steamships had begun to arrive also, cutting the voyage to ten weeks. The isolated outpost had become a magnet for enterprise, the world capital of greed in what promised to be a bigger and better version of the 1848–49 Californian rush. As Friedrich Engels recognised, writing to Karl Marx in August 1852, the Californian and Australian gold discoveries were two cases not foreseen in the Communist Manifesto; they would absorb surplus European population and create new markets, providing lymph for capitalism and decreasing the likelihood of revolution.

The spars of ships abandoned in Hobson's Bay stood gaunt against the wide sky, for the crews, usually paid £2 a month, had gone after gold. Seeing the marooned ships, an Englishman commented that even if most of the gold had been picked up, it could not have been carried away; the marauders had left for the quarry. As the 2,000-ton clippers could not negotiate the shallow Yarra Yarra River to the wharves abutting city streets, passengers were unloaded onto row boats which took them to a beach or eight miles upstream to the city. Carboni, eager to rip gold from the soil, complained he was charged £5 to land his luggage, which was only the first of a series of rip-offs when he fell into the 'unspeakable clutches of a shoal of land-sharks who ... swarmed the Yarra Yarra wharves'.[1]

He was also surprised there were no poor waiting for the coppers he had set aside. These were valuable lessons. Luck was needed not only to find gold but also to find someone to carry your luggage, and the carrier could become as rich as any master.

In the three years to 1852, Melbourne's population had trebled to 25,000 (of the 77,000 in Victoria), placing an acute strain on accommodation, especially as the town was without sewerage. In 1852, with the arrival of 100,000, the colony's population more than doubled. A canvas town had sprung up in Emerald Hill (South Melbourne) to house the transient gold seekers. Many suffered 'colonial small pox' because of the raids. of persistent mosquitoes.

Named after the British Prime Minister Lord Melbourne, the town had been founded only in 1835, but already in 1839 the Melbourne Club, preserve of the squattocracy, was established in Collins Street, which had shops, banks, hotels, churches, offices, stores and a flour mill. The city's administrative centre was in the William–Bourke Streets area. More than fifty per cent of the population was Church of England, but there were strong Catholic and Presbyterian communities. St James Anglican church, the Scots church and St Francis Catholic church were functioning by 1846. Although it was compared to an inferior English town because it was unpaved, unlit and muddy, traces of future developments were discernible; in 1846 land had been set aside for Botanic Gardens worthy of a major city; squatters were building town houses in Toorak, St Kilda and Brighton were pleasant seaside villages.

In 1850 the Port Phillip District was separated from New South Wales to create the colony of Victoria. As part of the celebration, the Yarra Yarra River was spanned by Prince's Bridge. Melbourne seemed assured of steady progress as capital of a vast sheep run, but the following year gold was found at Clunes and Warrandyte. Separation from New South Wales, followed immediately by gold strikes, created conditions for rapid socio-institutional changes. From spring 1851 a fearful epidemic raged, whose symptoms were recklessness and a conviction that circumstances could be transformed from one moment to the next: it was gold fever which threatened social order. When gold, in three drays each drawn by six horses, first arrived at the Treasury in William Street, all the survey department clerks left for the diggings. So many government workers deserted that salaries under £250 a year were increased by fifty per cent. To retain a few police and prison wardens, their pay was raised, respectively, to six and seven shillings a day. The sale of Virginia cradles to wash gold dirt was so brisk one commentator remarked that Melbourne seemed a huge lying-in settlement minus the babies. An undertaker was said to have used his stock of coffins to make Virginia cradles.

Unwashed, unshaven diggers appeared in Melbourne filling horse troughs with champagne, buying the best theatre boxes, lighting pipes with banknotes or eating them between bread and butter. 'This place is inevitably and irrevocably ruined', claimed the London *Times* correspondent, for, in his opinion, the wool industry was being wrecked 'to load with undeserved wealth the very dregs and off scourings of European civilization', men 'who can find no better use for £5 notes than to smoke them instead of tobacco'.

Servants walked out on their masters: the Lieutenant-Governor Charles La Trobe had to groom and feed his horses while the Anglican bishop's wife, Mrs Perry, was 'fagged' with curry-combing the horses, cooking, nursing and house-cleaning. Vandemonians (the word derived from an earlier name for Tasmania but was applied to all delinquents), headed for Melbourne; crime rapidly increased with daylight hold-ups even in the major thoroughfare, St Kilda Road. Especially in the Little Bourke Street–Flinders Lane underworld area, rough-house taverns and brothels thrived. It seemed normal society might disappear down the mine shafts. Labourers concluded that their picks and shovels would be more gainfully employed on the goldfields; barmen decided they could make more from solid than from liquid gold; even children set out for the gold gleaming beyond the Keilor plains.

In a pamphlet, the Victorian Chief Justice William a Beckett asked the Almighty to rescue men from the 'unholy hunger' which tempted Christians to exult in Mammon's sway. He deplored that gold had made men leave the 'legitimate highway of history', dispense with obedience and, enriched, give rein to their passions. Capital had been needed by pastoralists, not so much for their £10 annual-licence fee, but for acquiring flocks and herds and managing the huge runs. But on the goldfields, particularly in the first phase, little was needed apart from brawn and luck. In the course of a day, a battler could become a rich man. Ideals of steady wage-earning, or a social hierarchy based on birth and background, were subverted. What would become of thrift and industry if people were diverted from what were called 'their proper and more certain avocations'? There was a further, if generally unperceived, threat to the social order: many of the gold-seekers were well-educated and most had not been despatched to Australia, but chose to come. They expected civil rights and could protest articulately if these were denied.

By mid-1852 some were returning from the goldfields because wealth, 'although tantalisingly near, for most remained illusory. Nevertheless, stories of huge nuggets being unearthed gripped imaginations. Ten million ounces of gold were escorted to Melbourne in 1852, but food was scarce and prices soared. The money supply dried up. The Legislative Council had the temerity to petition London for a Melbourne Mint, but until it was established in 1869, gold made the long haul to London for minting. Topsy-turvy conditions rendered government arduous. 'The whole structure of society and the whole machinery of government is dislocated', complained Charles La Trobe, never a strong satrap.

La Trobe, a dedicated member of the Moravian Church, was intended for the ministry but became a teacher and mountaineer. He had published travel journals of Switzerland, where he was educated, and North America, where he joined forces with another author, Washington Irving, who was to describe him as 'a man of a thousand accomplishments: a botanist, a geologist, a hunter of beetles and butterflies; in short, a complete virtuoso'. After reporting for the British government on the conditions of emancipated slaves in the West Indies, in 1839 La Trobe had been appointed superintendent of the Port Phillip District. Although cultured and well-intentioned, he was not equipped to handle a rapidly changing society. Often slow to reach decisions, perhaps because he was waiting for the Lord to enlighten him, he was subject to scathing criticism by the merchant class and press who saw him as indecisive. He had not sought the Lieutenant-Governorship when, in August 1850, representative government was granted. In December 1852 he tendered his resignation; the *Argus* newspaper ran a standing advertisement: 'WANTED, a governor, apply to the people of Victoria'.

This 'extraordinary advertisement' caught the eye of Carboni, who described himself as 'a new chum in want of employment' as if he might consider the governorship. There was little point in staying in costly Melbourne, but he did have one firm and influential friend there, William Archer. Born in London in 1825, Archer was the elder son of a general dealer who, William wrote, spent his days 'walking all over London, laboriously doing nothing, in making what he calls bargains'.[2] Perhaps Carboni had met Archer in London;

there was a tenuous link between them. In 1841 frail, passionate Archer had converted to Catholicism under the guidance of Bishop Thomas Wiseman, rector of Rome's English College when Carboni's English teacher Vincent Eyre studied there. In a letter to Archer, Carboni was to refer to 'our dear Monsignor W.V. Eyre'.[3] Eyre may have put them in contact.

Statistics was the new science of the 1840s, hailed as a social panacea. For two years William Archer worked as statistician under Francis Nelson, manager of the London Medical, Invalid and General Assurance. At an annual salary of £50, he supported his parents and younger brother Alfred. Early in 1849 Archer became managing secretary, at £300 a year, of the newly established Catholic Assurance company. Science and his new faith were working nicely in harness.

Archer, who began work at 11, was concerned about his younger brother Alfred, for:

> he is nearly fourteen, and what he is most fit for, I know not. He loves reading, and seems to be ready at drawing, but he excels neither in writing nor in arithmetic, and without these, no youth who has to make his way in the world can possibly succeed now-a-days. But I shall not give him over yet, though his dullness is a hard trial – may God bless him and my endeavours for him!

Caroline Chisholm, in London in connection with her Family Colonisation Loan Society, adjudged dull Alfred 'just the boy for a Colonist'. In fact, Alfred wanted to migrate, for he would 'rather struggle in Australia for competence than secure it easily here ...' He wished to 'live in the open air and live a natural life as the Patriarchs did of old'. On his fifteenth birthday, 30 March 1850, Alfred set out to become a shepherd in Australia. He had 'upwards of a hundred of excellent works [books] of all descriptions', tools, ironmongery, several new suits and £3.10.

The re-establishment of the Catholic hierarchy in England in October 1850 had aroused hostility. It was construed as 'papal aggression', and Cardinal Wiseman's exultant pastoral 'From out of the Flaminian Gate', which spoke of his jurisdiction over 'the counties of Middlesex, Hertford and Essex ...', aggravated the 'awful state of excitement'. At York an effigy of Pio Nono (Pius IX), bearing the legend 'Oh No Pio No No', replaced Guy Fawkes.

Lord Winchelsea urged the government to declare war on the Papal States. The *Times* thundered, 'is it, then, here in Westminster, among ourselves and by the English throne, that an Italian priest is to parcel out the spiritual dominion of this country?'

Catholics felt besieged; hostility damaged the Catholic Life Assurance company, and William wrote to his brother Alfred, distressed and lonely in Port Phillip, that he might join him. Archer imagined that in Melbourne, of all places, there would be religious tolerance. Evidently he was unaware that Orangemen and Catholics had already clashed there or that the Anglican Bishop Charles Perry despised the Catholic Church as 'apostate and idolatrous'. In mid-1851, to talk about his brother, William went to the Bull and Mouth Hotel in Aldersgate Street to meet Bishop James Goold of Melbourne. Goold told William that he had found Alfred a 'person of very good disposition'.[4]

Concern for Alfred, as well as the downturn in the Catholic Life Assurance's fortunes, persuaded Archer to try his luck in Victoria. He collected books 'for mental food – in case I should ever be where there is no other store but my own'. Indeed he felt predestined to leave England:

> I have a strong presentiment that my lot is not cast here – that I shall have to play another part, in another clime. Is it to help in the Foundation of an Empire? Is it to die a poor unknown? God knows! To his holy keeping I recommend myself.

He sailed for Melbourne on the *Diadem,* taking his parents with him. Archer underwent a sea change: by the time he arrived in Melbourne, in November 1852, he had filled out, become tanned and sported a moustache. Carboni visited him at his Richmond home and borrowed money, leaving as surety a swordstick. After an informed letter on statistics to the *Herald,* Archer was asked to establish within the Department of the Colonial Secretary a Registrar General's office. All statistical information about the colony, and much else, was to flow to this friend of Carboni.

Nuggets galore

With a group, Carboni set out for Ballarat at Christmas 1852. Despite the heat, they traversed the almost 100 miles through Geelong loaded with tents and tools, part of a crowded pilgrimage with other hopefuls, bullock and horse drays, donkey, dog and goat carts. After the initial rush to Ballarat, many diggers had headed for new fields at Mount Alexander and Bendigo. Ballarat's population had plummeted but, unlike most other fields, it never emptied altogether. With new finds on the site, aptly called Eureka, and in Canadian Gully, once again the population was on the upswing, topping 5,000.

Ballarat nestled against spurs of the Great Dividing Range with the extinct volcanoes Warrenheip and Buninyong as 'the giant portals of the goldfields'. The Aboriginal word *Balla-arat* means 'elbow place'; an alluvial flat with permanent water where plain and wooded hills met, it had been an Aboriginal camping site. Kangaroos, emus and wombats were abundant. Over the centuries, ice and water had eroded quartz rock and the gold it contained was deposited among gravel, clay and other soil along the rivers. As the geological conformation had been violently reshaped many times over millions of years, it was difficult to unravel the skein of underground rivers. Lakes were submerged beneath layers of lava; basalt made the rivers dive or diverge. The diggers' tents were like sails plotting the erratic course of the underground rivers. It seemed as though the canvas had been transported from the spars of the deserted ships in Hobson's Bay.

A community was forming to serve the marooned fleet: tradesmen who doubled, for instance, as butchers and blacksmiths; surgeons who operated even though in huts. Tent stores, surmounted by distinctive flags, indicated confidence that the Ballarat diggings were not merely a flash in a few washing pans. Near the government encampment (the Camp) was a store, a Soda Water factory and a wood slab boarding house, a precursor of imposing hotels.

Carboni's party pitched their calico tent on Canadian Flat a couple of miles along the Geelong road, then dutifully went to the Camp on a rise above the Yarrowee river to pay 30 shillings each for a month's goldmining licence. They visited Golden Point Terrace, whose depiction in the *Illustrated London News* had convinced Carboni to cross the world. In September the previous year, Golden Point, half a mile long by 200 yards wide and once the inside bend of a swift river, had provoked the first Ballarat rush, for there nuggets seemed as frequent as nuts in nougat. But when Carboni's party arrived, the holes, mostly 5 to 8 feet deep, were abandoned; the plunderers had moved on leaving a scarred surface. Carboni and a companion jumped into a hole. Within five minutes, after a brief lesson in fossicking, Carboni pounced on the 'yellow boy' and received an emotional charge identical to a 'first declaration of love in bygone times'.

'Great Works!' he shouted, ablaze with joy, presumably abbreviating the Psalmist's 'great are the works of the Lord'. He must have used the expression frequently, for 'Great Works' became his nickname. The find was worth only a couple of pounds, but to earn half that sum in London he had to 'consume much time and shoe leather'. Here he had found the gold in a few minutes without 'crouching or crawling to Jew or Christian'; Jack indeed had no need of a master. Carboni had put his hands on the key to the monetary system, the source of Torlonia power; he was on a gold strike which seemed as prodigious as that of Spanish America, which had gilded Holy Trinity and Rome's other baroque churches. In the next decade, about fifty per cent of the world's gold production was from Victoria.

Writing almost two decades later, W.B. Withers was to describe Carboni as

> a shrewd, restless little man ... under the middle height, with reddish hair and red beard cut short, and small hazel eyes that had ever a fiery twinkle beneath a broad forehead and rather shaggy eyebrows.

The redhead was an eager recruit for the army which seemed to be fighting the landscape. Their fox holes and trenches were emblems of war, and they had also begun an assault on trees which was to denude nearby hills. From the diggings washed in it, the Yarrowee was as muddy yellow as the Tiber in flood. A journalist described Golden Point as 'deep yellow earth-yellow clothes-yellow hands-yellow faces-yellow everything'. The diggers not only had the back-breaking task of extracting the soil (which could be spongy or cementlike, soapy or smelly and perhaps all these in successive layers), but they had to carry it in sacks or trundle it in wheelbarrows to a creek, then wash it by stages with puddling tubs, cradles and dishes. It was torrid work when the northerly blew: one newcomer compared it to standing in front of a brick kiln emitting hot ashes.

There was more gold in Golden Point's abandoned holes but, with success, Carboni's expectations soared; he wanted his own gold-choked hole. He ascended the right side of Canadian Gully, swung his 'darling' pick and, sure enough, at 10 feet, found 17½ ounces of the lovely stuff worth just over £70. The word was that Canadian Gully was as rich in nuggets as other fields in gold dust.

Carboni was at work each day by 5 am before the worst of the January heat. Previously he had never worn a woollen shirt, moleskin trousers and thick boots; a pick and a shovel, and the calluses they caused, were also an abrupt change from wielding a quill or translating. As he worked one morning, his dog Bonaparte, disturbed by rattling in the bush, began to bark. 'What's up?' asked Carboni. A six-foot-tall 'ruffian' with carbine and fixed bayonet emerged.

'Your licence, mate.'

Carboni extracted it. With an 'all right', the trooper set off for other game, but Carboni did not resume work. He felt that after crossing the world he was again subject to the loathsome 'law of the sword'. He was to find others made the same complaint.

Towards the end of January, miners following the Canadian lead struck a lump of gold 20 inches long, 6½ inches wide and 5 inches thick, then another slightly smaller. In early February they unearthed a nugget weighing almost as much as a sack of potatoes, although only a third the size. Nowhere in the world had such finds been made; 1853 was Ballarat's *annus mirabilis*, but for Carboni, after his initial luck, the nuggets remained near but yet so far.

As cooler weather came, he joined a rush for Magpie Gully halfway to Buninyong, a surveyed town 7 miles south of Ballarat. He studied the run of the ranges, marked his claim and, 'safe as the Bank of England' struck 'bung on the gutter', meaning the course of the underground river. However the run was not rich and he was tortured by news of abundant 'yellow boy', of underground 'jewellers' shops' being found along the buried rivers on the Canadian and Prince Regent Flats.

Diggers were constantly teased by word of fabulous strikes elsewhere, from the field they had just left, from the next gully or halfway across the world. To save time they kept their dwellings makeshift, did not shave, and conceded themselves little leisure; Mammon, whom Carboni was conscious of serving, was an exacting God. Hard toil by day, a ritual firing of guns at sundown, then, at night, blazing fires and quarrels on all sides. By now Carboni was used to the diggers' life but his bones ached from the frequent winter weather changes, wet clothes and damp blankets. Gold and rheumatism were partners.

The Canadian and Prince Regent finds were at 110 and 140 feet. Diggers dug even deeper, fording buried rivers. They were sinking shafts, which increased both the work and the danger, for sometimes they were suddenly flooded by 20 feet of water, and once a 19-inch-long live eel emerged. In a letter written on Sunday, 28 August to Archer in Melbourne, Carboni commented that he could not tackle any such hell holes. He was having trouble enough at 60 feet. The shoulder of one of his workmates had been disabled when their hole was swamped because an 'Irish fool out of Vandemonian spite' diverted a creek from his hole to theirs. 'All the shafts in the gully', Carboni told Archer, 'are giving in with fearful hollow cracks'.

As they sank deeper, diggers used split eucalyptus slab casings, with clay mortar, to prevent infiltration of drift sand and water. Even using these casings and bailing steadily with windlasses and 18-gallon wood or bullock-hide buckets, shafts deepened slowly and always under threat of swamping. Some diggers drowned, others were poisoned by carbonised gas from buried trees. The shafts were giant barometers and when air pressure dropped, gas escaped. To carry away the gas, air holes were surmounted by calico windsails modelled on ships' ventilators, but working in a muddy barometer was still uncomfortable.

Hoping to hit the gutter again, Carboni and his mates decided to sink a new shaft with double slabbing. 'Hard, hard work', Carboni wrote to Archer, but he was putting gold aside. He instructed Archer to sell his swordstick for part-payment of a £9 debt but to keep carefully the gold already forwarded. He asked to be remembered to Archer's parents, and said he was expecting a letter from his brother Antonio; Mammon's acolyte retained other pieties.

At least at Magpie Gully there were no licence hunts. Carboni attributed it to the Bendigo diggers' 'sheer moral force, in the shape of ten thousand in a mob'. In fact, on the day before he wrote to Archer, thousands had met in Bendigo, further inland, under torrential rain to protest against 'the bloody licence tax'. After the New South Wales gold strikes, the Victorian government, with private interests, had offered rewards for the' discovery of gold to prevent the workforce stampeding to New South Wales. In August 1851, La Trobe decreed that all gold, even on private lands, belonged to the crown. Fearing an uncontrollable flood of miners would be drawn by Victorian gold strikes, he then introduced a licence fee. Diggers, dubbing La Trobe a 'Victorian Czar', protested against taxation without representation (they could not vote for the squatter-dominated Legislative Council in which one-third were government nominees and there was a property qualification for the remainder).

As Latrobe's second name was Joseph, diggers greeted police (either 'troopers' on horseback or traps on foot) collecting licence fees with cries of 'Joe'. When, in December, it was proposed to double the licence fee to £3 monthly, Ballarat diggers began gathering arms and the government desisted. By July the following year, diggers in Bendigo formed an Anti-Gold Licence Association. They sent a delegation to La Trobe asking for abolition of the fee. He argued that the law had to be obeyed until changed, but they had no right to representation, which would enable them to change it. The mayor of Melbourne convened a meeting which agreed that the goldminers' disaffection 'is caused by the residents of the goldfields being denied their political and social rights'.[5]

La Trobe's treatment of the Bendigo miners' delegation strengthened the Red Ribbon League of diggers whose opposition to the licence was advertised by a red hat ribbon. The 15,000 protesting diggers who met in Bendigo on 27 August 1853 resolved that if the licence were not abolished, they would no longer pay it. Moreover, they demanded Legislative Council representation and talked of raising 'volunteers'. Joseph Anderson Panton, 21-year-old senior assistant to the Bendigo goldfields commissioner, advised La Trobe that unless the licence fee was reduced, bloodshed was predictable. Impulsively La Trobe decided to waive the licence fee, but within a week, before the diggers' celebrations were over, he instituted new fees of £1 a month, £2 for three months, £4 for six months, £8 for a year. Although lower, the reimposed fees were bitterly resented.

In Ballarat it was rumoured that the government was stalling until it had troops to enforce the previous licence fees at bayonet point. On 21 November, at Ballarat's Eureka Hill, a protest meeting was held against harsh new goldfields regulations being debated in the Legislative Council. These even contained a clause providing for confiscation of all goods and property of unlicensed miners. About 400 diggers, including Carboni, attended the protest meeting. Flags flew, a band played, sly grog-sellers were busy. More turned out for Bendigo protests. Ballarat diggers were considered too opportunistic, too prosperous and too tired to engage in concerted political action. One Bendigo sympathiser called Ballarat diggers 'people with their mouths stuffed with pudding'.

At the protest meeting, little Alfred Carr, surgeon, gold-buyer and correspondent for the Melbourne newspaper the *Argus*, who had arrived at Geelong from Liverpool the previous October, predicted the new regulations would provoke armed rebellion. Warmly cheered, he added they would give powers not even dreamed of by the Russian Emperor. 'We won't have the bills', diggers chanted.

John Basson Humffray, a robust, well-read 29-year-old Chartist who had been a clerk in legal offices in his native Wales and in Wellington, New Zealand, ridiculed goldfields officials as discarded aristocrats whose indolence contrasted with the diggers' vigour. Humffray, who had arrived in Victoria only two months earlier, charged that the officials were

> thrust into position not through merit but to secure their support and rid their relatives at home of an encumbrance ... they thought of their situation merely as an introduction to gold lace, insolence and idleness.

Although Humffray's persuasive tenor voice alarmed officials, he favoured negotiation rather than force: his diary on board *The Star of the East* as well as his subsequent actions, shows he was imbued with edifying maxims.

> We should ... cultivate the sentiment of Universal Brotherhood, considering the world our house and mankind our Brethren – Let us not be influenced by anything in the shape of national prejudices, perish all conventionalisms.[6]

Carboni, for 'the fun of the thing', also spoke to the diggers, earning Dr Carr's congratulations and the information *'nous allons bientôt avoir la République australienne signore!'* (Sir, soon we'll have an Australian Republic!)

'Quelle farce!', Carboni replied, not specifying whether he was commenting on the idea itself or on Carr, whom he cast later as 'founder of a republic for thumb-sucking babes'. A republic to end papal despotism in Rome enthused Carboni but probably he saw no reason for Victoria to break from England, which he identified with the rule of law and as a refuge for political exiles. Carboni considered that there was a great 'waste of yabber-yabber' at the meeting about representation in the Legislative Council and squatters' privileges. To him it sounded mere rhetoric, 'fustian', for, he was to admit, 'the shoe had not pinched my toe yet'.

With the hot weather Carboni returned to mine the Ballarat Flat. In a brawl over rights to the adjacent hole, a digger was killed by miners from Eureka, mainly Irishmen with fearful reputations for fighting. Frequently Carboni denounced widespread drunkenness which led to brawls in this 'bullock drivers land.'

With others Carboni sank a deeper hole than any before and bought wooden slabs for it at £8 a hundred. But at 65 feet Carboni's party hit a mouldering gum tree; the hole was a 'shicer' (duffer). Carboni and his fellow miner knew the slabs, if salvaged, would not now be worth even £1 a hundred; they consoled themselves with drink.

Carboni and his workmate then decided to separate. In December, a year after his arrival in Melbourne, while preparations were underway for a Gravel Pits versus Canadian Flat Boxing Day cricket match, with the losers to pay for a meal at Bath's Hotel, Carboni set out to walk the 65 kilometres to Bryant's Ranges near present-day Maldon. Carboni, who was one of the first thirty diggers to arrive, shaped his Bryant's Ranges hole like a bathing tub and once again dropped directly onto the gold gutter; it was no longer beginner's luck but miner's skill. A disadvantage of the field, however, apart from abundant granite, was lack of drinking water. In Ballarat, channels cut from the Yarrowee brought water to the Flat, but in the ranges, where muddy drinking water cost a shilling a bucket, diggings had to be carted to the Loddon river for washing. Carboni paid £2 for cartage, leaving two other loads 'snug and wet with the sweat' of his brow over the hole. He obtained 28 pennyweights from the load but on return found a landslide had covered the other loads, his tools and even the hole. He sank a new hole, thankful there were no searches for licences, as he had none.

He planned a poem-riddle, 'The Cherry Earrings'. The theme was that an even number of cherries brought luck (lovers united, a Statute for Italy), whereas uneven numbers meant lovers' misunderstandings, spinsterhood, tyrannical husbands ... Carboni himself must have had an uneven number, for his health gave out; he was blinded by conjunctivitis and prostrated by dysentery. The wanderer had to stop, the invader was invaded by the land, its shifting aromas, its sounds sharp against silence. As he saw for only brief periods after he cleaned his eyes, he was at the land's mercy, but it proved inoffensive.

Gradually his sight and strength returned. One sleepless night he decided to walk to Bendigo, about 32 kilometres away. He did so but his only comment was on the Bendigo Chinese; he did not dislike them, he said, but deplored their 'tartaric water'.

Carboni became a shepherd, the role in which he depicted the Carboni figure Pastorello in his play *La Santola*. Mosquitoes were a torture but, with sight restored, it was as if he were reborn as a native, for he now saw the land as his own and the Loddon countryside reminded him of Bella Italia, the highest possible praise. In the scorching winds he found bathing in Loddon waterholes 'superb', tea made with Loddon water 'magnificent'. In a dream he turned the water into wine – a Loddon tumbler. Perhaps it induced a deep sleep, for he lost his whole flock. He seemed as Arcadian a shepherd as Pastorello.

Then Carboni went walkabout himself. He spent some time with the Tarrang tribe, even witnessing their corroboree. 'What a rum sight' he commented, 'for an old European traveller.' The Aborigines may also have considered rum the redhead they found wandering near the Loddon. They probably knew there were other white men burrowing at Ballarat like a swarm of demented bandicoots. These rapacious nomads had pushed aside the Aborigines.

Carboni found his sheep again – a bit worse for dingoes – or perhaps they found him. But rather than return to shepherding, as 1854 began he preferred to stay with the 'very humane' Tarrang tribe. He 'picked-up pretty soon' on their 'yabber-yabber', and pencilled notes which became the basis for a small glossary. He began 'pouncing on frogs every couple of minutes'. He found the women, the 'lubras', ugly enough in contrast with the slender arms and small hands of the young girls, whose fingers, however, he adjudged too long. It was a tantalisingly brief comment; the experience would later prompt Carboni to write his second extensive work set in Australia, *Gilburnia*.

The pastoral idyll was at an end; among the tribe, he had reached the farthest point of his wanderings from Rome. His gold fever returned in 'that portion of my brain called "acquisitiveness"'. He set out for, as he called it, 'old Ballaarat'.

Traps on all sides

Carboni's arrival in Ballarat towards Easter 1854 was a homecoming; by now he was a senior digger. He considered the miners and storekeepers more decent than elsewhere and, moreover, females were more frequent. Ballarat had grown in his absence. Victoria's first gold city had been surveyed at the beginning of 1852 but began to take shape along its 3-chain wide main streets only in 1854. As deep-sinking implied stability, solicitors, auctioneers and brokers established offices. Lydiard Street had a hotel, a post office, banks, stores and gold brokers, as well as private houses. The hotel that Thomas Bath, formerly a Geelong butcher, had hastily erected the previous year had been replaced by a fine two-storey building with a clock tower and stables. The mining camp was becoming a substantial town.

Market gardening, whose produce would reduce the incidence of scurvy, was underway close to the town while nearby farms geared production to it. Some diggers' tents were replaced by log huts while others added turf chimneys or other amenities to the starkly functional rough table, treestump chairs, bunks, frying pan and kettle. Methodists, Catholics, Anglicans and Presbyterians built churches; several state and denominational schools served a population which within the year reached 25,000. A quarter was female.

The first theatre had opened the previous December in a tent on the Gravel Pits, the field nearest the Camp. The leading actress was Clara Maria Lodge. In Dublin her father had arranged a ball for her seventeenth birthday where Clara Maria was given a belt with seventeen sovereigns for her seventeen-inch waist. After the ball she was presented to Queen Victoria but, despite her father's attentions, Clara Maria ran away with and married an artist, Claude du Val. Following his death she married Henry Seekamp, a prescient, thick-set man who, in March 1854, established the weekly *Ballarat Times*. A four-page broadsheet, it sold at a shilling and some weeks brought him £130 profit.

Not all the gold was underground. This was recognised by those who made Red Hill an entertainment area: there were concert halls in hotels such as the Charlie Napier, which was like an English coaching inn; the Star; and the United States. An American Mrs Hamner was the star of the wooden Adelphi theatre, and there was a circus.

The sawdust-strewn general stores carried a range of goods from pickles, blue for washing, clothes pegs and liquorice to mining equipment such as picks, shovels and leather buckets. Carboni could find the snuff he used 'especially imported to the Ballarat diggings by Clark Brothers' in tins at four shillings and sixpence each. Diggers worked in the dark, often waist – deep in water, but if successful they could now buy delicacies such as fresh oysters, preserved partridge, grouse, woodcock, lark, plover and freshly roasted coffee. They could also obtain the works of England's most popular novelists.

In a refreshment room, Carboni met an 'old mate' and they decided to resume gold grubbing together. On Easter Monday Carboni pitched his tent on Eureka Hill where he claimed the gold dust was 'finer, purer, brighter, immensely darling'. At its top end, Eureka was enclosed like an amphitheatre by a spur of the Great Divide, crescent-shaped Brown Hill Range and Black Hill's outriders. The Irishmen, some with Californian experience, who were predominant on Eureka since it was opened up in mid-1852, had followed the underground riverbed or gutter downhill towards the flat where it divided.

Sundays, which were observed respectfully on the goldfields, Carboni kept for himself. His clay-spattered moleskin trousers and precious watertight boots were set aside, and he changed his sweat-stained blue flannel shirt. During the week he tried to update his diary and accounts book so that on Sunday, invigorated by snuff and fortified by tipples of brandy, he could work at his plays and poems which, he was convinced, would bring him renown in Italy. Writing was his secret life, for most of his workmates were unaware of his literary ambitions. They knew him as a flamboyant character, a freedom fighter in his homeland who sometimes claimed to be 'of the ancient Roman family of de Carbonari Carbonis which gave two proconsuls under the Roman Republic'. Carboni would refer anyone rash enough to inquire further to histories of Rome by Gibbon and Niebuhr.

Countless colourful goldfield characters created whatever past they chose; taken with the appropriate grain of salt, these stories added to the gaiety of nations. What counted was the daily performance tracking the Eureka vein, which descended, twisting and turning, at 120 feet. Because diggers were not allowed to hold more than one claim at a time, disputes became inevitable as they staked out new claims over what they believed was the gutter. The location of a claim meant the difference between fortune and failure. Those merely guarding claims were called 'shepherds' because they dug shallow holes, then watched over the site until convinced, from strikes in line with them, that the buried gold-stream traversed their ground. They were gamblers sitting on their hands until sure it was worth playing.

Carboni had a neighbour who camouflaged himself to avoid the no-two-claims rule. Before breakfast, garbed as an Irishman, he worked one hole; after breakfast, donning a red shirt and cap (a Garibaldian?) he worked a second hole in the gully; on the pretext that damp matches would not light his pipe, the chameleon returned to his tent to dress as a Yankee, then worked a third hole.

The one-party-one-hole rule inspired not only ingenuity, but also clashes. Carboni saw a party of British diggers leave their hole because of a reported find in the gully below. On return, they found Yankees armed with revolvers and Mexican knives had dismounted the windlass and claimed possession. To settle the dispute, the Goldfields Resident Commissioner Robert Rede was summoned. He decided in favour of the Yankees which, Carboni claimed, was the beginning of his unpopularity.

The privately educated son of a naval officer, for some years Rede had studied medicine, which explained his nickname 'the little doctor'. He travelled extensively in Europe before arriving in Victoria in November 1851. He had joined the rush to Bendigo where, in October 1852, he obtained employment in the Goldfields Commission. On the Korong goldfield he was known as an opponent of the licence system. In May 1854, at the age of 39, he became Chief Resident Commissioner of Ballarat. Under him, senior commissioners and assistant commissioners each controlled portions of the Ballarat goldfields.

Stout, grey-haired with a large moustache, Rede had been encouraging when Carboni and a mate, Paul Brentano, had proposed manufacturing bricks from Gravel Pits clay. Perhaps Carboni dreamed of becoming wealthy by making Ballarat as bricky as Urbino, but nothing came of the proposal. Rede, who had spent nine years in Paris, spoke to Carboni and Brentano in French.

Carboni was gaining further first-hand experience of the 'bloody licence tax'. He called his Virginia cradle after a renowned Swedish opera singer, Jenny Lind. He was at his 'rattling Jenny Lind' at a waterhole in Eureka Gully when he had to produce his licence. He then climbed a quarter-of-a-mile to the hole for more wash dirt. Once more he was challenged: 'All serene governor'. Descending again, up to his knees in mullock, loaded like a camel, he was stopped a third time.

The licence hunts seemed a surrogate for war or riding at hounds. 'Joe! Joe!': the blasting hot wind blowing from the Gravel Pits towards Eureka would bring the cry of diggers signalling troops hunting licences. Soon a regiment at full gallop would surround the Eureka field. As police went among the holes, those without licences scrambled underground, slipped into the bush, hid under tent bunks or, hastily dressed as women, cooked and washed clothes. The search for those in the bush was like a game hunt. If captured, the miners might be chained to a tree while others were hunted.

Eventually they were taken to the Camp where they were gaoled or, if the log gaol was full, tree-chained until a commissioner heard their case, perhaps the following day. If a register had been kept of licences granted, the innocent could have been released immediately. The fine was usually £5, but the guilty could also be sentenced to hard labour.

Even when they went to pay their fee, diggers were humiliated, as one of them recounted in a letter to the *Ballarat Times*:

> Permit me to call your attention to the miserable accommodation provided for the miner, who may have occasion to go to the Camp to take out a licence. Surely, with the thousands of pounds that have been expended in government buildings, a little better accommodation might be afforded to the well-disposed digger who is willing to pay the odious tax imposed on him by the government, and not be compelled to stand in the rain or sun, or treated as if the 'distinguished government official' feared that the digger was a thing that would contaminate him by closer proximity; so the 'fellah' is kept by a wooden rail from approaching within a couple of yards of the tent In consequence of so many persons mistaking the licence-office for the commissioner's water-closet, a placard has been placed over the door.

I am, Sir, yours &c
FELLAH DIGGER.

The *Times* editor Henry Seekamp commented:

> … the audacity of this Digger Correspondent! Not only grumbling at the accommodation afforded but also desiring to remedy the nuisance! It is beyond all precedent! … Does he want a Crystal Palace to pay his taxes in? There is a better state of things coming, when the 'digger fellah' will know his own importance and make the imbeciles who misgovern him also know it.

The humiliating trials of diggers were described by John Manning, a balding Irish patriot, in a report from the local police court for the same paper:

> Five of these fellows (diggers) were fined the mitigated trifle of £5, for being without licence. The nicest thing imaginable is to see one of these clumsy fellows with great beards, shaggy hair, and oh! such nasty rough hands, stand before a fine gentleman on the bench with hands of shiny whiteness, and the odour of whose cambric rivals the Alpine snow. There the clumsy fellow stands, faltering out an awkward apology, 'my licence is only just expired, sir – I've only been one day from town, sir – I have no money, sir, for I had to borrow half a bag of flour the other day, for my wife and children.' 'Ahem/ says his worship, 'the law makes no distinctions – fined £5.' Now our reporter enjoys this exceedingly, for he is sometimes scarce of news; and from a strong aberration of intellect with which, poor fellow, he is afflicted, has sometimes no news at all for us; but he is sure of not being *dead beat* at any time, for digger-hunting is a standing case at the police office, and our reporter is growing so precocious with long practice, that he can tell the number of diggers fined every morning, without going to that sanctuary at all.

As a Marchigiano (a native of the Marches, the Papal States' eastern zone) Carboni would have been aware that tax collectors were universally loathed. Marchigiani had a reputation as the Papal States' tax collectors, which probably accounted for the saying 'better a corpse in the house than a Marchigiano at the door'. Diggers resented being treated as mere rent-producers without representation. But there was an added motive for hating the licence-hunters – the fee was extracted from both those who hit pay dirt and those who bottomed on mullock. In the diggers' eyes, it fined the unlucky; they were more equal than others. It was not an income tax, but a work permit levy tolerable when alluvial gold lay close to the surface but provocative as shafts went deeper and prolonged work could prove fruitless. It might take nine months to reach a gutter. Sometimes eight men worked on such shafts, cutting slabs, winding the windlass, digging in twenty-four-hour shifts; if, after nine months, they bottomed on mullock, they would have paid out £72 in fees alone for nothing.

Another source of irritation was the size of claims, usually only 8 square feet, which was much smaller than the size diggers, following the Californian pattern, had allowed themselves before regulation. The smallness of the claims caused crowding and frequent rushes as new ones were opened. As many as twelve men were needed for deep sinking but, no matter how big the party, 24 square feet was the biggest claim permitted.

An excise tax would have been more acceptable than the licence, but authorities feared it would lead to uncontrollable smuggling. Diggers pointed out that for £10 yearly squatters obtained huge runs. However authorities regarded squatters as permanent settlers and diggers as temporary marauders, a nomad tribe, vagrants likely at any moment to light out for the next strike be it in New South Wales, New Zealand or Peru. They could have encouraged these vagrants to become settlers if they had opened up farm lands, but failed to do so.

Some of the mounted police and foot police who collected licence fees envied the diggers' supposed wealth. Police entrance standards were low, for the most resourceful men preferred to mine. Many police were drunkards, several were sadistic and corrupt. 'Some of our shipmates had no money nor any inclination to hard work', a digger wrote to the historian W.B. Withers, recalling his arrival in Ballarat in November 1852, 'so they accepted billets as policemen at the Camp. They and others of the force then were a ragged, ununiformed Falstaffian sort of crowd, with arms to match'. The police were the diggers' point of contact with authority and contributed to its poor repute.

The Goldfields Commissioners had the wide powers of their prototypes, the Crown Land Commissioners. However they were dealing not with scattered squatters but a heavy concentration of miners, a significant proportion of them well-educated and politically aware. As diggers did not have political rights, their political activity was frowned upon; diggers could not modify laws in their favour; they could not unlock lands, which would enable them to have freeholders' voting rights. A newspaper such as the *Ballarat Times* which argued for diggers' political rights was considered a troublemaker. Diggers were trapped by the situation, but so were the authorities.

A distinctive feature of Ballarat was its compactness. The diggings, which lay beneath the Camp where the administration and the forces of order were quartered, were contained within the two arms of the Canadian Gully and Eureka. The Camp, which stood at the edge of the town, consisted of administrative buildings and quarters not only for soldiers and police, but also for the clerks, gold receivers and gold escort personnel. There was a police cantonment with a small gaol and the logs to which prisoners were chained when it was full. The Camp had 230 employees who lived in, increasing its enclave air even though it was unfortified. It was a sanctuary of order opposed to the underlying turbulent diggers' world. The Union Jack flew from Commissioner Rede's office while the diggers' tents were often surmounted by the occupants' national flags; at night the Southern Cross embraced all the flags.

The 1852 survey had created an unfortunate division between town dwellers and diggers by making the Yarrowee River Ballarat's eastern boundary. Legally no business could be established within a mile of the township, nor land sold east of the river. Despite this, pubs, stores and workshops thronged the Gravel Pits, Gum Tree Flat and Eureka. They were 'beyond the Pale', but also the area's growing point as if to illustrate the law was an ass and regulations could not keep pace with life. Town shopkeepers, mainly English, who had bought their freeholds, resented the storekeepers on the fields who did livelier business but paid only a licence fee.

The gap between town and diggers, however, was not as wide as that between the Government Camp and the diggers. Few interests were shared by the rulers and ruled. Diggers complained of 'boy commissioners' with foppish manners. Younger sons of aristocrats and other well-connected, but not necessarily qualified, people easily obtained positions as officials. They turkey- or possum-hunted, hobnobbed with squatters or visitors, but did not mix with diggers.

The Chief Commissariat Clerk Sam Huyghue was a keen observer. Born on Prince Edward Island in 1815, he had published two novels based on his experience with Canadian Indians before coming through London to Victoria in 1852. Also a painter, Huyghue, a 'young gentleman of much taste', disapproved the attempt to make the Commission aristocratic and exclusive. He was not impressed by the 'braided, gold-laced, perfumed, lofty' officials.[7] Their aristocratic-military airs cut even less ice with hard-working diggers, who had developed a strong group identity. Although mining was competitive for deep-sinking diggers, they banded into what were virtually small cooperatives, often involving storekeepers who staked them for provisions or even capital.

Diggers complained the Camp showed itself less interested in ensuring order than in squeezing money from them. Storekeepers, who paid a £50 annual licence, made the same complaint. So little protection was provided against theft from their canvas stores that they formed vigilante groups which held revolver practice in the hills.

Even more friction was caused by prohibition, which led to widespread sly grog-selling and fines for those who did not bribe the police. Incentives were given to police by allowing them to pocket half of the fines. This practice reached its nadir when a newcomer from Geelong was introduced to Shanahan's hotel-restaurant by one of its boarders. Although Shanahan did not have a liquor licence, when the boarder requested drinks for his friend, Mrs Shanahan obliged. The newcomer then hastened to the Camp, swore in as a policeman, returned and fined Shanahan £50 for grog-selling. The improvised policeman was burnt in effigy and driven from the goldfield, but his exploit illustrated the absurdity of a system which embarrassed magistrates also, for if they did not exact fines, they reduced police income, which was another name for morale.

As in the case of Rede adjudicating the Yankees–British claim clash, commissioners were involved in deciding heated disputes on the spot. There were no fixed rules to guide them; only by-laws, which made their decisions seem arbitrary. The fact that commissioners were also magistrates robbed the judiciary of independence while all the justices of the peace were drawn from goldfields officials. Miners were not represented in the administration of justice.

The Goldfields Commission could have been designed to foment a pre-revolutionary situation. The Camp was authority without the sanction of tradition, the sympathy of its subjects or the charisma of respect.

The diggers' Charley

Carboni had descended a hell hole. He was working in damp and dark and danger at a greater depth (140 feet) than ever before, as he recounted in an excited note to Archer written on a freezing Sunday, 25 June:

> ... through worlds of [indecipherable] and mire, double Oceans of water and treble torments of our old bones, we worry right-doggedly the rebellious gusts [sic] of Mammon, below at a depth of 140 feet in a 100! pounds weight Golden Hole. We had the pluck to grapple with old Belzebub face to face on his own ground. 'Well done my covy, roared long-tail Satan, thou art a lion of the old stamp, like the cock on a dung-hill, in the midst of my chosen ... Hold your blastedphenious jaw you d(cursed)d old curl, get ye up and let's have a cut at your gouty gall bladder – this will do –
> Without Gammon, my dear Mr Archer, (I got) again, Thank God, on a bit of Gold.

Carboni intended to send the bits of gold to the Torlonia bank. And he would follow them home. In August he informed Archer he wanted to leave the goldfields in late October and would certainly be in Melbourne, where he would repay Archer's loan, before Christmas. He planned to pass through the East Indies and visit Jerusalem on his way back to Italy.

Then he heard from Antonio that his father had died. Some weeks later writing to Archer, he was to describe himself pathetically as a 'friendless outcast since wandering from my Father's house ...' It was as if Urbino hills had been superimposed on Warrenheip and Carboni saw himself as a young man, setting off 'peeved' from home, but aware now that he had seen his father for the last time. He was moving up the queue towards death.

He asked Antonio for a memento of his father.[8] The letter, the first Carboni had received from his family since leaving Italy, may have reminded him of forgotten ties and roused latent resentments. Antonio asked his assistance as if Raffaello were the elder brother and heir to all responsibilities; home news threatened an end to freedom.

Carboni responded evasively to Antonio's request. Using French, he pedantically claimed his brother's letter was full of errors. And called him 'donkey'. But he also poured out the story of his wanderings, underlining his penury in Germany and England, stressing the dangers of goldmining, the threat to his health, his leg pains. He blamed Antonio for his troubles; home was where the hurt was. Gold, he wrote, was being sent through Archer. Twenty-five ounces of 'choice gold plus other specimens, small precious stones, carbuncle and rubies' were going care of the Torlonia bank; and all the remaining gold, plus a Napoleon, a Louis d'Or and 1844, '50, '51 and '52 sovereigns were for his brother. His poor but honest relatives, he told Archer, 'are immensely dear to me'. But Antonio's letter may have made Raffaello aware he was missing them as an ascetic would miss his hair shirt.

Three days before Carboni wrote to Archer announcing his find at 140 feet, the Governor's position, which he had seen advertised on his arrival, at last had been filled. The man who was to detain him in Victoria, Sir Charles Hotham, was greeted on arrival in Melbourne with the slogan 'VICTORIA WELCOMES VICTORIA'S CHOICE'. At Prince's Bridge spanning the Yarra, a crowd of 10,000 greeted the procession accompanying Hotham from the port to the government offices in William Street. In the eighteen months since tendering his resignation, La Trobe had taken no initiatives. Everyone expected more vigorous leadership from his successor, Commodore Hotham RN. The diggers anticipated he would correct the Goldfields Commission's defects.

The new governor was the eldest son of the Reverend Francis Hotham, prebendary of Rochester. It was a naval family and, at 12, Charles entered the peacetime navy. Carboni was probably unaware of it but Hotham had deprived his hero Garibaldi of one chance of glory. On 10 November 1845, preceding Garibaldi, Hotham led 325 seamen and marines against Puente del Obligado fort to break a blockade of the Parana River by the Argentinean dictator Juan Manuel de Rosas. Hotham's men captured the fort and threw most of the heavy cannons into the river.

Hotham had also negotiated a trade and friendship treaty with Paraguay. Perhaps because of this, against his wishes, he was nominated Lieutenant-Governor of Victoria when a major war, which would have enabled him to confirm his military skills, loomed in the Crimea. In fact, the ship which brought him to Melbourne carried the ten-week-old news that Queen Victoria had declared war against the Czar of all the Russians. The previous December at the age of 47, Hotham had married a widow at fashionable St George's in Hanover square. Balding Hotham with swarthy complexion, small dark eyes and thin lips was a contrast to blond Jane Sarah Holbech who was almost the same height.

Hotham's new government house at Toorak was a white-stone, two-storey building in extensive grounds above the Yarra, but he had not been able to find out from London whether his residence was furnished. He had brought all his own furniture but, as Toorak House was chock-a-block, had to sell it. He was hit with the bill for the furnishings – plus £400 for the pigsty! The Secretary of State for the Colonies, the Duke of Newcastle, had warned him of the colony's enormous, extravagant expenses, and here was evidence in his own backyard. Yet, in the stables the horses were up to their hocks in mud, and there were no rooms for the servants. Lady Hotham's maid had to be lodged in a cramped tower. It was too much. Hotham was away on the wrong foot; a bad start was inauspicious for someone who, in any case, would have preferred to be in the Crimea where England, France and Piedmont, to aid Turkish despotism, had begun to fight Russian despotism.

In a speech in Geelong, the energetic Yorkshireman affirmed that all power proceeds from the people: 'it is on that principle that I intend to conduct my administration'. His popularity increased when, with Lady Hotham, he visited Ballarat on Saturday, 26 August. Wiry Hotham, in dark tweed shooting jacket and pepper-and-salt trousers, surprised the diggers by inspecting, at about 5 p.m., a shaft on the Gravel Pits behind the Ballarat Dining Rooms. A crowd soon gathered. Hotham heeded their comments on goldfield conditions. Here was vice-regal authority with naval cachet, and, unlike Camp officials, manly and accessible. Hotham, careless of the mud which splattered his trousers, did not need to give himself airs. Nor did Lady Hotham, in a red-striped plain plaid dress, who held his arm.

> A tall young woman, with fine symmetrical figure, very active, no mock delicacy about her, blond complexion, fine liquid ox eyes, teeth white and regular as a greyhound, an affable and conciliatory manner …

was one digger's description. She broke the lumps of clay given to her, asking diggers about mining. Their Excellencies were shown a lump of black clay studded with gold. The diggers named a 98½-pound nugget found at that time after Lady Hotham.

As the one-and-a-half miles back to the Camp were muddy, Carboni and other diggers improvised a wooden slab path for the cordial vice-regal couple. Amid laughter, a hulking Irish miner Big Larry took Lady Hotham in his arms to save her from a crab hole. For the remainder of the walk, as if he had acquired a proprietary interest, Larry kept other diggers at bay with a switch. Perhaps he was buoyant because, under Hotham's eyes, his party had washed 6 pounds of gold to a tub. At the Camp, Hotham told the diggers he was delighted by their reception; he would not neglect their interests and welfare. He looked the type to make things shipshape. The 500 blue shirts, who were sure he would shake up the goldfields administration, gave the Governor three hearty cheers. They dubbed him the 'diggers' Charley'.

A 'Constantly Grumbling Digger', in a letter to the *Ballarat Times*, expressed his appreciation of the Hotham visit:

> Here is the Governor and people chatting and talking to another, as familiarly as two old chums; the Governor and his lady are laughing heartily at the rough but hearty welcome the diggers are giving themselves; and the diggers, with dirty hands and dirty faces, are doing their best to make the Governor and his lady be in good humor – each party does everything possible to please the other; that's the right way; I'll grumble no more.

Even the *Times,* the scourge of Camp officials, was convinced:

> a bold vigorous and far-seeing man has been amongst us, and the many grievances and useless restrictions by which a digger's success is impeded will be swept away.

In his diary, Carboni recorded that all had gone to drink a nobbler to Hotham's health and success; writing up the event in his snug tent prompted Carboni to take another drink. And perhaps to ask himself whether he had seen Lady Jane before. Had it been at a Torlonia Palace reception? At that time he had been a young blade and interpreter for the bank, not a mud-spattered miner. Perhaps he had known her even before Charley Hotham; during her previous marriage to Hugh Holbech she had visited Rome. Carboni could look forward to returning soon to those same Roman sites, to similar women, and no longer as a mere bank clerk, but with his pockets full of gold.

His planned departure was delayed, however, because water infiltrated the shaft: 'we have to fight day and night to keep down the water', he told Archer. And hopes in Hotham shipwrecked when, in September, instead of licence searches being reduced, they were stepped up to twice weekly. As the areas under each commissioner's control were not clearly defined, hunts which took place on different days in different zones overlapped. In pubs and over fires diggers swapped tales of harassment, which seemed almost continuous. What had happened? Hotham had reported to the English Colonial Secretary, Henry Grey, on his triumphal August–September goldfields visit. In Ballarat, he wrote, he found

> an orderly, well-conducted people … For some time I was enabled to walk undiscovered among them, and thus I gathered their real feelings towards the government, and obtained an insight into some minor causes on which they desired redress.

He described his welcome when the diggers 'burst forth [in] shouts of loyalty to Her Majesty, and cries of attachment to the old country, such as can hardly be imagined …' Noting that the Ballarat miner was now sinking shafts which took five or six months, Hotham commented 'he will always be a lover of order and good government and, provided he is kindly treated, will be found in the path of loyalty and duty'.

In Bendigo, he told Grey, he had tackled the licence-fee issue head-on, warning the diggers they 'must pay for liberty and order, and on concluding [I] was loudly cheered'. He had cast a military man's eye on the diggings:

> no amount of military force at the disposal of Her Majesty's Government can coerce the diggers, as gold fields may be likened to a network of rabbit burrows. For miles the holes adjoin each other; each is a fortification, and frequently there is

> an extensive underground communication; nowhere can four men move abreast, so that the soldier is powerless against the digger, who, well-armed and sheltering himself by the earth thrown up around him, can easily pick off his opponent. By tact and management must these men be governed; amenable to reason, they are deaf to force, but discreet officers will always possess that influence which education and manners everywhere obtain.

In his report he was Hotham the straightforward, yet when he opened the Legislative Council session, he was a changed man. Or rather, as the *Argus* commented, he had 'sunk the man in the Governor ... either distrusting himself, his audience or his assistants'.[9] Moving the levers of government was more difficult than meeting diggers face-to-face. Despite his encouraging words on the goldfields, he did not mention to the Legislative Council the diggers' problems, as if silence would exorcise them.

An *Argus* comment, made during Hotham's goldfields trip, no longer seemed fanciful; inspired by news that Captain Charles MacMahon was drilling police in Bendigo, the Melbourne daily had suggested: 'perhaps provision is being made for a possible Russian attack – or a rising of the diggers is apprehended.'[10]

There was a fund of goodwill on the diggings, but Hotham squandered it. The gold rush meant disruption of services and a strain on resources, while the benefits would come only with time. But in Downing Street, Hotham had been told to put the colony's finances in order and warned that he would probably have to fight over the licence fee. London had not. forgotten nor forgiven La Trobe's September 1853 'mistake' in halving the fee, which had brought an immediate protest to the Secretary of State from Governor Charles FitzRoy of New South Wales who had served at Waterloo. The Colonial Office wanted 'no more yielding to intimidation'. On the voyage to Australia, according to Hotham's secretary Captain Kay, the colony's finances had been a constant topic. In Melbourne, said Kay, 'how to get revenue and how to curtail expenditure were the unceasing object of his [Hotham's] daily thoughts'.[11]

During Hotham's goldfields trip, he had been told that only 60 per cent of all diggers in Victoriaa paid the licence fee. Ballarat diggers had a reputation as the most evasive, but he had seen them picking chunks of gold from the ground. What could be more logical, then, than to insist the recalcitrant pay the fee to replenish government coffers? Hotham had not understood that the goldfields administration was seen not as ensuring order but as extorting an unjust tax. He did not realise his goldfields' welcome was largely due to a conviction that he, unlike the local officials, would heed the diggers' complaints. The diggers had greeted him as a friend, but he acted like a tax inspector to whom they had incautiously shown their wealth.

Scobie collides with a spade

'Below!'

'Haloo!'

'Jim, the miners of Ballaarat demand an investigation.'

'And they must have it, Joe.'

Carboni used this exchange to show that indignation crackled like a lit fuse as news streaked through Eureka and the Gravel Pits that a digger-prisoner had died because denied medical care. The victim had cut his head falling on a broken bottle. His raving caused by loss of blood was taken as drunkenness. Transferred from the Camp hospital to gaol where, for ten hours, he was left lying on the floor, finally he was brought back to the hospital but died two hours later. For Carboni and other diggers, he was a victim of the inhumanity of the 'silver and gold lace' officials.

* * *

The troopers' horses galloping as if at his tent woke Carboni in panic. Foot police tramped towards it too. He rolled off his stretcher, then stumbled into the dark where other diggers in nightcaps and underclothes were asking what the devil was going on. Troopers surrounded a hilltop store flanked by a tent.

'Whose tent is that?' asked Commissioner Rede.

Carboni knew it was the storekeeper's and crammed with grog because his sleep was often disturbed by the tent's rowdy clients. A spy, he concluded, had tipped off the Camp that valuable stock had arrived.

'I don't know', the storekeeper lied.

'Who lives in it? Who owns it? Is anyone in?'

'An old man but he's gone to town on business and left it to the care of his mate who's on the nightshift.'

'I won't peck that chaff of yours, sir. Halloo! Who is in? Open the tent.' Rede's command brought no response.

'Cut down this tent and we'll see who's in'.

Two troopers' swords slashed the tent. As £200 worth of grog was carted to the Camp, the diggers protested ineffectually. For them, the raid was further proof that the administration was not interested in their needs but only in applying those laws which brought gain. Carboni maintained that miners working in wet and cold needed nobblers. However, prohibition prevailed on the goldfields until May 1854, even though, from the previous year, licensed hotels were permitted in the towns. In these circumstances sly groggers, dispensing mainly rum, thrived. Carboni took his argument a step further. Prohibition bred spies because those who denounced sly grog-sellers collected half of the £50 fine. Spies bred, he added, because the 'paternals' of Toorak needed revenue. Moreover diggers suspected that Camp officials who granted licences accepted bribes.

One of the most hated Camp officials was overbearing, corrupt Sergeant-Major Robert Milne. Whenever he and his men approached the Excelsior Restaurant, run by an American, Frank Carey, they were subject to catcalls. Using plain-clothes police, Milne framed Carey and obtained his conviction to six months' imprisonment for selling two glasses of grog. This particularly angered the Americans who resented their Excelsior meeting place being described in court as a gamblers' resort. They successfully petitioned Hotham for Carey's release.

Following a Californian slump in mid-1853, Americans had come in strength. Not only did Californian miners apply their skills in Ballarat, but American businessmen made their mark. Americans were prominent in transportation – from the fast clippers, bringing men and materials such as building facades which made the Australian goldfields resemble their American counterparts, to swift Concord coaches and even an undertaker, or mortician, whose flag showed a black coffin on a white field. (Not only were mine accidents often fatal, but so was drinking; grog took some off and the unfiltered water could cause fatal dysentery.)

Grog was the background of a still sharper clash with authorities than the Carey case. While working as a confectioner in Melbourne, James Bentley, a former convict, had made influential friends, including the Ballarat magistrate John D'Ewes. Prominent Melbourne and Geelong citizens had provided references when he set out to establish a hotel in Ballarat. His hotel, which occupied a half-acre corner site on Eureka Hill, was the first on the goldfields and the most lavish, with gaudily painted weatherboard walls, a shingle roof and sash windows. It was valued at over £20,000, and a concert hall and billiard room were being added. At the back were livery stables and a bowling alley like a canvas worm. Nearby were auction rooms, stores and a pharmacy.

Some diggers called Bentley's hotel a 'slaughterhouse'. They alleged that drunks there were cheated, robbed and thrown into the street. About 1 a.m. on Tuesday, 7 October, Scotsmen James Scobie and James Martin, tipsy after celebrating their reunion, vainly tried to enter the hotel. They kicked in a glass panel of its front door and called Mrs Bentley a 'whore', before staggering away. They were followed by Bentley, his wife, his clerk Hance, the night-watchman Thomas Mooney and another employee, John Farrell, an ex-convict who had been chief constable at Castlemaine. At about 100 yards from the hotel, Farrell picked up a puddling spade and smashed Scobie's skull, killing him. Martin had already been knocked down but managed to flee. An inquest brought in an open verdict that the 'deceased had died from injuries of persons unknown', but in a letter to the *Ballarat Times,* nine of the twelve jurors confessed their misgivings.

Two Irish diggers whose claim adjoined that of Scobie attended the inquest. One of them attested later that the proceedings seemed rigged. He was a long-faced, black-whiskered engineer who, with three others of his thirteen-member family, had arrived in Melbourne in October 1852. His name was Peter Lalor, the son of a one-time member of the House of Commons and younger brother of one of the most radical Irish nationalists. He had set up a wine-and-spirits store in Melbourne before trying his luck on the goldfields. With him at the inquest was Timothy Hayes, stout and suave, who had his wife and six children in Ballarat.

In a local court, with Assistant Commissioner Johnstone dissenting, Resident Commissioner Rede and Police Magistrate John D'Ewes (who was also president of the licensing bench) exonerated Bentley. (At this point the involvement of his employees in the killing was not known.) Spectators who considered that D'Ewes, a friend of Bentley, was patently partial to him, hissed the verdict.

However Johnstone, who had been a miner in Bendigo for six months before joining the Goldfields Commission, fomented hostility to officials in a licence hunt he directed. A trooper demanded a licence from Johann Gregorius, a crippled Armenian who was the servant of Father Patrick Smyth, while he was visiting a sick friend. The Armenian was not obliged to have a licence but could not make himself understood. After railing against the Armenian's employer, the trooper seized the cripple's shirt and he finished on the ground.

Father Smyth ran to the scene. Johnstone would not heed Smyth but accepted £5 bail. Johnstone's version of events was unconvincing; after admitting the trooper seized the cripple by the collar, tearing his shirt, he continued:

> the man [the Armenian] struggled with him and tried to get away and during the struggle either the horse's chest had come against him and shoved him down or the man had thrown himself down.

The police court fined the Armenian £5 for being without a licence. Johnstone explained that this had not been the charge and then had the Armenian fined £5 for resisting arrest. Catholics, mainly Irish, took the incident as an insult to their priest and were as disaffected as the Americans over the Carey case, and the Scots because of the Scobie inquest verdict.

Reports such as that in the *Ballarat Times* of 16 September 1854 would make old wounds ache for Carboni:

> His Holiness [Pius IX] ... has resolved to execute those who have been convicted, by a most impartial tribunal, of the murder of [Pellegrino] Rossi.

The item would have reminded Carboni sharply of his time in Rome when Rossi had been killed but also of a Holiness who could condemn to death. (Pius IX received from Australian miners 100 ounces of gold used for medals to commemorate proclamation of the doctrine of the Immaculate Conception in 1854.)

In Ballarat, however, the Irish priest Patrick Smyth was not an oppressor but a victim. With intense eyes, brushed-back curly hair and a high forehead, sensitive Smyth was unlikely to find the goldfields' rough-and-tumble congenial. Evidently Carboni gave up some of his precious Sunday hours to attend

Mass at the Bakery Hill Church, for he commented that Smyth's preaching, 'though not remarkable for much eloquence, does not lull to sleep'. Unlike the Italian clerics who had fed Carboni's anti-clericalism, Smyth was from a tradition in which priests shared their flocks' nationalism. But he was also cast in the Roman mould transmitted through Maynooth, the world's first national seminary. Carboni admired Smyth's lack of cant and unimpeachable conduct, but also suspected rigidity:

> He scorns any conversation with Voltaire and would see the fellow burnt ... he forgets not that he belongs to the priesthood of Ireland, the 'proved gold of the Catholic Church'.

Carboni was on good terms also with a strong-faced, balding Kerryman, Father Matthew Downing. He had entrusted messages for Archer to Downing, an Augustinian who, while still a seminarian, had assisted cholera victims in Naples in 1836–37. Subsequently, as prior of a Roman monastery, Downing had been on good terms with Pope Gregory XVI. He had volunteered as a convict chaplain, arriving in Port Arthur, Tasmania, early in 1849. In February 1853 he pegged out part of God's claim in Ballarat, building a 90-foot long timber and canvas school and church as well as helping to found the first cemetery. Then he had transferred to Keilor, making way for Smyth, but was still seen occasionally in Ballarat.

Profound ditch of perdition

A searing northerly frayed tempers and carried dust as about 3,500 diggers assembled, towards midday on Tuesday, 17 October, where James Scobie had been killed. It was only five minutes from the tent of Carboni, who attended. Convinced that authorities favoured Bentley, whom they believed was the murderer, the diggers hooted at his name. Tom Kennedy, a fiery, red-haired Scot who had his wife and four children on the field, told the crowd that the ghost of his friend Scobie haunted the site seeking revenge. A fundraising committee, with Peter Lalor as secretary, was formed to ensure conviction of Scobie's murderer. Carboni contributed.

A detachment of foot police stood near Bentley's hotel, where the owner stayed out of sight, while mounted police rode provocatively through the crowd. (The previous day Bentley had requested police protection. He said there were 'lying rumors' about the Scobie case and that he had been warned that the owner of a 'notorious Sly Grog shop was instigating the miners to set fire to my place'.)[12] Diggers taunted the unarmed police. As the meeting dispersed, the crowd moved towards the hotel, the police falling back before them. A youth threw a stone which smashed a fine lamp over the hotel's front door. It was as if all restraint had been shattered with the lamp. Vengeful diggers broke windows with stones and sticks. To cheers, they tossed out bedding, curtains and furniture. Edmund Westerby gave a lead in ripping away weatherboards; other diggers drank Bentley's grog; a Californian smashed crockery. The mounted police struggled to control their frightened horses.

Commissioner Rede had asked a Gold Receiver, John Green, to read the Riot Act if trouble threatened, but Green adjudged the police insufficient, so he refrained. Rede, who had watched proceedings from Commissioner Gilbert Amos's Eureka station, hurried over at about 2.30. Mounting a window sill, he tried to assert his authority. An egg splashed against the wall behind him. Rede ordered apprehension of the egg-thrower but troops, wary of the angry mob, were reluctant. Stones were thrown at Rede. Diggers shouted that destruction would cease if he ordered Bentley's arrest. He refused. Carboni, within six yards of Rede, could not hear a word he was shouting but could see 'his wild looks, the firocious blinking of his eyes and reddening of countenance, his passionate fisting with the buttend of his whip', which brought to mind 'a scion of Marshal Haynau fencing to frighten away in confusion a whole town of Italy'. Carboni considered Rede, whom he compared to an Austrian bull dog, had 'accelerated the fury of the Destroyers to the fever heat by his bravadoes'.[13]

A police officer hoped the mob would be drawn away if the diggers saw Bentley on horseback, but he escaped without them noticing him. As Bentley galloped toward the Camp past the Gravel Pits, diggers left work to rush to the hotel, where the crowd more than doubled.

Irritated by Rede, diggers called for the more popular Amos. But when he had had his say they gave him short shrift too. Rede then handed his whip, symbol of authority, to a digger, Andrew McIntyre, in the hope that he could calm the mob, but he was no more successful. Smoke issued from a ground-floor room, someone called 'Fire' and a horse shied. Police extinguished the fire and tried to throw a cordon around the building while word spread that Rede had summoned about fifty soldiers of the 40th Regiment. Another hotel lamp crashed and troopers struggled to control their horses.

As the redcoats, with swords drawn, lined up in front of the hotel, flames rose from the bowling alley. McIntyre and police who ran to quell the blaze were thwarted because the rising wind acted as a bellows. Shavings and loose wood of the partly built billiard and concert rooms, windward of the hotel, were lit. A corner of the hotel blazed. 'Hip, hip, hoorah', shouted the crowd.

Carboni had seen London crowds make sport of similar occasions and perhaps thought of the Bishopsgate pawnbroker where he had lost his mother's ring. There was another cheer as, at a maidservant's request, a young man rushed into the hotel and retrieved her treasure box' (he later married her).[14] Looters handed out grog: 'here's porter and ale with the chill off'. It was impossible to say whether those who quaffed it were sweating from the broiling sun or the blaze. Troopers caracoled their wild-eyed horses. Fire crested along the roof's ridge before, with a whoosh, it fell in. Sparks leapt towards the burning sun as, within twenty minutes, Bentley's and nearby shops and tents were destroyed.

The roar of flames as they devoured the hotel could have been the diggers' hot anger. The authority of the Camp officials, who impotently witnessed the riot and destruction, collapsed as spectacularly as the hotel roof. Ridiculed by the diggers, officials, troops and police withdrew to the Camp leaving a smoking ruin, which was the pyre of their prestige.

Sam Huyghue, the chief of the seven Commissariat clerks, wrote that in the Camp 'the general feeling was one of angry humiliation'. Now the Camp dreaded being overrun.[15] It was rumoured that the diggers planned to burn it that same night. Guards to the approaches were doubled, the garrison was under arms, and women unable to leave took refuge in the thick-walled Commissariat. Rede asked Hotham for reinforcements. The Camp had wanted to arrest more than three for the hotel burning, but desisted for fear of the reaction. On the arrest of the trio, a menacing crowd had gathered outside the Camp. Nevertheless Rede had insisted on a bail of £500 each, compared to the £200 set for Bentley on a far graver charge. It prepared the ground for further trouble.

The authorities' every move that Tuesday afternoon had been mistaken. Although Rede was responsible, his conclusion, apparently inspired by hurt pride, was not that greater firmness should have been shown, but, as he wrote to the Chief Commissioner, that the diggers should be taught 'a fearful lesson'.[16] He did not spell it out, but the lesson would be that Robert Rede commanded and that his name should not be taken in vain. It would be a lesson not only for diggers, but also for other commissioners and officials, the troops and traps, Camp employees and townies – Rede ruled. It would be designed also for Commodore Hotham in Melbourne, proof that Rede, resolute and implacable, ran a tight ship, even though subversives stormed.

If the 'little doctor' had nightmares, one may have been of himself as Aunt Sally at Bentley's, mouthing words to a jeering mob, in danger of apoplexy, impotently banging the butt-end of his whip on his palm when he wanted to lash the rioters. Earlier Rede had not believed in the licence system, but once trouble arose, he insisted on coercion, as he told Melbourne, 'the sooner the miners are shown that coercion can be used successfully the better'.[17]

Carboni was an old hand but in touch with many newcomers, particularly foreigners who needed his translation skills and sometimes turned his tent into a Babel. However, he recognised few faces in the Bentley's hotel mob. Since September Eureka had slumped. Carboni wrote to Archer that diggers were

> embittered by disastrous disappointment in these deep sinkings; idle perhaps for want of Capital, but averse to a death from starvation or a life in a work-house, hence desperate and must do something desperate, and can not afford to pay any more 'Licence' for sinking to try their luck, many of them working night and day like Niggers on an American plantation. This after all is the general feeling on the late hooting pelting and ridiculing of the Camp Officials on this Ballarat, a Nuggety Eldorado for the few, a ruinous Field of hard labour for many, a profound ditch of Perdition for Body and Soul to all.

The previous year diggers had lost track of the Eureka lead for eight months. Now the trouble seemed to be that four unworked claims were blocking progress. The erratic leads' zigzags had stymied diggers once again. This may have contributed to the huge turnout of Eureka miners for the earlier Scobie protest meeting. In contrast many at the thriving Gravel Pits had kept working until Bentley galloped past.

Diggers always worked upper slopes in winter to avoid the flooding frequent in the flat and then, in spring, returned to the basin. But in spring 1854, the Eureka-lead population dropped far more than usual. Late in September the *Ballarat Times* reported the effects on business:

> Many of them [the storekeepers] are shifting down to the Gravel Pits ... There is not a tithe of the population of last winter now left ... at present the storekeepers are hardly able to pay their licences ... we have never seen business so dull or businessmen so care-worn and dispirited as they are at present on the Eureka.

It added that storekeepers had asked the commissioners to forego odious prosecution. It was a reminder that storekeepers were nomadic like the diggers, and shared their fortunes and their licence preoccupations. At this inauspicious moment, when less money was available, Hotham pressed for more levies.

The economic downturn was accompanied by lawlessness which worried Carboni. 'All friends of Freedom, order and progress must lament when the

Law is turned into a Sow left weltering in the mire', he wrote to Archer on 18 October about the hotel incident. He was upset enough to change his metaphor as he continued, 'and the Law officers ridiculed as decrepit diseased harlots'. Four days later he again wrote to Archer of the 'deplorable work of destruction', describing the hotel site as a 'vast charcoal hearth and a scene of desolation all around'. He mentioned rumours that the hotel night-watchman 'has got the pluck to jump the golden hole'. In fact, the night-watchman Tom Mooney was to receive a reward for testifying against Bentley and Farrell.

Carboni referred to the 'fermentation for evil' in Ballarat. As a former bank clerk, he may have been shocked by the robbery of £15,000 in gold and notes from the Ballarat Bank of Victoria at noon the day before Bentley's burnt. Four men, dressed as diggers wearing sou'westers and black masks, had bound the manager and his assistant, then made a getaway. Carboni noted that a £1600 reward was offered for the apprehension of the bank robbers compared to £500 for Scobie's killer. Carboni had taken out a new three-month licence from Amos; the day of his departure was receding and he wanted to be able to grub for gold in peace. An incident he recounted to Archer, however, was more typical than the robbery and more irritating – a clash, with pistol shots, between two parties of diggers because one group had swum in the other's waterhole. 'I am sick of these scenes of blood', Carboni wrote. 'There is a rare Mob quite of Marat's cast on this Ditch of Ballarat and they mean to raise the Cain!! and pay no more for licences.'

Carboni had law-and-order instincts, but he may also have considered Archer would appreciate these sentiments. His description of himself as a 'friendless outcast since wandering from my father's house' in the letter written after receiving news of his father's death suggests Archer reassured him. Carboni sent excited reports of his adventures to that paternal figure. But Archer had turned down a Carboni proposal, perhaps a request for Archer to stake him, and Carboni had responded rather facetiously as if he had run head-on against English reserve.[18] Carboni still wrote to Archer but perhaps his expectations of the Englishman had been disappointed.

There was a more important event than the waterhole shootout that Sunday. After Mass, Catholics decided to protest to Rede the following day against the fining of Father Smyth's servant. Eureka men were the bulk of the Catholic deputation which met Rede on Monday morning. He told them to petition the Governor to re-open the case of the priest's servant, but they thought he was merely stalling. The acting police commissioner, Charles MacMahon, a Dubliner who was up from Melbourne, described them as 'the Tipperary mob, one of the most powerful and troublesome to contend with and who seem bent on mischief'. MacMahon was worried not only about the Tipperary mob, but also about the drunks among his police and the fact, as he complained to Hotham, that the police were forced to act 'like a military barracks for coercion'. He asked his representative in Ballarat, Inspector Gordon Evans, who would police the police. Evans responded that he had recently been sent thirty ex-soldiers of whom nearly twenty were inveterate drunks. Because understaffed, he explained, he had not been able to dismiss all. He added that they were accommodated in miserable tents, often without stretchers or blankets, and sometimes, after night-time guard duty, had to search for licences.

There were ample reasons for the police to be disgruntled, but they contributed to the diggers' anger as thousands of diggers gathered at Bakery Hill to protest the charges against Henry Westerby, Thomas Fletcher and Andrew McIntyre for the hotel burning. Westerby, a hard drinker, had been a riot ringleader, but the role of Fletcher, a printer who produced many of the diggers' protest posters, was not clear, while McIntyre had pleaded for order and tried to quell the flames. But the diggers' stand was not based on the trio's degree of guilt, but on a feeling that the rank injustice of the Bentley verdict had provoked the hotel fire.

Prominent at the meeting were three Chartists who intended to establish a Ballarat Reform League – Henry Thomas Holyoake, a storekeeper; George Black, editor of the *Digger's Advocate;* and John Basson Humffray, who, according to Carboni, inclined to a 'John Bull' build. The meeting decided to gather funds for the defence of the 'arsonists'; both Humffray and Tom Kennedy, the Scot who had addressed the crowd about his friend Scobie before the burning of Bentley's, trenchantly criticised the Camp. A committee formed to collect evidence included Kennedy, Peter Lalor's mate Timothy Hayes, John Manning of the *Ballarat Times* and Samuel Irwin, the *Geelong Advertiser* correspondent and secretary of the Ballarat Glee Club. Frederick Vern lent £100 to the committee and was then enrolled.

Vern, who had arrived in Melbourne as a first mate, had all the *bragadoccio* attributed to Italians, but claimed to be from Hanover. Perhaps Carboni's time there made him doubt Vern's claim, for he suspected him of Mexico-

Peruvian provenance. According to Carboni, Vern spoke bad English, worse German, abominable French and belonged to the school of 'Illuminated Cosmopolitans'. He admitted that clean-shaven Vern, who often carried a large sword, had a fine physique, with a 'splendid' chest, broad shoulders and long legs which made him 'a lion among the fair sex.' But Carboni added that he had 'opposum eyes', was an inveterate blatherer and believed in 'nothing except the gratification of [his] silly vanity'. When Vern was working with a mate in a 132-foot hole, a party led by Commissioner Johnstone demanded their licences. Vern produced his but that of his mate was in his tent one-and-a-half miles away. Vern lent him £5 as bail. The next morning they waited at the Police Court from 9.30 to midday, but the case was not called. The clerk told them no licence cases had been called that morning. However, outside the court they saw Johnstone, who said that as they had not been present at 10 a.m., the bail was forfeited.[19] No wonder Vern was spoiling for a fight. He was not the only resentful digger which was ominous when many of those who enforced order were drunkards.

Sullen excitement

The Catholics, who had been cold-shouldered by Rede, met on Wednesday, 25 October. Protest meetings were all the rage as if mining itself had become a secondary concern. Several currents of protest were beginning to converge but still sought constitutional channels for redress of wrongs rather than resorting to direct action. But how long would diggers be satisfied with these if no heed was paid to the editorial in the 28 October *Ballarat Times:* 'The corruption of every department connected with the government in Ballarat is become so notorious and barefaced that public indignation is thoroughly aroused.'

Hotham, evidently concerned by the stirring of the motley crew marooned above Ballarat's rivers of gold, moved to restore respect for law. Heeding Johnstone's dissenting opinion on the Bentley trial verdict, he had ordered retrial of the hotel keeper and his accomplices. On 30 October he appointed a three-man Board of Enquiry into the burning of Bentley's, the murder of Scobie and the charges of corruption against officials.

But the diggers wanted more: they demanded release of their three mates held since Bentley's burnt. On the same day as Hotham appointed the Board of Enquiry, placards went up all over the Ballarat fields announcing a Bakery Hill meeting to discuss the imprisoned trio. A brass band played as a crowd of more than 8,000 assembled on Wednesday, 1 November. Speakers such as Humffray advocated reliance on moral rather than physical force, while George Black of the *Digger's Advocate* expressed the hope that, unlike the Americans, diggers would obtain their rights without being forced to take up the sword. Recommendations against violence, however, were not as rousing as the message of Tom Kennedy who, after seeing the killer of his mate Scobie absolved, now advocated that the diggers take the law into their own hands. He reminded them that:

'Moral persuasion is all humbug
Nothing convinces like a "lick in the lug".'

Vern raved about 'red republicanism'. The diggers elected Humffray, Black and Kennedy as a deputation to demand from Hotham the release of the trio awaiting trial.

The Board of Enquiry interviewed fifty-eight men in the week to 10 November and received a submission from the group about to form the Ballarat Reform League. The submission, which suggested the group was a nascent political movement, detailed the diggers' grievances and blamed the Camp for the hotel burning.

Carboni attended the Bakery Hill meeting on 11 November when the Reform League was launched. Doubtless frightening the wits out of authorities from the Camp to Toorak and London, the *Ballarat Times* wrote:

> The League is not more or less than the germ of Australian independence ... we know what it means, the principles it would inculcate, and that eventually it will resolve itself into an Australian Congress.

Republicanism was only a distant threat; as one speaker said, the League did not want to effect any immediate separation of the colony from the parent county provided the whole free community enjoyed equal laws and rights. Humffray, the secretary, was a moderate while the League's programme was for full and fair political representation, manhood suffrage, abolition of property qualifications for parliament and payment of members.

Although the League speakers received an enthusiastic reception, Carboni was not impressed by its programme. He considered it a mere echo of London Chartism and his Mazzinian background made him scornful of gradualism. Morereover he suspected that Humffray, with his eloquence and cool smiles, was a friend of everyone and no one. But he approved the League's immediate aims: to disband the Goldfields Commission and abolish the licence fee.

Carboni's reaction indicates he did not transpose his nationalism or republicanism wholesale to Australia. Nationalism meant achieving Italian unity by ridding it of the foreigners who occupied many of its northern regions; he did not see the English as foreigners in Australia nor, as did some at Ballarat, look at Queen Victoria with republican eyes. While many Irish in Ballarat identified repression with the British flag, Carboni had high expectations of British rule and, when these were disappointed, felt it had declined to Austrian standards. It was this which reawakened his fighting instincts: his impatience with overweening authority had survived the long sea voyage.

The day after the Reform League was launched, the *Ballarat Times*, probably in the person of John Manning, lambasted local magistrates:

> Notwithstanding the host of magistrates on the Camp, every man of whom is in the pay of the government, in some capacity or another, there appears to be an absolute scarcity of these men after all. For the last week the public has been stultified and humbugged, waiting till eleven and sometimes two o'clock in the afternoon ... in such a community as ours, where every man has some important business, brooking no delay, to attend to, it is rather presumptuous in the hired servants of the public to neglect their business ...
>
> Occasionally we see such a crowd of the 'profanum vulgus', as Horace has it, collected about the sacred precincts of the Court House, waiting for the temple to be opened, that if seen on any other part of the diggings [it] would be construed into a serious riot. The magistrates may have the power but most certainly they have not the right to treat the public cavalierly.

Commissioner Johnstone was pilloried:

> Where there is such an abundance of magistrates it savours something of indecency to see a magistrate making a practice of popping down from the bench, on which he has been immediately administering the law, to become a prosecutor in some other case, and take the holy bible in his hand with as much nonchalance as if it were a number of the 'Parlour Library'. This is a practice with Mr Commissioner Johnson [*sic*] who, of all the gold laced in the Camp, is certainly the most 'generally useful' in this respect. One time adjudicating with all the state of magisterial display, and immediately after, tripping nimbly down, and becoming a prosecutor. If there be a necessity for his being a prosecutor, let him in the name of decency, confine himself to that congenial avocation; but while there are magistrates ad nauseam on the Camp let him not sit on the bench. Let him on the other hand, take the bench if,

despite of popular feeling, the Government wills it; but let him not continue the avocation of the prosecutor and the responsible functions of the magistrate in his own person: or let him be removed hence altogether, as a person who was an eyesore to the people, and it will meet with our unqualified approval.

The Board of Enquiry found the Bench astray in the Bentley verdict. It considered the decision 'opposed to the evidence and facts' and Bentley's discharge a 'perversion of justice resulting from partiality or venal motives'. It reported evidence that some publicans discounted bills for D'Ewes, and Sergeant-Major Robert Milne took 'hush money' from sly groggers.

D'Ewes was sacked, Milne prosecuted and dismissed. A trial of Bentley and his employees Farrell and Hance was ordered. But rather than act directly on the criticism of the licence-fee system and the police, Hotham appointed a commission to see whether law administration and revenue collection could be improved and whether diggers' complaints were justified. At the same time, he established with Rede, who was in Melbourne for much of November, a system for the speedy exchange of coded messages. This may have been because they had decided to pursue licence hunts even though Rede recognised their risk. Before setting out for Melbourne he had written, 'I look upon all direct taxation now as impolitic ... the miners have no personal ill-feeling to the police but they detest the system ... being hunted-up'.[20] The code Hotham installed was in keeping with the highly personal links he established with some officials. Huyghue accused him of 'jesuitically' making officials spy on one another; certainly the code implied there were officials he did not trust. Moreover it was deciphered and resented in the Colonial Secretary's office. Hotham tended to run the colony as his personal fief while insisting on the impersonality of law.

On Saturday, 25 November, the *Ballarat Times* carried the verdicts the diggers awaited. Mrs Bentley was freed but her husband, Farrell and Hance, found guilty of manslaughter, were sentenced to three years imprisonment with hard labour. In the other Supreme Court verdict (on the trio held since the burning of Bentley's hotel), McIntyre received three months, Fletcher four and Westerby six. The jury added a telling rider, that it 'would never have had that painful duty [to hand down the verdict] to perform if those entrusted with the government offices, at Ballarat had done theirs properly'.

The diggers had been vindicated by both trials but their three mates were still in gaol. The law had been upheld, commented the *Argus*, 'but the government had been disgraced'.

Humffray, in Melbourne to prepare briefs for the trio's defence, met Hotham, who indicated he might favourably consider a petition for the prisoners. But the Reform League committee decided by one vote to 'demand' rather than 'request' their release. When the deputation of Humffray, Black and Kennedy met the Lieutenant-Governor, the Colonial Secretary and the Attorney-General at the government offices on 27 November, Hotham bridled at the word 'demand'. He pointed out that when the Americans, through their consul, petitioned for Frank Carey he had ordered his release. The Reform Leaguers, however, had no consul. The deputation argued ably but Hotham, looking over his shoulder towards London, felt he was being forced into a corner:

> You have placed me in a position which renders the release of these men impossible … we all have to give an account to those above us, and it cannot be. I am sorry for it … we are all in a false position altogether.[21]

An opportunity to calm the waters had been missed. The discussion broadened to issues such as the availability of land and parliamentary representation for diggers. Hotham insisted he had the diggers' interests at heart and adduced his appointment of the Commission of Enquiry:

> Tell the diggers from me, and tell them carefully, that this commission will enquire into everything and everybody … you have only to come forward and state your grievances, and, in what relates to me, they shall be redressed.

He seemed more sympathetic than the cousins John Fitzgerald Leslie Foster, the Colonial Secretary, and William Stawell, the Attorney-General, who shared the siege mentality of many of the Anglo-Irish ascendancy fearful that their minority privileges could be threatened by a popular movement. The other side of this fear was contempt, as reflected by Stawell describing the diggers as 'wandering vagabonds' and 'vagrants'.

While Hotham was pledging himself to redress the grievances of the 'wandering vagabonds', Robert Rede was writing an anxious report to his superior, Sandburst-trained William Henry Wright, Chief Commissioner of the Goldfields. Rede wrote from a Camp in which, against an anticipated attack, key buildings such as the Officer's Mess, the doctors' quarters and the hospital had new fortifications of bags of oats and bran. He repeated his previous advice that, if law and order were to exist, 'nothing but crushing the agitation movement can do it'. However he did not have the necessary forces. He asked that 'Captain Thomas or some officer of known capability be sent up without delay', and predicted that under attack, 'every man will do his duty'. It was most ominous, he wrote, that despite 'trying to make use of money according to your instructions', he had great difficulty in getting information. The diggers appeared 'quiet and well-disposed'.

Father Smyth, however, had come, Rede reported, bearing a different tale:

> that we are in a most dangerous position, that measures had been arranged so as to make us the aggressors in which case it was determined to make a general assault on the Camp, he says the people are better organised than we imagine, that 1,000 rifles can be brought to one spot and that on one occasion when an intention had been formed of attacking the camp 900 had been assembled ... that things were in a dreadful state and much worse than we could possibly have any idea of, the only people not mixed up in it he says are the English.

If such scare stories came from Smyth, who needed paid informers? But was Rede reporting fully? This was after he showed no particular interest in redressing the insult to Smyth suffered through the treatment of his servant and shortly before Smyth was accused in the Camp of being on the diggers' side. It is likely that Smyth brought his alarmed report to persuade Rede to make some concessions, but no mention of these is made in the letter. It had a postscript which seemed to confirm all Rede's fears: 'As I was folding this dispatch Mr Commissioner Amos has sent in to say the mob have taken his horse out of the stable.' He added what can only be called a dramatic rider: 'they are trying to get up a cavalry corp.'[22]

Rede's reference to an 'agitation movement' could confirm Melbourne authorities' conviction that the main body of diggers was content. Like de Tocqueville's French nobles, the authorities believed the people had acquiesced in their ascendancy. They were insensitive to protests until the diggers became violent, in which case they attributed those protests to agitators. 'The government understands nothing but Irish hints', wrote a Bendigo correspondent of the *Argus*. 'If we are not in open revolution, we are perfectly content … we are not dissatisfied unless we are agitating …'[23]

The day after Rede's alarmed report the goldfields remained quiet, but by this stage he considered that odd. Nevertheless he decided to accept an invitation to attend a dinner in honour of the American Consul, James M. Tarleton. Speaking with the Union Jack and the Stars and Stripes as background, Tarleton recommended obedience to the law. Despite this, Rede was to tell Wright:

> I cannot help thinking that the Americans are playing a deep game … they are in a most insidious manner urging on the mob without showing themselves and I can only suppose it is with the view of Americanising this Colony.[24]

Rede had been called away from the dinner before he could respond to the loyal toast. An Englishman who took his place showed that scorn for the authorities was not confined to mud-spattered, sweat-stained 'vagrants':

> While I and my fellow colonists claim to be and are thoroughly loyal to our sovereign lady the Queen, we do not and will not respect her men servants, her maid servants, her oxen or [gesturing to the chair vacated by Rede] her ASSES.

The diners applauded.

Rede had been called away because diggers had attacked the troop reinforcements. At 7.00 that evening the first of the reinforcements Rede had requested reached Ballarat. As soon as they were in sight of the diggers' tents, the detachment of about fifty men of the 40th Regiment descended from their horse-drawn carts. With fixed bayonets, led by Captain Wise and other officers with drawn swords, they marched along the road flanked by diggers who jeered them.

The diggers then heard that a larger force was following and that the Humffray–Black–Kennedy deputation to Hotham had been thrown into prison. (The rumour was as false as the Melbourne one that diggers had taken Rede and other hostages to ransom Westerby, Fletcher and McIntyre.) At 8 p.m. a detachment of eighty men of the 12th Regiment, accompanied by eight drays with baggage and ammunition, left the road and crossed the Eureka diggings either deliberately or by mistake. Previously the 12th had been popular, not least because it escorted gold to Melbourne. Diggers asked the commander if the carts contained cannon to be used against them. 'I have no information for rebels', was his answer.

In his tent, Carboni heard cries of 'Joe'; when he rushed out he saw soldiers of the 12th Regiment being pelted with mud, tree stumps, stones and broken bottles. Carboni and others had some success in placating spirits but farther up Eureka Hill diggers pulled soldiers out of carts and took their arms and ammunition. A drummer boy was seriously wounded, and a storekeeper, an American and some soldiers were injured. As Carboni and his mates discussed the attack, which they considered cowardly, an officer with drawn sword arrived and began to berate them. They offered to look for missing soldiers and soon found them. Mounted troops sent from the Camp to aid the shocked reinforcements were met by a volley of stones and pistol shots. They charged with drawn swords, chasing the diggers among their tents. The exhausted 12th finally reached the refuge of the Camp. There were wounded on both sides. Throughout the pitch-dark night guns and pistols were fired on the goldfields, where diggers lit countless fires.

The 12th's reception must have convinced soldiers such as Felix Boyle that they had to quell rebels. After fourteen years with the 10th Regiment in India, Boyle had been pensioned off and returned, unscathed, to his home town, Belfast. But as most of his friends were dispersed, some of them to the Australian goldfields, he joined the 12th a month before it sailed for Australia.

Late on the night the reinforcements were attacked, Rede wrote to Wright that, for the next day's Bakery Hill meeting, he was so convinced 'that active measures must be employed to maintain order and give confidence to the well-disposed, that I am determined to act in the most energetic manner'. But what if his energy was judged excessive? It was all very well communicating with Hotham in cypher but there had been an independent assessment of his behavior because of the Bentley trial.

> I hope that under the very peculiar and pressing circumstances in which I now find myself placed that should I overstep the exact line I may confidently look for the support of His Excellency the Lieutenant-Governor. It would have been a great assistance to me had I received some instructions or the opinion of the law officers of the crown on the exact extent on which I am legally empowered to go in a case of sedition.

Now that just over 300 extra troops had reached the Camp, he was uneasy about the consequences of employing them but sure the troublemaker Henry Seekamp should be removed:

> I cannot too strongly urge that the Editor of the *Ballarat Times* should be arrested and sent to Melbourne for his seditious article in the copy I sent down.[25]

Authorities claimed that, as constitutional changes giving diggers greater rights were on the way, agitators must have intended to foment unrest. But, by the same token, if authorities wanted to avoid clashes, they could have refrained from enforcing regulations which were likely to be changed. Miners' militancy could be justified because, after previous protests, the government had stalled until diggers left for new fields. Concessions had come under the threat of direct action.

The 29 November public meeting, to hear the report from the deputation to Hotham, would determine whether diggers continued to negotiate or resorted to direct action. The posters advertising it advised diggers to 'bring your licences, they may be wanted'. Two days earlier Father Smyth had written to Bishop James Goold's vicar-general at St Francis in Melbourne that:

> considering the sullen excitement prevalent over the whole of these diggings, I don't and cannot augur a peaceful conclusion … everything tends to an insurrection … What am I to do?[26]

Although he was about to lay St Patrick's College foundation stone, Goold lost no time in leaving Melbourne. Like the American Consul Tarleton, he hoped to keep his people out of trouble. In 1837 the Benedictine William Ullathorne, in Rome on a visit from Sydney, had met Goold on the steps of Santa Maria del Popolo church and recruited the earnest young Irish monk for the Australian mission. Chubby-faced Goold, dour and zealous, was both physically strong and strong-willed. When appointed bishop of Melbourne in 1847, he drove a buggy and four horses there from Campbelltown, outside Sydney. He was the first man to do so. He made a horseback pastoral visits to many goldfields: in November he had been in Ballarat, where he found Father Downing's tent 'the most miserable apology for a dwelling I have been in'. On receipt of Smyth's call for help, he headed for Geelong where he picked up Downing, who could be invaluable in a crisis pitting many Catholic diggers against authorities. Hiring a carriage and pair at Christy's hotel-stables in Geelong, they set out at 11.30 p.m., reaching Ballarat at 10 a.m. the following morning.

Goold must have feared the worst. He was to describe Hotham as 'mentally unfit for the high and responsible position of civil governor', and seemed to lack confidence also in the 29-year-old newcomer Smyth. He wrote in his diary on the day he arrived in Ballarat:

> The inquiry into the insult offered to Fr Smith [*sic*] in the person of his servant & the illegal fine in which the latter was mulcted has terminated in a most unjust discision [*sic*] approved by the Ex. & communicated to the clergyman in a most offensive manner. This slight which the Government put upon the clergyman & the unjust fine he was forced to pay for his servant together with the silent contempt with which the address of the Catholics approved at a public meeting [was received] have forced them into the ranks of the dissafeced [*sic*].[27]

The bishop vainly tried to dissuade two digger leaders from holding the meeting. 'I think a little kindness & forebearance on the part of the officials & Police would have gone far in conciliating them', he confided to his diary. 'It is however now too late.'

Goold did not attend the Wednesday, 29 November Bakery Hill meeting, but Smyth and Downing were there to argue for conciliation. With them on the platform when the meeting began at 2 p.m. were the Reform League leaders, reporters, and the deputation which had just returned, by Cobb and Co. coach, from meeting Hotham. Under the burning sun a sly grog-seller did good business on the platform, as did others among the 10,000-strong crowd. The chairman was Timothy Hayes who, according to one onlooker, imbibed gin and soda water. A hurriedly made flag, a stylised Southern Cross on a blue field, flew for the first time from an 80-foot-high flagpole. This 'rebel flag' was visible from the Camp, as was the crowd; Graham Webster and another commissioner recorded proceedings and could order their termination.

George Black, in his gentlemanly way, told the diggers of Hotham's objection to the word 'demand', adding that the Lieutenant-Governor was surrounded by injudicious advisers. Humffray argued that Hotham aimed to end the diggers' grievances and suggested sending him a memorial for the release of Westerby, Fletcher and McIntyre. But these counsels of moderation did not have the impact of Tom Kennedy's philippic. For a few seconds, rubbing his fingernails together, he surveyed the silent crowd, then shouted his rousing slogan: 'Brother diggers, moral persuasion is humbug. Nothing convinces like a lick in the lug.' After reporting the failure of the delegation, he denounced officials from the Governor down, concluding, to the diggers' roar of support, 'Follow me and I'll lead you to death or glory'.

A fat Aberdeen-educated lawyer wearing a gamekeeper's coat, Fraser, clambered on the platform shouting, 'the glorious British constitution', but was upended. In his first public speech Peter Lalor, who saw the importance of digger unity, proposed that the Reform League meet the following Sunday at the Adelphi to elect a central committee. Carboni seconded the resolution and Lalor bent to haul him to the platform. They were friends; they shared the same work and faith and were quite close neighbours on Eureka. Another link may have been that Carboni was in the Young Italy movement while Lalor, although not a member of the Young Ireland movement, had an elder brother, James, who was one of its leaders.

Carboni had had little peace as the goldfields tension mounted, for diggers with inadequate English were always asking him for explanations. That morning he had translated for them from the *Ballarat Times* and the *Geelong Advertiser,* but also jotted notes because friends had suggested he should speak on behalf of foreigners at the meeting. And wasn't he a descendant of the Roman consul who, in 63 BC, was a leader of the opposition to tyranny? His notes began:

> I come from old Europe, 16,000 miles across the ocean and I thought it a respectable distance from the hated Austrian rule. Why, then, this monster meeting today, at the antipodes? We wrote petitions, signed memorials, made remonstrances by dozens; no go; we are compelled to demand and must prepare for the consequences.
>
> The old style: oppressors and oppressed. A sad reflection, very sad reflection, for an educated and honest man.
>
> For what did we come into this colony? *Chi sta bene non si muove* [who's content doesn't budge], is an old Roman proverb. If then in old Europe, we had a bird in hand, what silly fools we were to venture across two oceans, and try to catch two jackasses in the bush of Australia!
>
> I had a dream, a happy dream. I dreamed that we had met here together to render thanks unto our Father in heaven for a plentiful harvest, such that for the first time in this, our adopted land, we had our own food for the year; and so each of us holding in our hands a tumbler of Victorian wine, you called on me for a song. My harp was tuned and in good order: I cheerfully struck up.
>
> Oh, let us be happy together.

After offering the vision of a Ballarat fiesta, Mazzinian rhetoric may have spurred on Carboni when he tackled 'in right earnest with our silver and gold lace':

> We must meet as in old Europe – old style-improved by far in the south – for the redress of grievances inflicted on us, not by crowned heads, but blockheads, aristocratical incapables, who never did a day's work in their life. I hate the oppressor, let him wear a red, blue, white or black coat.

He called on the diggers to salute the Southern Cross flag as refuge of all the oppressed from all nations on earth. One digger later claimed Carboni preached '*i sacri diritti dell'insurrezione*' ('the sacred rights of insurrection'). Tom Kennedy, who was no slouch himself as a rabble-rouser, accused him of a 'suicidal rant'. The political shoe had begun to pinch at last and the pain may have been partly that of old muscles coming into play again.

Carboni had been distant from the Reform League's gradualism; he did not share Seekamp's intimations of republican nationalism; the colony, he had implied, was a quarry rather than a theatre of politics. His aim had been to get gold and get out. But then he came to feel that the authorities were as oppressive as the hated Austrians. And he became an actor, his words winning acclaim as if he were performing in one of the plays burgeoning in his tent. By the Leddon he had learnt to love the land; now he realised he could fight oppression in Ballarat as in Rome. He was no longer simply a foreign observer.

Grog flowed, the sun scalded, Carboni and others paid the two shillings and sixpence Reform League membership fee. Frederick Vern proposed that they abolish licences by burning them and collectively resist the arrest of unlicensed League members. Father Matthew Downing advised against burning licences but was not heeded – the diggers believed themselves untameable lions. The Catholics among them acted according to Daniel O'Connell's 'we take our religion from Rome and our politics from home'.

Chairman Timothy Hayes drove home the implications of pledging to collectively resist arrest of unlicensed diggers. 'Should any member of the League', he asked the thousands who had given up an afternoon's work, 'be dragged to the lock-up for not having a licence, will a thousand of you volunteer to liberate the man?'

'Yes! Yes!'

'Will two thousand of you come forward?'

'Yes! Yes! Yes!'

'Will four thousand of you volunteer to march up to the Camp and open the lock-up to liberate the man?'

The roar of yeses was deafening.

'Are you ready to die?' shouted Hayes, thrusting out his clenched right hand towards the Southern Cross. 'Are you ready to die?'

'Yes, yes! Hurrah!'

Hayes was intoxicated by their enthusiasm. He boomed as if he hoped to be heard in Toorak:

On to the field,
our doom is sealed,
To conquer or be slaves;
The sun shall see our country free,
Or set upon our graves!

There had been nothing quite like it since Romans trundled the Torlonia cannon to the Quirinale and trained it on the government camp in Rome, Pius IX's palace. Licences were burnt, pistols fired. The 'physical force' party had carried the day but aims could be further clarified at the meeting Lalor had convoked prudently for the following Sunday.

A mere cloak to cover a democratic revolution

The atmosphere was still electric. Although Rede had opposed Hotham's increase in licence hunts, he marshalled all armed soldiers and police for just such a hunt. The diggers, who had pledged to die rather than be treated like felons, were once again to be hunted, paraded through the diggings, locked up with common thieves. Under a scorching northerly, Commissioner Johnstone, still chasing people despite the requests of Catholics and 4,000 Canadian Gully miners for his transfer, led police into the Gravel Pits. They were pelted with stones. Rede was summoned and was nearly hit by a lump of quartz. He told diggers that while there was a law he would enforce it, then gabbled the Riot Act and sent for troops who, flanked by cavalry, advanced in skirmishing order, one man forward, one man back.

On a police officer's orders, troops fired at a fleeing miner. Diggers responded with pistols, but on both sides casualties were slight. Rede claimed that 'at the risk of considerable slaughter', the Camp's forces, who took eight prisoners, maintained the law. As Rede left after what was to be the last armed licence hunt, he saw John Humffray and called, 'see the consequences of your agitation!' 'No', replied the Welshman, 'but I see the consequences of your impolitic coercion.'

Carboni was not only a protesting digger, but also corresponded with a man who had Hotham's ear. That morning, after an early start at the shaft, Carboni had gone to his tent to finish a letter to Archer with sound advice on how Hotham could head off trouble. He admitted that people always 'growled' at taxes but said the licence fee was an 'abomination ... the whole Camp had better be changed at once ... there will be eternal discontent as long as Rede and fraternity are lodging over that way.' Archer may have shown some of these letters to Hotham.

As Carboni was about to set off to post the lettter, he heard cries that a licence hunt was underway on the Gravel Pits. 'The traps are out for licences and playing hell with the diggers', he added hurriedly. 'If that be the case, I am not inclined to give a half-a-crown for the whole fixtures of the Camp.

I must go and see what's up.'

Nearby Peter Lalor was working at the bottom of a 140-foot shaft. He broke off when Timothy Hayes, who was at the windlass, called down the news. Other diggers were clambering out of shafts, grabbing weapons and running downhill towards the Gravel Pits, but the troops had retreated. The diggers decided to meet at Bakery Hill at 4.00 that afternoon. When they assembled, the Southern Cross hoisted at the previous day's meeting still flew. The men milled in angry confusion until Lalor, wearing dark tweed trousers and blue shirt, mounted a stump. Until that moment, handsome Lalor, 26, who topped six feet, had been a secondary figure: Vern was more belligerent, Humffray more eminent. But when the diggers needed a commander, Lalor surprisingly emerged. He thought of the Camp's latest brutal attack and the frustration of poor diggers for whom farming land was not available. With 'the burning feelings of an injured man',[28] he proclaimed 'Liberty!' and told the diggers to fall into ranks according to their arms and choose captains. George Black's younger brother Alfred noted the names of the divisions and their captains. Lalor threatened to shoot the first man who took any property except what was necessary for defence. Many diggers asked Lalor for arms.

Carboni, who had brought a sword from his tent, went to Lalor, who grasped his hand. 'I want you, Signore, to tell these gentlemen,' Lalor indicated the non-English speakers, 'that if they can't provide themselves with firearms, let each procure a five- or six-inch long piece of steel. Attached to a pole, that'll pierce the tyrant's heart.' Carboni relayed the message in other languages to the international brigade.

Lalor's left hand held the muzzle of his rifle whose butt rested at his foot. The setting sun gilded the clouds as, raising his right hand, Lalor told the diggers that those who did not intend to take a solemn oath to the Southern Cross should leave. Next he ordered the diggers to 'fall in'. After each divisional captain saluted Lalor, the Irishman knelt, removed his hat, and with his right hand pointing to the flag vowed: 'We swear by the Southern Cross to stand truly by each other and fight to defend our rights and liberties'.

'Amen', responded the diggers with religious solemnity. Their right hands, like Lalor's, extended towards the cross on a blue deeper than that of the sky glimpsed between clouds. An historic moment, thought Carboni, who had already lived a few; for him this was the climax of all the Eureka events. Perhaps he recalled the pledge of mutual solidarity by the crowd at the Colosseum before volunteers left to tackle the Austrians. They had stood with their right hands extended towards the Cross; here hands had been extended towards the Southern Cross flag. The shaggy-headed diggers' faces reminded Carboni of the Crusaders; at the Colosseum the reference to the Crusaders was explicit. His Rome experience shaped his perception.

But the mood was disturbed by a loud-mouth shouting that the diggers should fight for their rights and burn down the Camp like Bentley's hotel. A drunkard, Carboni first thought, but then, as his contacts with conspirators in Rome had made him hypersensitive to spies, he suspected the shouter could be an agent provocateur. Carboni gave the fellow 'a respectable kick in a less respectable region with a most respectable boot', which silenced him. Carboni was to learn his name, in dramatic circumstances, only later.

At the foot of the flagstaff, sword in hand, stood Carboni's former workmate, forceful Lieutenant Charles Ross of Toronto, surrounded by his rifle division. He hauled down the Southern Cross and fastened it to a short pole to lead the column of diggers who, two abreast, marched towards Eureka where they were to drill. Patrick Curtain, a robust Irish digger turned shopkeeper, exchanged his pike for Carboni's sword. He captained the pikemen, who included Carboni and John Manning. Some men were armed with pick and shovel. At Father Smyth's church, St Alipius, they turned to cross the gully. When Ross reached the Eureka road on the other side of the gully, Carboni looked back – the column was so long its tail was at St Alipius.

At Eureka, Lalor told the diggers that if government forces attacked immediately, they should fight them on the Gravel Pits and, if necessary, retreat to the Canadian Gully heights for a final stand. However, that morning's Gravel Pits sally had been enough for Rede. Lalor summoned the divisional captains and other prominent diggers to a meeting in a room of Diamond's store. Drawing on his experience at the Falcone restaurant in Rome, Carboni took precautions against spies and sudden raids. Bottles and tumblers were placed on the table as a blind. Among those present with Lalor and Carboni were Timothy Hayes, John Manning, Patrick Curtain, Frederick Vern and small, bearded Edward Thonen, a Prussian lemonade seller and skilled chess player Carboni had first met at Sailor's Gully. He praised Thonen as a man whose word whas his bond.

Carboni and Manning presented a motion that Lalor be temporary president until a commander-in-chief was elected. Although the Lalor family had a centuries-old fighting tradition, Peter confessed he had no military knowledge. Unfortunately he was to show this was all too true. He added that he did not seek the chief command but, if appointed, would do his duty manfully: 'I tell you, gentlemen, if once I pledge my hand to the diggers, I'll neither defile it with treachery nor render it contemptible by cowardice.'

John Manning then proposed Carboni as commander-in-chief, pointing to his scars as evidence of pluck against aggressors in his homeland. It was flattering to be cast as the diggers' Garibaldi, but Carboni declined, claiming to be weakened by working in the damp at over 100 feet. Perhaps he was shrewd enough to realise that, if troubles were in store, the commander-in-chief should be British.

Vern, whom the Camp considered the troublemakers' leader since he had advocated licence-burning, launched into a lecture on military tactics. He claimed he had a posse of about 100 men and promised a 500-strong German rifle brigade, but Lalor's questions about it did not evince clear answers. After praising Lalor's comportment under pressure from the Camp, Carboni argued that, as he enjoyed the men's confidence, he should be their commander. The Edward Thonen seconded the motion, which was carried eleven to one. Possibly Vern, who saw himself as the diggers' leader and was peeved at Lalor's popularity, cast the contrary vote.

A prolonged 'hurrah' from the waiting diggers greeted the announcement that Lalor was commander. Many diggers were keen to use force. Lalor asked Carboni to tell them in various languages that the Council had to meet again. 'Go ahead, Great Works!', shouted the excited diggers.

Father Smyth and George Black joined those who had elected Lalor in the Diamond store Council room. Black, a carroty-haired beanpole, proposed a deputation be sent to the Camp to demand both the immediate release of those arrested during that morning's licence hunt and a pledge that hunts would cease. As delegates, Smyth proposed Black, and Lalor nominated Carboni; the diggers waiting outside approved.

As they descended towards the Camp, Father Smyth, who accompanied them, whispered to Black. Perhaps he was coaching Black because he did not trust impetuous Carboni. After the. recent heat, it was a cold night with the moon huge in a clear, starry sky. Drinkers could be heard cursing and shouting. Groups of diggers, discussing the day's events, asked the deputation for information as it passed them. At the Yarrowee Bridge police stopped the trio, but Smyth was allowed through to explain the mission.

Cork-born Sub-Inspector Taylor, in silver-lace cap and blue uniform with jingling sword, came to accompany Black and Carboni, whom he recognised. 'We've always been on good terms with the diggers', said Taylor, whose manners Carboni found French, 'and we hope we may keep friends still.' He climbed with the deputation towards Commissioner Rede who stood in the moonlight with an arm tucked, Napoleon-like, in his jacket. Rede impressed Carboni who recalled that he had helped honest diggers out of trouble. At Rede's left was Police Magistrate Charles Hackett who had mean eyes but splendid blond whiskers, a good heart and an amiable manner. Carboni called him the only Camp official who was not detested.

Rede told the deputation he was meeting them in the open as a digger onslaught was anticipated. It would have taken more than Rede's Napoleonic pose to daunt Black, who had not been overawed by Hotham. 'It was very imprudent of you, Mr Rede, to challenge the diggers at the point of the bayonet', he said referring to that morning's Gravel Pits sweep. 'Englishmen'll not put up with your shooting-down any of our mates because they haven't a licence.'

Rede's version was that shots had been fired at troops checking licences and three of the mob's ringleaders were held on riot charges. Black vindicated the diggers and presented their first demand.

'Demand!' echoed Rede, startled. The word was as offensive to his dignity as necessary to that of the diggers. He affirmed he obeyed only the government and repeated that the men had not been arrested for lacking licences.

> This is the way honest diggers are misled. Bad characters get up a false report: it finds its way into certain newspapers and Camp officials are held up as the cause of all the mischief ... these men are charged with rioting and it's out of my power to interfere with the course of justice.

But Rede agreed to release two on bail, which Smyth would bring the following morning. Black presented the second demand that licence hunts be abandoned. 'What do you think, gentlemen, Sir Charles Hotham would say if I were to give such a pledge?' asked Rede, and then answered himself: 'Why Sir Charles would have at once to appoint another Resident Commissioner in my place!' To Carboni, Rede now seemed a marionette jerked by wires from Toorak. And he was about to appeal to 'dooty', which Carboni considered a poor substitute for brains: 'I have a dooty to perform, I know my dooty, I must *nolens volens* adhere to it'.

Black's argument that suppressing licence hunts would avert bloodshed forced the Commissioner to show his hand:

> It's all nonsense that the present agitation is intended solely to abolish the licence. Do you really wish me to believe that the Ballarat diggers will no longer pay two pounds for three months? The licence [protest] is a mere cloak to cover a democratic revolution.

These words disclosed the authorities' ultimate fear. No doubt confirming Rede's worst suspicions, Black admitted that the licence issue was not the only grievance, for the diggers wanted parliamentary representation and to 'unlock the land'. Realising this would frighten Rede, Carboni said the diggers' immediate aim was to avoid further licence hunts.

> I speak for the foreign diggers who I here represent. We object to Austrian rule under the British flag. If you'd pledge yourself not to come out any more for the licence until you've communicated with Son Excellence, I'd give you my pledge.

'Give no pledge sir,' interrupted Father Smyth, 'you've no power to do so.'

Later Carboni explained he merely intended to make the sensible suggestion that he would try to calm the diggers until Hotham responded, but Smyth's interruption, which may have stirred memories of other censorious clerics, silenced him. Carboni recalled that, on the way to the camp, Smyth had excluded him from conversation as if distrustful. Rede leant forward and his forefinger tapped Carboni's clenched hands as he said, 'My dear fellow, the licence's a mere watchword of the day and they make a cat's paw of you'.

Black spoke up for Carboni, who may have been asking himself if, as in Rome, he was part of a larger political design which he would not see until arrested. Moreover, here, as a foreigner, he was even more vulnerable.

Rede consulted with Hackett, who argued the Commissioner should assess the advisability of a licence hunt the following day. 'But, gentlemen,' Rede warned, 'I give no pledge.'

Taylor, looking to Carboni like a puss-in-boots, accompanied the disappointed trio to the bridge. As best he could, Black calmed the diggers who had descended Main Street to hear the result, then at Eureka he reported Rede's reaction. Carboni added the prediction that even if Rede were for moderation, the redcoats would override him and licences would be hunted the following day, or rather the same day, for it was dawn, 5 a.m. Friday, 1 December, before the diggers dispersed.

That night Father Smyth retraced the road to the Camp, presented himself again to the sentry and was accompanied once more to Rede. Dignity did not require him to make demands; he was simply appealing to avoid violence. He 'pressed me very much', Rede wrote to Wright the following day, 'assuring me that would I do so [desist from licence hunts] every man would return to his work'.

'I refused', reported Rede, who foolishly interpreted such requests as a sign of weakness:

> I should not mention this but I think it shows they are frightened ... I should be sorry to see them return to their work as by their present conduct they are disgusting the majority with mob law, total stagnation of trade and the ruin of some of the best claims after seven or eight months work ... we may be able to crush ... the democratic agitation at one blow which can only be done if we find them with arms in their hands and acting in direct opposition to the laws.

Short on facts and lacking empathy, Rede was now enjoying the brinkmanship, for he was confident he could isolate the 'troublemakers'. Rebuffed by Rede, that same long night Smyth dashed off a letter to Hotham pleading temporary suspension of the licence laws.

Soon after sunrise on Friday, armed diggers arrived at Eureka from all directions and began drilling. About 9.00 they demonstrated at Bakery Hill but, as many diggers had drifted into town in small groups, the Camp did not ride out for fear of an attack from the rear. At 10.00 came word that redcoats were under arms and about to hunt licences. The Camp was carrying the fight to the diggers. Lalor ordered a stockade be built.[29] Vern, still wearing his huge sword, was in charge. *'Wo ist der Raffaello?'* he shouted, *'Du Barrikaden bauen.'*[30] ('Where's Rafffaello? The palisade has to be built.')

At gunpoint, but also with an illusory promise of payment, the Tipperary boys pressed into service a circus brass band lodged at the Charlie Napier Saloon.[31] As they played marches such as 'Ben Bolt' on their way from the Gravel Pits to the Stockade site, they were joined by miners in flannel and moleskins straight from their shafts, and dandies in colourful, extravagant clothes. Some volunteered, others were conscripted at gunpoint. The band played on as, at three-foot intervals, outward sloping shaft slabs were driven into the ground. Other slabs, boulders, tree stumps, carts were criss-crossed between these teeth to form a four-foot-high breastwork. The roughly rectangular palisade enclosed about an acre, and included Patrick Curtain's licensed store, Thomas Allen's store and coffee house, Lalor's hut, several tents and the smithy of John Hafele from Wurttemberg who boasted of his valour in the Mexican wars. Hafele was hammering pikes as fast as his strong arms allowed and promised they would 'fix red-toads and blue pissants' but Carboni doubted if his coarse handiwork, usually meant for kangaroos and wild dogs, would even skewer an opossum. The Stockade looked formidable, but Carboni could have asked if Garibaldi would have gathered his forces in an enclosure where the enemy could concentrate its attack.

Towards 5 p.m., about 300 reinforcements, unarmed and exhausted, arrived from Creswick goldfield 9 miles away. After meeting Rede, George Black had headed for Creswick to rouse support there with Tom Kennedy who, sword brandished above his head, led the newcomers. The ragged Creswick diggers had been assured that arms, ammunition and provisions were available in Ballarat where all miners' grievances were about to be redressed. Their arrival was a complication. Resourceful Edward Thonen organised drays of bread and provisions, while Eureka butchers donated meat to be cooked on the Stockade fire. But there were not even enough arms or ammunition for the original Stockaders.

At sunset diggers cheered as Alfred Black read a Declaration of Independence. There was talk of taking the Camp, the banks, then Melbourne. Henry Nicholls, a Chartist poet who had edited the *Digger's Advocate* with George Black, was drinking tea with his brother and others in his Red Hill tent when his former workmate, Lieutenant Ross, arrived with two files of armed Stockaders. Ross said that if Nicholls were not prepared to fight in the Stockade, he should hand over his rifle and his brother's. Nicholls avoided requisition of the arms by promising to bring them to the Stockade and to decide there whether to join Lalor's forces. However, not all out 'pressing' were as gentlemanly as Ross. Some demanded arms and ammunition at gunpoint without giving receipts. Others plundered in the name of the Stockaders. The belligerence and confusion estranged many diggers. Humffray and Smyth, whose negotiation attempts looked like betrayal to the extremists, were threatened. Humffray was told he would be hanged, Smyth that he would be shot (the Camp also told him to choose sides; there was little space left for mediation).

John Manning told Carboni a committee meeting at the Star Hotel was pushing for more aggressive action. There was word of troops marching from Melbourne. Nealson, an American carpenter who had the best armed corps, led his men, as did Ross, through the bush in a vain attempt to ambush the reinforcements.

In a 2 December letter to Wright, Rede claimed the Rioters were divided into six companies. 'About five hundred of them are determined men and the greatest scoundrels in the Colony – they are now entrenching themselves on the Eureka.'

Presumably using information supplied by his spies, Rede reported that instructors were telling their troops to shoot officers first. 'Mr Johnstone and myself are looked on by diggers as doomed.' He added that diggers in search of arms were stopping drays on the Geelong road and that Captain Thomas had warned officers against ambushes; the wounds from the diggers' 28 November attack were still raw. J. Wellesley Thomas, whose father had fought at Trafalgar, had acquired his commission by merit, not money. His first assignment with the 40th Regiment had been in India and Afghanistan where, in December 1841, 14,000 soldiers and hostages had died in snow-covered passes. He had sustained a leg wound in the march on Kabul and fought also at Maharajapore in India. His cool behaviour, as commander of forty crack mounted troops, during the anti-licence troubles in Bendigo the previous year had helped defuse that situation. But Ballarat was more ominous.

Rede told Wright that, to save the Colony, exemplary repression was needed:

> I am convinced that the future welfare of the Colony and the peace and prosperity of all the gold Fields depends on the

crushing of this movement in such a manner that it may act as a warning.[32]

Rede's view coincided with the assessment of Charles Pasley, a 30-year-old engineer who, after missing out on promotion, had asked on 25 November to go to Ballarat. Pasley, the eldest son of General Sir Charles William Pasley, had seen service in Canada and Bermuda before joining the staff of the Crystal Palace Exhibition in 1851. On 30 November, Pasley had written to the Colonial Secretary that 'conciliatory measures will only do harm at so late a period of the disturbances ... the disaffected must be coerced'.[33] If Ballarat fell, he thought, the diggers could take over the colony; strong measures were the answer. Pasley feared that although all Camp civilians were armed from 1 December, they could not long withstand the constant tension and sleeplessness.

In the Stockade also, on that surprisingly cold Friday night, there had been spasmodic tension with almost hourly alarms about the arrival of troop reinforcements. Despite a digger's threat to shoot him, at 8.00 on Saturday morning Father Smyth arrived during Carboni's watch and obtained Lalor's permission to address the Catholics. Looking 'very earnest', probably without sleep, Smyth told them there were 700 to 800 armed men in the Camp with more due from Melbourne. Warning against shedding blood uselessly, he invited them to Mass the following morning.

As licence hunts never took place on Saturday afternoon, at midday Carboni and Manning went 'to get a bite' at Carboni's tent, the second from the Stockade on the hill west of it. While Manning peeled an onion, Carboni fried a steak at his chimney facing the Stockade and noted that only a hundred diggers were left inside.

Towards 4 p.m. on that hot north-wind day, diggers returned and resumed drilling enthusiastically. Suddenly Vern, who had extended the stockade higgledy-piggledy across the Melbourne road and down Warrenheip Gully in the mistaken belief that this strengthened it, shouted, 'Here they're coming, the boys; now I'll lead you to death or. victory!' A couple of hundred men were marching towards the Stockade. However they were not the German Rifle Brigade Vern had promised, but the Independent Californian Rangers' Revolver Brigade, who all had large Colts and some, at their hips, Mexican knives. By ensuring their autonomy, Lalor had convinced the Americans, many of whom had fought in Mexico in 1846–47, to drill in the Stockade.

That afternoon two other Americans arrived: pale, alert James McGill in his early twenties, who was said to be a West Point Military Academy graduate, and immediately began imposing discipline; and a surgeon, Dr Kenworthy. Bell-toppered Kenworthy had a letter of presentation from J.B. Humffray who had not been seen since the previous Wednesday. For Carboni, Kenworthy's arrival must have been particularly welcome for they chatted about Mazzini and a mutual acquaintance Captain Forbes who, in Rome, with Carboni had resisted the French forces on the Janiculum.

Thomas Allen, 59, a Waterloo veteran who ran a store and coffee house enclosed in the Stockade, returned from Melbourne Saturday evening with a drayload of stock. He was waylaid by Stockaders who took his gun, then he found that diggers from Creswick had robbed his store. He was busy there when diggers burst in and tried to thrust a pike in his hand. Allen told them the pike was so damned ugly he would not touch it. A digger sought to convince him to join them but Allen said a £50 bounty would be little enough for a Waterloo man. He was made prisoner with three pikemen at his door. He saw the diggers drill 'like an awkward squad' and heard pikemen instructed to poke their pikes into the horses' guts then draw them out from their tails. He escaped, reported to Captain Evans at the Camp on the Stockaders' preparations, and returned unseen to his tent.

Carboni, leaving the Stockade to check on rumours of reinforcements on the Melbourne road, saw 200 armed redcoats at the foot of Black Hill. He returned to report to Lalor but, as the password had been changed, unknown Californians refused him admittance to the committee room. Diggers rode in bearing requisitioned gunpowder, bags of shot, firearms and boxes of caps. Some, such as James Esmond, an Irishman whose Californian experience had helped him find the first gold in Victoria, were requisitioning conscientiously, but others continued to take it as an excuse for looting. A burst of shouting greeted Lieutenant Ross and his men as they entered with Commissioner Gilbert Amos as prisoner. Amos, who was on comparatively good terms with the diggers, had been rash enough to visit his Eureka station. Lalor ordered his release but Amos had time to note the Stockade layout. Lalor also expelled a sly grogger selling nips of brandy out of a keg hanging from his neck.

Two men on horseback were crossing the gully below the Stockade. George Black's younger brother Alfred, coming from the committee room, ordered Carboni to requisition the horses. Carboni said angrily that he was not yet a bushranger. Others armed with revolvers, however, forced the horsemen to enter the Stockade. Carboni, disgusted by the coercion, asked Vern the password. It was 'Vinegar hill', which could have been a reference to a suppressed 1798 uprising in Ireland or to a convict revolt in Sydney in 1804. Carboni left the Stockade, giving vent in French, German, Spanish, Latin and Italian to his annoyance at the devilish confusion there.

Henry Nicholls, fulfilling his promise to Ross, visited the Stockade. Lalor, he considered, hardly knew what he was doing, while Vern was doing 'nothing but mak[ing] a noise'. Nicholls claimed Lalor told him 'plump and plain' that he aimed at independence. About 10 p.m., Nicholls went to see if those, who were to give advance notice of a Camp attack, were on duty. He found them in a grog hut, playing cribbage and drinking. Nicholls, like some other diggers who deplored the indiscipline and extremism, returned home.

Carboni headed for the Prince Albert Hotel on Bakery Hill to meet friends. The German proprietor Carl Wiesenhavern had been eight months on the diggings. After a brief spell as a miner, he had run a store at Eureka before opening his hotel. Carboni, seated in the bar, knew trouble was brewing when he saw enter a bulldog-headed ruffian who growled, 'Who's the landlord here?' Like his nine henchmen, the sunburnt ringleader was heavily armed. Carboni detested such foul-mouthed boozers renowned for their 'black-eye-giving, nose-smashing and knocking-in of teeth'.

'Here I am', answered Carl Wiesenhavern coolly. 'What do you want?'

'Nobblers round.'

'If that's what you want, you'll have it with pleasure.'

'We got no money.'

'I didn't ask you for any: understand me well though.' With the forefinger of his clenched right hand, Wiesenhavern pointed at each in turn. 'You'll have a nobbler apiece and no more; afterwards you'll go your way. Are you satisfied with my conditions?'

'Yes, yes! We agree to that: go on you bugger.'

Wiesenhavern placed two brandy decanters with tumblers on the counter.

'Help yourself gentlemen.'

When they had, the ringleader said: 'Well landlord, your brandy's damned good – the real sort of stuff, and no bloody mistake. You shouted nobblers round for all hands – that's all right; it's no more than fair and square now for the boys to shout for you. Fill up the bottles, let's have another round.'

One of the ruffians tried to enter the bar to serve his mates. Wiesenhavern calmly dissuaded him by promising to fetch from his room 'something rowdy, the right old *stuff – champagne cognac très vieux*'. The ruffians, presuming Wiesenhavern was scared, were in high spirits awaiting his return.

Instead of cognac, Wiesenhavern fetched a lodger, John Brandt, a short, broad-shouldered German who looked formidable even when he was not, as now, bearing a double-barrelled gun. Wiesenhavern, with his habitual precision, placed a brandy decanter on the bar and, holding cocked pistols in both hands, said, 'Touch it if you dare: if anyone of you has the pluck to put in his tumbler one drop out of that bottle there, he's a dead man'.

'I'll shoot the fellow like a dog', added Brandt matter-of-factly. By this time regular customers were arriving to give Wiesenhavern support. The ruffians fled.

The customers said other groups were looting in the name of the Stockade committee. A gang of four had entered O'Connor's Golden Point store demanding, in the committee's name, powder and shot. They ransacked the store, eating Yorkshire hams, drinking coffee and stealing £20 from the cash box.

Although sure Lalor had not sanctioned such deplorable behaviour, Carboni ran uphill to the Stockade to remonstrate with him. It was about midnight when he arrived. The diggers who were still awake were warming themselves by a fire. In German, Carboni told Edward Thonen he had to speak with Lalor, but the response was that the commander had to sleep at least a few hours. As Carboni had not slept since Thursday, he decided to follow suit. Thonen gave word to the outlying Californian guard to let the Italian pass. The password was necessary as there was fear that too many had departed, leaving fewer than 200 armed men. It was a moonlit night, still and cool after the day's searing north wind. Carboni lay on his stretcher, perhaps recalling the questions posed at his Urbino College: 'What is Democratic government?', 'What is Despotism?', 'What does Anarchy mean?' All was quiet. Soon he slept.

Massacre Hill

The reinforcements from Melbourne, whose arrival in Ballarat had been expected hourly, were also asleep. Before setting out they had waited for days, perhaps while wheels were fitted to cannon from Her Majesty's ships *Electra* and *Fantone* lying in Port Phillip. Tars from these ships and the main body of the 12th and 40th Regiments (only advanced detachments were already in Ballarat) added up to more than 800 men. The operations were directed by 68-year-old Major-General Sir Robert Nickle, assisted by Deputy Adjutant-General Edward Macarthur, son of John who had introduced merino sheep to Australia. They were operating under plans originally prepared to quell trouble from convicts. Nickle, who had fought in the Peninsular War and in the Americas, was in charge of all military forces in Australia. He was in Melbourne to build Victoria Barracks as replacement for the army's temporary quarters in Spencer Street.

The troops, who were to put down the rioters before they marched on Melbourne, had set out from Flemington Bridge about 6 p.m. on Friday. Instead of taking the Geelong route, they passed through the flourishing township of Essendon to Keilor, where daily twelve coaches bound for Ballarat or Castlemaine changed horses. The troops camped in a field near the main inn. About 4 a.m. on Saturday morning, they broke camp. Dawn coolness gave way to a scorching northerly as the troops dragged the four cannons (two field guns and two howitzers) uphill towards the bare Keilor plains. The land seemed hostile to the penetration of Her Majesty's forces.

The recently arrived members of the 12th Regiment, in shell jackets and red-striped doe-skin trousers, suffered particularly but the whole force began to wilt. Many collapsed. Carts and bullock drays were requisitioned for them and also took the other troops' knapsacks. The wide cracks in the road made it difficult for the guns and drays. One officer found the parched, monotonous countryside a 'boundless waste'. At 2 p.m. the reinforcements stopped by a creek at Rocky Bank; they had covered only nine miles in ten hours. At the Rocky Bank hotel, wine or spirits cost a shilling a nobbler, ale or porter 3 shillings a bottle, but colonial beer only a shilling. Despite warnings against 'imbibing more than was sufficient for refreshment', the thirsty troops drank huge quantities of sour colonial beer. It was more insidious than insurgents. After an hour, an officer recounted, those who had indulged

> became the victims of the most excruciating pains and suffering ... in every form of internal bodily commotion did this deleterious compound operate; and the contortionist might have derived many an instructive lesson for his guidance.[34]

Eventually the debilitated troops resumed their march. After Melton, the countryside became more pleasant with trees 'whose umbrageous branches offer protection to the shepherd in his pastoral occupations'. All that was needed, suggested the officer, was 'erection of a suitable mansion to render it a fitting residence for the noblest of our aristocracy'. The weary troops finally reached Bacchus Marsh township, where they spent Saturday night in the government paddock. They had covered only 32 miles, less than half the distance to Ballarat, but it must have seemed they had crossed the Gobi desert at the summer solstice. There was not a hint of a breeze as the leg-sore 800 slept.

However, at the Ballarat Camp, Rede, Thomas, Pasley and Amos were still awake. Pasley had further fuel for his fear that the diggers' aim was 'Ballarat today, the whole colony tomorrow,' because that day Alfred Black had issued a receipt: 'this is to certify that a horse branded H.H. was pressed by order of the Commander-in-Chief for the use of diggers under arms'. The threat had been brought closer by a stray bullet hitting a jug Rede held in the officers' mess. Moreover, storekeepers were unreliable; Camp authorities feared they might cut off supplies.

As well as reports on the Stockade layout from Amos and Thomas Allen, informers brought word that Stockaders intended to ambush the Melbourne reinforcements. However now there were only about 150 in the Stockade and not all were armed. A successful attack would not only save the Melbourne contingent, but show that, despite doubts, Rede ruled.

It was decided to attack before dawn. At about 3.30 a.m. the troops were roused and marshalled as discreetly as possible for fear that the diggers had informers within the Camp. In all there were 176 infantry and 100 cavalry under Thomas, who had Pasley as aide-de-camp. Captain Wise, with eighty-seven men of the 40th who had 1842 Pattern muskets, led the main attacking party. Police Magistrate Charles Hackett and Commissioners Amos and Webster rode with Thomas; somehow, in the dark, the Riot Act calling on the Stockaders to disperse was to be read. (As Eureka was Amos's bailiwick, he would serve as guide.)

Silently the force left the back of the Camp and skirted the flanking hills where, in the still night, stringy barks stood motionless. On the moonlit flat, gums gleamed bone white. There was a haze which did not conceal, but without being spotted, Thomas brought his foot and mounted troops within 300 yards of the Stockade.

The 40th took up skirmishing order and began to move on the Stockade. Cavalry were on their left, mounted police on their right, with riflemen providing cover from higher ground. A shot rang out: a sentry, Harry de Longville, had fired it, waking Lalor who shouted to his men to prepare for an attack. Ross commanded the northern defences, Thonen the southern.

At 150-yards range, the two groups joined fire. In his coffee house tent within the stockade, Thomas Allen heard what he described as 'pop, pop, pop', which might have recalled Waterloo, and prudently decided to stay in bed. Half a mile off, John Bullas, a digger from Sheffield, England, stirred in his sleep, surmised an attack was under way but decided to breakfast before going to the site.[35] In half light on the Court House verandah, Sam Huyghue stood with other Camp inhabitants peering anxiously towards Eureka in Warrenheip's pyramidal shadow.

The firing might have inspired swift dreams of repulsing French forces from the Janiculum hill for Carboni, but as bullets whizzed past his tent, he rushed to his turf chimney overlooking the Stockade. The Stockaders' fire was so rapid and precise that the attackers wavered. A young bugler rallied the troops, who wheeled on an angle and regrouped to his left, then Captain Wise led them in a determined frontal charge.

The Stockaders were running out of ammunition. Carboni lost sight of Vern, who fled. Lalor, standing on the first logged-up hole in line with the main brunt of the attack, ordered the musketeers to shelter in shallow 'shepherd's' holes and called on Patrick Curtain's pikemen to skewer the advancing cavalry. But several shots smashed Lalor's left arm and shoulder. He fell, bleeding profusely. Those who had their heads above the barricade were mowed down by a discharge of musketry. Ross was hit in the groin; Thonen, who jumped on the barricade to repulse the assault, was hit in the mouth; the pikemen were hardest hit of all.

The attackers were hit also. Captain Wise, shot in the knee, fell, rose again and was hit a second time. He told his men his dancing days were over. Felix Boyle's lower jaw was shattered by a bullet. With fixed bayonets and swords, redcoats stormed through the front of the Stockade, cutting down diggers while cavalry broke through the rear. To cheers, trooper John King of County Mayo, Ireland, scaled the flag pole and tore down the insolent Southern Cross flag, which was thrown from man to man, then trampled upon. Later Hotham referred to it as 'the Australian flag of independence'. To see it in this way, transformed a riot into a revolution.

The mounted police, perhaps too well primed with rum, skewered the dead and wounded. One pikeman's corpse had fifteen wounds. A terrier sat on his breast and howled. Although removed time and again it returned to its dead master, even as he, with others, was carted away. Pasley had to restrain troops from bayoneting prisoners.

From his tent Carboni saw troopers dismount, take brands from the fire in the middle of the Stockade and set tents ablaze. For him they were devils. Near Diamond's store, where Carboni had met with others of the Digger's Council, he saw a powerfully-built trooper strike matches to set a tent alight. The wounded who had sought refuge in tents howled and yelled as they were burnt to death. Thomas Allen, smoked out of his Waterloo Coffee House, was made prisoner. A trooper and a soldier entered the tent of the Shanahans who in 1851 had come from Kilmarney, Ireland, because their landlord had burnt tenants' houses to evict them. Woken by the firing, Mrs Shanahan had told her husband to take his gun and fight, but he hid in the outhouse. The trooper told the soldier to shoot Mrs Shanahan, but he refused. They ordered her out, then set fire to the tent, but she managed to douse it before much damage was done.

The mayhem spread beyond the Stockade. Quinn's tent, next to Carboni's, burnt merrily. Carboni's could have been the next with him leaving the chimney in a red blaze. He grabbed his most important papers, jammed on his floppy, broad-brimmed cabbage-tree hat and rushed out to remonstrate. Sub-Inspector Carter, who commanded the twenty-four-foot police, pointing with his pistol told the indignant redhead to fall in with a batch of prisoners. Halfway down the gully, Carboni complained about his arrest to Captain Thomas, who asked if he had been made a prisoner within the Stockade.

'No sir.' After a few more words, Thomas gave Carboni a gentle stroke with his sword: 'If you really are an honest digger, I don't want you, sir; you may return to your tent.' Carboni was released, along with Gordon, a storekeeper who had likewise been made prisoner outside the Stockade.

As Carboni, relieved but still distressed, climbed the gully towards his tent, a trooper on the Ballarat road took aim with his Minie rifle, which had a 900-metre range. The shot knocked off Carboni's cabbage-tree hat. A Mrs Davis, who stood outside her tent nearby, ducked for cover. The troops could have been hunting game; they were more murderous than the French in Rome five years earlier.

'Raffaello!'

It was Dr Carr, an early advocate of Republicanism whom. many diggers suspected as a turncoat, calling from the Stockade. Father Smyth, standing near Carr, gestured to Carboni that his help was needed.

What a sight! Teddy Moore, Carboni's neighbour and workmate, with both thighs smashed, pleaded for water; poor dead Thonen's mouth was choked with bullets. Blood streaming from under slabs led to Lalor, who seemed in a death agony. The smell of powder and burning flesh ruined the blue morning. As the injured breathed, blood pumped from their wounds, or bubbled, burst and trickled away. John Hafele, the blacksmith from Wurttemberg, his chest smashed, had died in the arms of a woman while begging for water. Anne Diamond, who had fled from her store tent at the first shots, returned after forty-five minutes to find her husband's bayoneted, sword-slashed body and their store a blackened ruin. 'God saw', she said, '... and they will pay for it on the Last Day'. Ross, shot after being a prisoner for ten minutes, was carried to the Star Hotel, where he died.[36] When Carboni returned with a pannikin of water for Teddy Moore, he was amazed by the apathy of the diggers who, perhaps because under shock, merely watched the wounded. Father Smyth, however, with his anointed-of-the-Lord air, gave extreme unction to the dying until troopers, who threatened him several times, forced him to desist. But he returned later to take the hidden Lalor away on horseback.

With a few neighbours Carboni procured stretchers and, under Dr Carr's direction, converted the London Hotel, 100 yards from the Stockade, into a hospital. Carr asked Carboni to fetch his surgical instruments from Dr Glendenning's hospital two miles away on Pennyweight Hill. On his way back with Glendenning, Carboni met a certain Binney, an acquaintance from his early Canadian Gully days. Binney took him warmly by the hand: 'Old fellow I'm glad to see you alive! Everybody thinks', Binney pointed to a dead digger, red-bearded Johnny Robertson, 'that's poor Great Works!' Carboni took little notice of the incident but later was to realise witnesses might have confused him with Robertson. At the improvised hospital, Carboni dressed diggers' wounds; it was as if he were back in the Holy Trinity convalescent wards.

Towards 9 a.m. Carboni, whose Christian name meant 'God's healer', was bandaging the thigh of an American, who had been hit frontally at least half-a-dozen times, when a patrol of seven traps and troopers stopped outside. The fellow Carboni had kicked for his inflammatory shouting after the Eureka oath-taking rushed in and thrust a cocked pistol at his face. Carboni's suspicion that he was an agent provocateur became sickening certainty. His name was Henry Goodenough, which Carboni considered the equivalent of Judas Iscariot.

'I want you', said Goodenough from behind his eager pistol.

'What for?'

'None of your damned nonsense or I'll shoot you down like a rat.'

'My good fellow, don't you see? I'm assisting Dr Carr dress my friends' wounds.'

Goodenough continued to threaten. Carboni appealed to Carr, who said not a word in his defence. The fact that Carr, who had not been seen on Eureka during the agitations, was the first into the Stockade after the carnage, and that he took charge of the wounded, now appeared sinister to Carboni. He would have known the accusation that Carr was partial to Bentley both at the Scobie inquest and in the hotel owner's trial. Carboni was dragged out, hobbled to other prisoners and marched to the Camp. The main drama was over, but his own, a wholly unexpected epilogue, was just beginning.

He had walked the mile and more to the Camp many times as a free man but now he was hobbled, humiliated, at the whim of malice incarnate, Henry Goodenough, who clearly would relish shooting him like a rat. If only he had kicked the foul fellow harder at the meeting where Goodenough, paid informer, had pretended to take the pledge of solidarity. It was a replay of the

Holy Trinity priest's denunciation of him in Rome, but must have rankled all the more because this time he had been succouring the wounded.

That was the task the American Dr Kenworthy, who had brought Humffray's letter of presentation to the Stockade, had promised to fulfil. But when Carboni, with the other forlorn captives, arrived at the Camp, Kenworthy was there. Carboni gave Kenworthy a fearful look, for the American could have reported and also distorted every word of their earlier conversation about the fight for the Roman Republic in 1849. Goodenough, Carr, Kenworthy – he was betrayed on every side, victim once more of spies and double agents, a doomed man.

To Carboni, the victorious Camp seemed part emergency hospital, part boozy bedlam. John King allowed anyone to tear portions from the ragged end of what was now called the 'Revolutionary League' banner, the Southern Cross. The excited soldiers, drinking from a pannikin dipped into a bucket of brandy, verbally abused the prisoners while their dead comrades lay stiff in carts and, at the end of the Commissariat, the wounded sprawled half-naked and panting, the blue holes in their flesh already swelling. Inspector Henry Foster, who knew Carboni, told the prisoners to strip. A clerk misspelt Carboni's name. He pulled out a little bag of gold and his licence. Foster took the gold and Carboni handed his licence to the clerk for his name's correct spelling. As fresh prisoners arrived, Foster was called outside. Carboni wanted to keep his waistcoat for the money and papers in its breast pocket. A trooper accused him of being one of the Bakery Hill meeting speakers. His clothes (wide-awake cap, waistcoat, red shirt, moleskin trousers and watertight boots) were 'torn from him'. He protested but was kicked and knocked down.

He woke in the lock-up, naked, but was able to dress because a thoughtful friend had sent him clothes. It was so cramped prisoners had to take turns lying down. Carboni recoiled from the company of thieves and horse-stealers but still more from the fleas and lice which feasted on him. Stifling heat increased the stench of sweat, urine, shit; why was it always broiling hot, as it had been in Rome, when he was imprisoned? Towards midnight of that long, long day, Carboni was delirious and may have imagined himself in the hands of an antipodean Inquisition. In the confusion, those arrested under arms were mixed with those taken without them, which was to have serious consequences.

That night there was another scare in the Camp, which was edgy because digger leaders such as Vern and Lalor had escaped and insurgents were said to be gathering in the hills. Bullets struck the sacks of bran protecting the mess room. In an officer's tent a bullet cut a candle, which, falling, set the tent afire. Sentinels responded, nearly hitting startled J.B. Humffray, who crouched for cover, and wounding three other passers-by. Either because of this or the prisoners' howls of protest at conditions, about 2 a.m. Stockaders were removed, between two files of soldiers, to the spacious, zinc-lined, well-ventilated Camp store.

Rede, apparently sympathetic rather than exultant, visited them. He passed before Carboni, who told him in French that he had been wrongly arrested.

'Je ne manquerai pas de parler au Docteur Carr', promised Rede as if he had run into Carboni promenading on the Boulevard Saint Germain, *'et si ce que vous venez de me dire se trouve vrai, je veux bien m'interesser pour vous'* ('I'll certainly speak to Dr Carr, and if what you've just told me is true, I intend to do something for you').

'Vous êtes bien bon, Monsieur le Commissaire' ('You're very good, Mr Commissioner').

Carboni asked himself whether his Camp enemies acted for money or sheer malice. He would have given anything to know; but whichever it was, he felt he could never pardon them. The 128 prisoners were handcuffed in couples and lay in rows on the bare floor. A rampart of hay trusses and sandbags separated them from guards with levelled muskets.

Next morning, to derisive cries of 'The *Times*! The *Times*!', the paper's editor Henry Seekamp was brought in on sedition charges, mainly for hailing the Ballarat Reform League as the germ of Australian independence. Sardonic Seekamp looked contemptuously at the jeerers. Carboni, who admired Seekamp's courage and pitied his condition, spoke with him in French and, as he wrote later, felt that he was then and there classified as his accomplice. Seekamp had been arrested just as he completed an editorial on the Eureka 'massacre'.

Towards 10 a.m., the prisoners were ordered to fall in four rows. Camp officials chose some for further investigation. Not only did Carboni's 'red hair, fizzing red beard and fizzing mustachios' make him look inflammatory, but he was considered as one of the leading agitators. He was chosen; next to him was the 'nigger rebel' John Joseph, thought to have been a freed slave from America's eastern seaboard.[37] Athletic, dignified Joseph, who had arrived in Ballarat from nearby Avoca only a few days before the Stockade clash, was believed to have killed Captain Wise.

Word was that redcoats were sinking a large pit in the Camp. 'Are they going to bury us alive without fighting?' Carboni, frightened, asked an Irish fellow prisoner. 'That's not half as merciful as Haynau's rule in Austria.'

'Where did you read in history that the British lion was ever merciful to a fallen foe?' replied the Irishman earnestly.

The 14th would be Carboni's birthday. Was he to succeed in emulating Raphael only in dying, as had his fellow Urbinite, at 37? His situation was bleak but the Camp's victory was pyrrhic. On the goldfields flags flew at half-mast, diggers wore black ribbon in mourning but also red ribbon in defiance of the licence tax. Authorities spoke of 'salutary bloodletting', of having 'broken the neck of rebellion'. However, diggers persisted in their grievances.

A Bakery Hill meeting deplored even-handedly 'the sacrifice of so many lives', but pledged to take the diggers' complaints to the Legislative Council. John Humffray and Father Smyth were among those deputed to place the resolutions before Rede. He rejected them and arrested Humffray, even if for only a day. Rede ruled and would not tolerate even those who protested peaceably; they disproved that the contented majority was merely goaded by agitators.

On Sunday Melbourne had trembled at rumours that armed miners were about to sack it. But by Tuesday news of the slaughter in Ballarat (twenty-two diggers, four soldiers and two bystanders were reported killed, as well as scores wounded, with considerable destruction of property, but Captain Thomas estimated that 30 diggers were killed and others died of wounds) caused an anti-government revulsion. The diggers' mistake in gathering in a stockade had been topped by the attackers' in running amok. Somehow Hotham had to justify this to the Colonial Office, which already doubted his competence. Hotham enrolled special constables to ensure 'rioting and sedition would be speedily put down'. A public meeting called in Melbourne to express support for the government condemned it, instead, as a 'set of wholesale butchers'. *The Age,* founded only the previous month but already winning a reputation as the 'Diggers' daily', deplored that 'the lifeblood of nearly thirty brave men had stained the sod of this Victorian land …' It concluded: 'military despotism holds rule'.[38]

A scapegoat had to be found. It was assumed that the unpopular Colonial Secretary John Fitzgerald Foster, who had been the colony's administrator for a short time before Hotham's arrival, still decided policy, and he was blamed. People did not realise that in the Queen's name, Hotham could do more than the Queen would dare, exercising a disguised but very personal fiat. It was to emerge later that Hotham, 'so self-willed that he was indisposed to take counsel',[39] was responsible for goldfields' policy. However he did appoint a Royal Commission to review it. News of the resignation of Foster, whom Carboni considered 'Jesuitical', was balm for him in prison.

The reinforcements, with their cumbersome artillery and baggage wagons, finally arrived in Ballarat on Thursday afternoon. As martial law had been declared, Major-General Nickle ruled. Many preferred this to the semi-military dictates of the Camp civilians. Nickle moved freely among diggers and also visited the prisoners. Formerly a commander of the famous Irish 39th Regiment, the Connaught Rangers, Nickle noted the predominance of Irish prisoners and expressed sympathy. He told them he would prefer to be with them before the walls of Sebastopol and asked why, as Britons, they had not settled their differences without allowing foreigners to meddle. It was well-meant but must have turned Carboni's blood to ice.

Already, along with Seekamp, Timothy Hayes, John Manning and the self-possessed John Joseph, Carboni was the object of particular police enmity.[40] Seekamp, Manning, Hayes and Carboni were considered to have acted irresponsibly by inciting others to fight, although without participating themselves.

In a court crammed with uniformed witnesses, Carboni's preliminary trial began on Friday before the plump magistrate Evelyn Sturt, whose brother Charles became an explorer. Trooper Goodenough claimed that on the 30th he had seen Carboni, whom he took to be a captain, drill a company which seemed to be 'half foreigners, Germans and Frenchmen' armed with swords or long knives. Goodenough said Carboni told his men:

> Gentlemen soldiers those that cannot provide themselves with fire arms let them provide themselves with a piece of steel, if it is only six inches long and attached to a pole, and that will pierce the tyrant's heart.

This was Lalor's instruction which Carboni had relayed in various languages.

Trooper Andrew Peters, whom Carboni dubbed 'Sub-spy' as if he were an assistant to Goodenough, swore he had seen Carboni on that same day 'armed with a sword, a pistol and a revolver'.

Carboni had expected Goodenough and Peters, who could swear holes through iron pots, to accuse him, but was dismayed when other witnesses he had never seen asserted 'with savage eagerness' that he had been in the Stockade. Constable John Badcock testified that, when he jumped over the Stockade slabs, he had seen Carboni 'running around a corner of a tent'. Badcock said he had tried to fire at Carboni but his pistol snapped. Private John Donnelly, of the 40th, said he had seen Carboni in the Stockade holding a weapon; Private John Gower, also of the 40th, swore Carboni, pike in hand, had chased him from the Stockade; another Private, Patrick Synott, confirmed Carboni had chased Gower. Trooper John Dougherty swore he had seen Carboni taken prisoner in the Stockade, and Sergeant Hagerty said he was in the guard which took Carboni from Stockade to Camp.

Some may have mistaken Carboni for his red-bearded look-alike who had been killed during the attack, but he was convinced that the witnesses were mercenaries competing for the perjurer's prize. He pointed out contradictions and insisted that Sub-Inspector Carter, who had seen him emerge from his tent, and Dr Carr could vindicate him. It was so much wasted breath. Carter and Carr were not called. Sturt committed Carboni to trial for high treason along with twelve others. In addition, Seekamp was committed for sedition. In the lock-up Carboni had been discriminated against for not fighting, now he was condemned to trial for allegedly doing so.

Only two of the other twelve, Timothy Hayes and John Manning, were well known to Carboni, who was hobbled to John Joseph. Of the others, young Michael Tuohy had brought a double-barrelled gun from Creswick to the Stockade and had fought valiantly, while robust Thomas Dignam of Sydney had saved the life of a soldier by challenging the mob during the 28 November ambush. Five days later, Dignam had fought like a tiger against the soldier and his mates. Carboni did not know the other seven companions in misfortune. One, Joseph Campbell, was a black Jamaican. On 9 December, a Camp official informed Melbourne: 'Hayes, Raffaello, Seekamp the editor, and Manning the reporter have been committed. These are the principal persons.'[41] Carboni had a distinction he did not mention at any stage: surely he was the only one who was not on his first high treason charge.

Sergeant Harris, in charge of the prisoners, obtained good drinking water, which was scarce, and if handcuffs were tight, he eased or changed them. But Carboni suspected his kindness to Joseph was because he 'wanted to draw worms from the black rebel', while Joseph, scratching his black wool hair, widening his nostrils, whistling unearthly doodle music, called Harris that 'goddammed hypocrite'. Harris tried to humble Hayes, the best dressed and most prepossessing prisoner, by assigning him to empty the sanitary tub. Hayes complied once but refused to continue. More irritating than Harris, however, were the lice: Hayes' plump body was bloated by them; Manning suffered even more, while Carboni may have suspected the disgusting vermin were Jesuit-trained. A pointer to the food provided is a figure given three years earlier for the daily cost of rations: prisoners 7½ pence; troopers 1 shilling 3¾ pence; horses 5 shillings 7 pence.

Sunday was a scorcher. In the late afternoon, some of the prisoners paced, cursing their fate, while others stared fixedly as if under shock. Carboni was broken-hearted; he had planned to be on his way to his brother by now. Antonio was so distant he would not understand if he received a letter from prison; indeed a letter from Australia would take so long that, by the time it arrived, the prisoners would be acquitted or … Carboni's hopes of a fair trial had decreased when an incident persuaded him political influence reached into the lock-up. One night he had been hobbled to a white American, young Charles Fergusson, whose blue blankets he had shared. Fergusson had been in the Stockade on Saturday afternoon when Peters had spied there. But Fergusson was released. Carboni was convinced Dr Kenworthy arranged this, but, in fact, he was only one of several who helped Fergusson obtain a discharge. Carboni was left with the blankets and the suspicion that had he been a white American, he too would be free.[42]

The still-handsome Anastasia Hayes arrived with clean clothing and provisions for her husband Timothy, as he was bound with the others for Melbourne. She was a woman of spirit. Seeing her husband under arrest the previous Sunday, she had told him that, if she were a man, she would not have let herself be taken. Turning to Lieutenant Richards, who had arrested Hayes, she added, 'why didn't you come yesterday when the men were ready for you?' When Lalor's arm was amputated at Father Smyth's, where he had found refuge, she had taken the priest's place when he was too nervous to hold a basin to collect blood. Six neatly dressed children, mirror images of their father, accompanied Anastasia Hayes in her prison visit, and at her breast she had a seventh child. Hayes's small daughter climbed his shoulders; he blessed his younger son; the eldest child, a boy of 12, cried as he kissed his father's hand. Carboni felt it was a scene to match anything painted by Raphael. He lacked his fellow Urbinite's pictorial skill to record it, but, as he later wrote, when his 'electric fluid' flowed his mind was a daguerreotype. The fluid had flowed fast when he had watched the Stockade attack from his chimney. It had fixed indelible images of what he was to call 'Massacre Hill'.

Foreign anarchist becomes hero

At 4 a.m. Tuesday morning troops woke the prisoners. They were told to fall in, hobbled. The Carboni–Joseph pair, red-haired Italian, black American, both aliens, heard Captain Thomas announce that they were bound for Melbourne under his charge. If anyone moved a finger or lip, especially as they crossed the diggings, Thomas threatened, he would be shot on the spot. 'God save the Queen,' shouted Carboni at this Austrian-type *diktat*.

Gammy-legged Inspector Foster sprang at Carboni, put on 'tighter darbies' (hand-cuffs) and sat him with Joseph in front of a cart, giving orders that both be shot if they so much as turned their heads. From that moment, Carboni's hatred for the repressive Austrian generals Haynau, Jellačić de Bužim and their ilk declined because it had found an object nearer at hand.

It was already daylight as they hurried along the main road, where Carboni noted only one digger. Passing through Eureka, Carboni saw his deserted tent. Thinking of himself writing there contentedly of a Sunday, his eyes filled with tears. However, the superb landscape along the Melbourne road reminded him of Italy; tiny blue flowers were thick among gently swaying grass. Parrots, crows and other birds could be heard. A dozen armed outriders accompanied the three carts while a score of troopers with unsheathed swords and cocked carbines rode so close that one collided with a gum tree.

At 8 a.m. they stopped at Ballan to change horses. The chained prisoners were forced to lie on the hot ground. Captain Thomas and a stout, black-whiskered man dressed as a digger sat on a tree stump outside a pub drinking bottled lager. The escorts were served biscuits, cheese and ale, but Carboni and his fellow prisoners had to plead with the pipe-smoking redcoats for a drink. Carboni had promised Archer he would come to Melbourne before Christmas but he had not planned to arrive as a hobbled prisoner who had to beg for water.

Shortly after the convoy resumed, the prisoners were hungry and thirsty again but the carts dragged interminably across the dusty black soil plain to Bacchus Marsh. The prisoners were thrown into a lock-up, which was dark but cool and clean by comparison with lice-ridden Ballarat gaol. Captain Thomas won the men's gratitude by sending them a gallon of porter with ample damper.

After a punishing day, smothered with dust, burning with thirst, at 8 p.m. they finally reached Melbourne, where the University and Public Library under construction indicated that the township was becoming a city. There was even Victoria's own Crystal Palace, the original two-storey Exhibition Building, which was proof of 'pretensions of civilisation'. Another innovation, one which must have made Carboni's heart fall, was the massive Melbourne Gaol. He had shifted from the realm of timber and canvas to bluestone, which embodied implacable authority. It was not Ballarat's log lock-up – this was serious. It was a fortress almost as formidable as Castel Sant'Angelo, where political prisoners languished in Rome. The Metropolitan Prison, as it was called, occupied a whole block, with the entrance, courtyard and chapel fronting Franklin Street and the three-tiered cell block on Russell Street. Although work on it had begun in 1841, it had been opened only the previous January; it was brand new and built to last.

The black-whiskered escort offered a glass of ale to all before handing them to the prison governor, Mr George Wintle, with such a good report that they were given bread and cheese. They underwent the humiliation of stripping, then were shown their cells, 12 feet by 3, which had board beds. Carboni's cell, shared with John Manning and Michael Tuohy, was number 33. When the cell doors were bolted inmates could feel they were at the core of confinement. At Pentonville prison he had interpreted for a young German and his desperate mother. Now he was worse off than the German, without relatives who knew his whereabouts, liable to a death sentence. Despite the endless, exhausting day, sleep would not come. In the dark, as he later recorded, he made the return journey to Eureka, to everything he had left, and replayed the drama of the previous two weeks.

Father Smyth, writing to Archer the following day, thought Carboni was still in Ballarat. At his presbytery he had given Matthew Downing a lobster lunch which the older priest found an 'opiate'. While Downing took a siesta,

Smyth wrote to Archer, recounting the threats he had received from both sides while trying to mediate, adding that he was even told in the Stockade not to tend the dead and dying:

> would not this make a granite rock imbedded [*sic*] in polar ice turn to fire & much more one of my temperament & disposition who stakes his life for peace & would stake it doubly for the weal of the dying.
>
> Raffaello is a prisoner: he is not wounded: I could say more but more will not say. If he remains home, he shall not want. If he go to Melbourne you shall look after him.[43]

Unaware of Carboni's whereabouts, presumably Smyth did not know either that Rede was asking Hotham to order Goold to transfer him.[44] Rede reported that he had Smyth's Reform League membership card and claimed the priest had advised diggers how to attack the Camp. Apparently he did not know Smyth's part in the salvation of Lalor, who had a £400 ransom on his head but was now in good hands in Geelong. Rede refrained from arresting Smyth only for fear of angering Catholics, but proposed he should be arrested if he refused transfer. Rede's odd suggestion was ignored. Smyth was transferred to Castlemaine only in 1856.

The first post-Eureka inquest damaged the government. It concerned James Powell, a Cornishman who on 2 December had come from Creswick to Ballarat to visit a friend. Woken by firing at 4 on Sunday morning, he had ventured 20 yards from his friend's tent when troops rode up. He had recognised the red-haired leader as the Clerk of Peace, Arthur Purcell Akehurst.

'Stand in the Queen's name' Akehurst had called, 'you're my prisoner.'

'Very good, Sir. Don't be in a hurry, there are plenty of you.'

For his pleasantry, Powell was knocked down by a head blow from a sheathed sabre. The troops fired at him and rode over him repeatedly.

The coroner declared that Powell's death was caused by sabre cuts and gun-shot wounds wilfully and feloniously inflicted with malice aforethought by Akehurst and other persons unknown. The jury expressed extreme horror at the brutal conduct of the mounted police in firing at and cutting down unarmed and innocent persons of both sexes at a distance from the scene of the disturbance.

It did nothing for the government's image as the preserver of law and order. Eureka seemed a further example of incompetent officialdom backed by a vindictive government as in the Harrison–MacKay case, which, the previous month, had caused huge protest meetings in Melbourne and Geelong. The *Geelong Advertiser* proprietor James Harrison had commented on the drunkenness in court of the Crown Prosecutor George Mackay. MacKay sued Harrison who, in November, was fined £800 damages plus costs. Carboni took this as a choice example of misgovernment but presumably did not know that Attorney-General Stawell had insisted on the anti-Harrison action. Similar vindictiveness threatened Carboni in particular.

Hotham persisted with his repressive policy. He even ordered another licence hunt in Ballarat (in fact it was bland because conducted apologetically by unarmed troops) and rejected public appeals for an amnesty of the state prisoners. What particularly menaced Carboni, the foreigners' spokesman, was Hotham's insistence that foreigners had caused the Eureka clash.

When Hotham wrote to Sir William Denison, Governor of Tasmania, on 4 December requesting 'as many companies of the 99th Regiment as can be spared', he explained that the Ballarat insurgents 'are principally foreigners'. At Government House on the 6th, he told the Legislative Council:

> The moment there is an outbreak, and that caused, not by Englishmen, but by foreigners – men who are not suffered to remain in their own countries in consequence of the violence of their characters and the deeds they have done – I, for one, say that whenever that happens, the Englishmen of Victoria must rally round the Government ... and put that outbreak down.

Receiving a delegation of 500 Melbourne bankers, merchants and other prominent citizens who offered their support, Hotham let them into the secret: 'we have active, designing, intriguing foreigners who ... desire to bring about disorder and confusion ...' On 20 December, he wrote from Toorak to Sir Henry Grey, Secretary of State for the Colonies, about the Eureka troublemakers: 'foreigners are to be found amongst the most active, and if they abuse the hospitality and protection they obtain here, have no right to expect clemency if convicted'.

Carboni thought of himself as representative of the international Republic of Letters but must also have been aware he was the only prominent foreigner in captivity. The German Vern was still at large; the American, whom Hotham's secretary had described as the leader of the revolt, was presumably McGill. Carboni said that 'he was smothered by bitterness' to learn that McGill had been pardoned by Hotham, which made nonsense of both his scaremongering and his air of relentless severity.[45] If Carboni walked the plank, it would prove there had been a quarterdeck rebellion fomented by foreigners and would justify its harsh repression – the slaughter of Britons by Britons.

The anti-foreigner cry was taken up. The *Ballarat Times* denounced it on New Year's Day:

> Official, semi-official, and other such twaddling journals in the different colonies who have not the independence, if they know it to be false, to contradict the assertion [of Hotham], nor the honesty and brains to assure themselves of the falsity or the veracity of such a statement, have echoed and re-echoed the word foreigners until it has become stereotyped and worn out.

'Poor Governor Hotham!' continued the paper, whose editor was in gaol for sedition, alongside his main reporter who was facing a high treason charge.

> Could you not have found some other and more truthful excuse for all the illegal and even murderous excesses committed by your soldiery and butchers? ... The cause assigned by you based on the well-known antipathy of the old Anglo-Saxon race to anything but English was very well chosen, and told with wonderful effect at the time, and went down admirably with some who, like the Pharisee of old, thanked God they were not as other men are – Irish, Scotch, Welsh, Americans, French, Germans, Italians and other such ungodly men.
>
> ... What is this country else than Australia? Is it any more England than it is Ireland or Scotland, France or America,

Italy or Germany? Is the population, wealth, intelligence, enterprise and learning wholly and solely English? ... No, the population of Australia is not English, but Australian and *sui generis*. Anyone who immigrates into this country, no matter from what clime or of what people and contributes towards the development of *its* resources and its wealth is no longer a foreigner but an Australian, a title fully as good, if not better than that of any of the inhabitants of the various geographical divisions of the world. The latest immigrant is the youngest Australian; and the moment before Sir Charles Hotham put his foot on our shores, he was as much, and more, a-foreigner, than any person in the country.

Carboni may have been struck by newspaper reports of a Sicilian anti-Bourbon insurrection and accompanying denunciation of the despotism of King 'Bomba' (Ferdinand II) of Naples, whose law courts condemned political prisoners to death. But he too was battling for his life and health in a Bourbonic prison. His brick barrel-vaulted cell was cramped; the gaol was crammed with hardened criminals; the exercise yard was narrow and the food revolting. He claimed it permanently impaired his health. Breakfast was grub-infested hominy (Indian meal); lunch was tepid water with half a dozen rice grains called soup, more or less high-flavoured dry bullock flesh, a couple of black potatoes and sour bread. Dinner was hominy as in the morning. For messmates there were bushrangers, horse-stealers or the robbers of the Ballarat Bank of Victoria who had been taken in Melbourne's Canvas Town when overheard discussing their success. Prisoners ate in a small yard, 30 yards by 8, without tables or benches; if they sat, the food was dust-covered. Carboni suffered almost continual dysentery.

Better food was available only in the death cell, which was one of the more sobering aspects of this high church of law enforcement with its intricate iron work on the galleries and the staircases which rang to the warders' steps. In addition, the gaol had a functioning treadmill and a flogging triangle. Twenty-five lashes was punishment for slight offences. Carboni had noted mining's demonic aspects, but here he was in one of hell's lower circles. He was convinced Sheriff Claude Farie, Inspector Price and Turnkey Hackett would qualify as devils, but stout Governor Wintle showed concern for his deteriorating health. Not all the warders were sadists either. Manning, in particular, missed a chew of tobacco. With Tuohy he encouraged Carboni to sing Italian opera arias. Carboni knew at least *The Barber of Seville*, for in Rome he had taught himself to write it note for note, word for word from memory. Surely he could not have sung the *'che bel vivere'* (what a lovely life) aria without bitter irony. The music's irrepressible vitality contrasted painfully with his confinement. And he may have reflected that he came from the same region as Rossini, from the same school of music, that they had mutual friends, but who could believe it here and now? When Carboni had sung, a tap on the cell door would announce that, from the crack below, they could collect as reward a stick of tobacco; even in hell, Carboni and his cellmates decided, there were some good devils.

The state prisoners wrote to the Sheriff of Victoria requesting improved treatment, as they were not hardened criminals. Carboni's hand seems evident in two passages: 'was there ever worse treatment, in the worst days of the Roman Inquisition, for men whose reputations had never been sullied with crime?', and:

> Some of us, for instance, could wile [*sic*] away several hours each day in writing, an occupation which, while it would fill up the dreary Vacuum of prison life, as would the moderate use of snuff and tobacco cheer it, and soothe that mental irritation consequent upon seclusion. But that system of discipline which would paralyse the mind and debilitate the body, that would destroy intellectual as well as physical energy and vigour, cannot certainly be of human origin.

Carboni obtained some paper, for he wrote a poem, a song, then a prayer inspired by the arch devils Goodenough and Peters. Using the notes he had taken while with the Tarrang tribe, he composed a glossary of Aboriginal words which was later criticised for inaccuracies.

At 3 p.m., the hottest hour of the day, prisoners were locked in their cells, except for a half-hour dinner break, until the following morning. They felt the confinement most cruelly of a Sunday, for they were locked in from 3 p.m. Saturday until 7 a.m. Monday unless they went to a church service Sunday. This was an inducement for Carboni to attend Mass, but it did not supply much spiritual consolation. If the priest arrived, he was always hurried, then gabbled his short sermon and once said half the Mass without an assistant. Carboni, who could have filled in, may have reflected that things were better managed at Holy Trinity. After Mass, the depressing cell again, spasms of dysentery, weakness and the wait for the trial.

Carboni was in the dusty yard when 'Fall in, hats off' announced a magistrate's visit. Carboni complained that the money and goods taken from him on arrival at the Camp had not been returned; John Joseph asked about the £8 taken from him. The magistrate answered that the gaoler who had received these monies had bolted. Robbery under arrest!

Carboni resolved to obtain compensation but feared he might yet lose his life as well as his money; perhaps he recalled that the Roman pro-consul he claimed as a forebear had been killed by his political enemies. Early in January, the state prisoners received what Carboni called a 'New Year's present': the high treason indictment. The Italian found it the 'coarsest fustian ever woven by Toorac spiders', but his solicitors warned him that the government meant to make an example; a guilty verdict could mean death or fifteen years imprisonment in the hulks standing off Williamstown. Carboni must have cursed the day he had sailed up the bay where he might now be put to death or marooned; would he limp out of a hulk, a 53-year-old wreck, in 1870?

'What'll be the end of us, Joe?' Carboni asked good-natured John Joseph.

'Why if the jury let us go, I guess we'll jump our holes again on the diggings. If the jury won't let us go, then ...', Joseph's head slumped over his left shoulder, then he poked his thumb between windpipe and collarbone, widened his eyes and gave an unearthly whistle.

Pointers to the trial prospects were contradictory. The state prisoners had press support while 4500 diggers petitioned Hotham for an amnesty. His refusal inspired a cogent letter from Humffray and the Chartist C.F. Nicholls, which, among other things, pointed out the inconsistency of condoning Americans of the right skin hue. (By various means the American Consul Tarleton had secured pardons for white Americans.) But the stronger the support for the prisoners, the more anxious the government was to obtain convictions.

It succeeded with Henry Seekamp, the first to be tried at the Supreme Court, a gothic-windowed, bluestone building with wooden verandahs on the corner of Russell and La Trobe Streets only a few steps from the prison. Found guilty of fomenting sedition and condemned to three months prison, Seekamp was released on bond. It looked ominous; if Seekamp had fomented sedition, the thirteen could well be condemned to death for high treason. That would vindicate the Attorney-General, William Stawell, who spurned the diggers and presumably advised Hotham to be implacable. The judge, William à Beckett, forebear of many talented artists such as the novelist Martin à Beckett Boyd and the painter Arthur Boyd, had incensed diggers by his contemptuous remarks about Irish rioters in a recent trial. But he might have favoured Carboni because, shortly before the Urbinite arrived in Rome, à Beckett had published a long, fond poem, *Recollections of Naples*.

The first of the thirteen tried on the high treason charge was John Joseph. Presumably it was thought he would arouse least sympathy both because he was black and because allegedly his shots had killed popular Captain Wise. The Crown rejected as jurors all publicans and men of 'doubtful exterior', but Joseph rejected gentlemen and merchants. By the time fifty potential jurors had been dismissed, repeated laughter rocked the courtroom, but the defence had made its point that workers should be tried by workers.

The defence maintained Joseph was a poor ignorant darkie incapable of plotting or even understanding the crime for which he had been charged. Joseph played the part, 'being all the time on the broad grin, and looking like the corner man in a company of Ethiopian serenaders'.[46] Within half an hour of retiring, the jury returned a 'Not Guilty' verdict. Jubilation was so great in court that à Beckett immediately sentenced two men to a week's gaol. For a few days, Joseph was the toast of Melbourne. At a benefit night for the actor George Seith Coppin at the Queen's Theatre, the verdict was celebrated to the tune of *Billy Barlow*:

> *I am told Mr Joseph of Ballarat fame*
> *Has this day been acquitted and freed of all blame,*
> *As the jury saw no harm in Joseph, why 'Joe'*
> *Ain't no longer seditious – says Billy Barlow.*

John Manning also was acquitted, then à Beckett fell ill. There was a month's delay before he was replaced by Redmond Barry, who had been a contemporary of Stawell and Foster at Trinity College, Dublin, but was less draconian. Born in County Cork in 1813, Barry had youthful sympathies for Daniel O'Connell. In his fifteen years in Australia he had proved public-spirited; among other things, he fostered establishment of the University, the

Public Library, the National Gallery and the Museum. Majestic in appearance, imperious in manner, sometimes sanctimonious, he was sympathetic towards Australian Aboriginals. He is best known for later sentencing the bushranger Ned Kelly.

Carboni's trial was postponed several times because of the unavailability of defence witnesses such as Dr Alfred Carr, the storekeeper Gordon who had been arrested outside his tent almost at the same time as Carboni, Sub-Inspector Carter who had made the arrests and Binney who had seen Carboni's look-alike corpse in the Stockade. It seemed that if the trial was further delayed, Carboni might die from dysentery as had so many on the goldfields. But the delay served some purpose: on 16 March, *The Age* published a letter which, although only initialled J.B., must have helped Carboni. *The Age* was more pro-digger than the *Argus* and *Herald* or, as Carboni put it 'it mustered a Roman courage in defence of the diggers, and jumped the claims of the *Herald* and *Argus*'. The letter writer recounted that he had met Carboni on the morning of 3 December and they accompanied Dr Glendenning to the Stockade,

> Raffaello bringing his [Glendenning's] surgical instruments. We entered the stockade, and saw many lying almost dead for want of assistance and from loss of blood, caused by gun-shot and bayonet wounds. I did not remain long in the stockade, fearing if found there at that time I would be arrested. I made my escape; but poor Raffaello, who remained rendering an act of mercy to the dying, would not leave. He might, during that time, have easily made his escape, if he wished to do so; and I am sure, ran no inconsiderable risk of being shot, through the constant explosion of firearms left in the stockade by the diggers in their retreat.

At last, on Monday, 19 March, the high treason trials resumed with Timothy Hayes in the dock. Despite what *The Age* described as Stawell's 'bloodthirsty' zeal and the 'bottomless depth of that Mephistophelian mind … with its hard incapacity for recognising the claims of simple truth, honor, honesty', Hayes was acquitted. Two days later, three-and-a-half months after his arrest, it was the turn of Carboni who, the *Argus* correspondent noted, betrayed 'a strange excitability which his professional adviser could scarce restrain'. Carboni was described as 'unshaven, haggard, careworn and dispirited'. Evidently anxiety and dysentery had taken a heavy toll. Timothy Hayes, who had just been through the same ordeal, was present to encourage him.

Carboni was pleased his defence lawyer was James McPherson Grant, a former Bendigo gold digger and radical activist, and his counsel bushy-whiskered, robust Richard Davis Ireland, a Trinity College contemporary of Redmond Barry and also a former supporter of the Irish Confederate Clubs. Carboni compared his eloquence with Daniel O'Connell's. Ireland had defended gratuitously the three diggers arrested after the burning of Bentley's Hotel. Another leading barrister who offered his services free for the state prisoners was caustic Butler Cole Aspinall, who had written for the London *Morning Chronicle* and was an ex-Melbourne *Morning Herald* editor. Grant, Ireland and Aspinall were all future Ministers of the Crown.

The accusation was that Carboni,

> with divers other false traitors at present unknown, armed and arrayed in a warlike manner that is to say with guns, pistols, muskets, blunderbusses, swords, bayonets, pikes and other weapons being then and there unlawfully, maliciously and traitorously assembled and gathered whether against our sovereign Lady the Queen and did afterwards to wit on the third day of December in the year aforesaid fire upon attack and kill certain troops of our Said Lady the Queen …

Shortly after 10 a.m., Redmond Barry took his seat and, after some contestations, the jury (Brag, Bartholomew, Black, Butt, Bell, Baines, Belford, Broadhurst, Berry, Boyle, Burnett and Bayes) was sworn in. It consisted of three gardeners, two farmers, two carpenters, a butcher, a baker, a grocer, a painter and a joiner. The Attorney-General addressed the jury, then called Goodenough as witness. Ireland cross-examined him about his presence at Bakery Hill on 30 November when, dressed as a digger, he had pledged solidarity and, until kicked by Carboni, had incited the others to attack the Camp.

'I did not take down all [Lalor's] words', responded Goodenough. 'I knelt down. I did not move my lips [when the pledge was taken]. I do not know the object the meeting had in view in kneeling down. My object was to be allowed to remain there. I did not say "amen". I do not remember whether I said that I did on Hayes' trial. I may have said so.'

Other witnesses who had caused Carboni's committal likewise crumbled under Ireland's questions. When Sergeant Hagerty swore he had taken Carboni directly from the Stockade to the Camp ('I was in the guard which took him to the Camp. The prisoner did not get away, I know'), Ireland pointed out that Goodenough swore he arrested Carboni later at the London Hotel. Hagerty said confusingly, 'I do not know that the prisoner did not escape on the way from the stockade to the lockup'.

Sparks flew between Ireland and Commissioner Graham Webster who claimed Carboni was the most violent speaker at the 29 November Bakery Hill meeting and that there he had torn up his licence and thrown it towards the fire. Webster affirmed there was good feeling towards the goldfields authorities 'except by a few agitators'. Attorney-General Stawell told Redmond Barry that this should be noted, for Webster's opinion as commissioner was 'very valuable'.

'But he has some novel ideas of the diggers', objected Ireland, 'and this is the first time I have ever heard such a statement made.'

'I should suppose truth at all times', responded Webster tartly, 'is a strange novelty to you.' He added that, unlike Ireland, he knew the diggings.

'I can read the newspapers though', Ireland objected.

'But the newspapers', said Webster, 'cannot be trusted.'[47]

Carboni was silent throughout the proceedings except for cross-examining Police Magistrate Charles Hackett, the only witness he considered honest. Hackett's account of Carboni's meeting with Rede, in the company of Father Smyth and Black, confirmed his own.

When the Crown case was concluded at 2.30, the court adjourned for half an hour. On reassembly, Ireland analysed the law of high treason which decreed the guilty be hung, drawn, quartered and displayed atop the town gates. Carboni consoled himself with the thought that as he and Paul Brentano, despite Rede's encouragement, had not set up the proposed brick-making business, Ballarat had no city walls and, consequently, no gates. How the deuce, then, Carboni asked himself, could they hang his hindquarters from them? He felt less threatened, particularly as he liked the look of the jury foreman.

Aspinall followed Ireland. He confessed riot but ridiculed the treason charge, claiming the diggers were justified in resisting unconstitutional force by force. As for Carboni's violent language, Aspinall explained Italians were

> a little more animated when speaking on any particular subject on which they were interested than an Englishman generally was ...
>
> The government had failed to ensure conviction in the case of the black man, the Irishman and the Englishman; and now they had got this poor Italian, this 'foreign anarchist' and they thought it would tell well to send home an account of his being hanged, drawn, and quartered. The jury would never assent to his coming sixteen thousand miles from Austrian tyranny to have less liberty than he had there ...

Although excited, Carboni, presumably obeying instructions, declined to add anything. Attorney-General Stawell began his reply, which was followed by Redmond Barry's summing up. Carboni remarked on Barry's 'parson's solemnity', but paid tribute to his kindness and impartiality. At 8.57, the jury retired.

Carboni found it very peculiar to be in a felon's dock while a jury discussed his fate. Despite the surge of confidence he had felt during Ireland's address, now he was acutely aware that his life hung on whether the foreman pronounced 'not' before 'guilty'. He prayed, then thought of friends in London and Rome who could not imagine what a bind he was in. If only he had a protector like Albani or Spada who could have saved him the trial agony and helped him leave for Italy. Archer, even though Assistant Registrar-General, could not work that kind of magic. Carboni was on tenterhooks, almost convinced he would be released, but probably also chilled by a sliver of dread. The minutes were leaden: 9.10, 9.11, 9.12, 9.13, 9.14, slow torture.

At 9.20, the jury returned. Their expressions reassured him. He was confident they had untied the knot tightening around him.

'Gentlemen of the jury, have you considered your verdict?'

'We have.'

'Do you find the prisoner at the bar Guilty or Not Guilty?'

'Not Guilty.'

Magna Opera Domini!: Carboni considered his acquittal one of God's Great Works.

As applause filled the courtroom the 5,000 who waited in Russell Street cheered. At the Supreme Court exit, some of the surging crowd hoisted Carboni on their shoulders, pushed money into his hand and shouted themselves hoarse. He called for silence, raised his right hand and intoned the prayer he had written in gaol:

> Lord God of Israel, our Father in heaven! We acknowledge our transgressions since we came to this our adopted land. Intemperance, greediness, the pampering of many bad passions have provoked Thee against us; yet, Oh, Lord our God, if in thy justice, Thou art called upon to chastise us, in thy mercy save this land of Victoria from the curse of the 'spy system'.

Timothy Hayes responded with a deep 'Amen' which others echoed. Some drank to Carboni's health. Many cried and embraced the hero.

Back to Ballarat

Immediately after the trial, Carboni was driven to the home of a Melbourne friend, presumably William Archer. Two days later he was in court again, no longer nervy but exuding confidence, for the trial of his cellmate Michael Tuohy and James Beattie. He sat between two barristers and, with nods and smiles, encouraged the prisoners. Ireland again cross-examined Commissioner Webster who repeated his claim that Carboni had torn up his licence and thrown it towards the fire. Suddenly the licence, issued on 17 October for three months, was produced.[48] Sensation in the court, no doubt hugely enjoyed by Carboni. 'I remember a party saying', Webster asserted, 'that they'd take care not to burn the current licences'. The farce, Carboni promised, would be produced at the Argentina theatre in Rome. Inspector Foster had given the licence to Father Smyth, who must have sent it to Carboni after his acquittal.[49]

Immediately after the trial, Carboni had boasted that, as attested by witnesses, he had put soldiers to flight. He was not sorry that 'Toorac spiders' had lent him 'the wings of a hero'.[50] But he was not resigned to being robbed: from Richmond, the suburb where Archer lived, on 31 March, Carboni wrote to the Colonial Secretary for restitution of the property taken at his arrest. He asked for replies to be sent care of Archer. The value of the money and goods taken from him, he declared, was at least £30.

> My clothes and watertight boots which were new, and my money which was in the breast pocket of my waistcoat were taken by Gaoler Nixon ... My mate, who supplied me with fresh clothing, applied at the Ballarat Camp for my property, but was told that nothing could be done, for Nixon the gaoler had 'bolted'.

Carboni would persist with his claim but the government had graver worries. Hotham's policy was in tatters. All the state prisoners were acquitted, and the Colonial Office questioned

> the expediency of bringing these rioters to trial under a charge of High Treason, being one so difficult of proof and so open to objections of the kind which appear to have prevailed with the jury.

Moreover, within 24 hours of the last state prisoners' acquittals, the Goldfields Commission of Enquiry brought in its report which found the diggers were governed three times over. Lack of political rights and self-elected local authority contributed to their dissatisfaction, it concluded, as well as the licence fee and the violence used in its collection. It recommended replacement of the Goldfields Commission by a warden system with reduced powers; introduction of a gold export duty instead of the licence; and a £1-a-year Miner's Right, which would be a title to vote. It further recommended establishment of local miners' courts, nomination and election of miners to the Legislative Council, and their appointment as honorary magistrates. Hotham may also have made a rough calculation of the high cost of the Eureka Stockade operation, which was to be estimated later at £26,733/18/6 plus £7110 in compensation for damages.

From Melbourne on Palm Sunday, 31 March, Carboni wrote again to his brother Antonio, including a letter for his more than 80-year-old aunt Veronica, abbess of a Rimini convent. He asked Antonio to send her, in his name, lemons and pastries. He included a waybill stating that three days earlier he had forwarded a box of specimens and gold dust for Antonio care of the Torlonia bank. This may have been the gold he had sent to Archer the previous year. He did not tell his brother he had been imprisoned and tried for high treason; instead he complained about his leg troubles.

Soon, however, he was to walk back to Ballarat: as the coach fee from Geelong was £3, it suggested he was low on funds. Yet he had just forwarded gold to his brother. This could have gone towards his ship passage home but evidently he had affairs to settle in Ballarat. He had left there his diary and manuscripts, his tent, tools and tubs, gold specimens and money belt. And probably he felt he could nab the 'yellow boy' more surely than when, twenty-eight months earlier, he had first trekked from Melbourne. He was an experienced miner now and, unlike the period preceding the stockade clash, work would not be interrupted by licence hunts and protest meetings.

Still debilitated by dysentery, he was reassured by what he considered the example of British justice provided by his trial. But his estimate of his fellow men nosedived before he reached Ballarat. First he asked one of the 'moral force' group, who had been 'spouting, stumping and blathering' for the state prisoners, to check whether his stretcher was still in his tent on Eureka. To Carboni's chagrin, the moralistic moral force man, who returned to Ballarat by coach, refused this simple favour.

Next, in Geelong, he saw Arthur Purcell Akehurst, condemned by the inquest jury for the brutal slaying of the Cornishman Jamie Powell, chatting with young women. Carboni was shocked, as Akehurst represented for him all the random violence of that 3 December. In fact, unknown to Carboni, Akehurst had been exonerated by the Supreme Court (Carboni would have been even more indignant if he had seen what an official had scrawled across the depositions against Akehurst: 'looks like a case of justifiable homicide'). And many were indignant that although Police Captain Gordon Evans had been warned by Dr William Wills, father of the future explorer, that Powell's death was imminent, he had not sworn Powell when he made his anti-Akehurst statement. Consequently it was not admissible as evidence. Akehurst himself may not have killed Powell, but he had a position of authority over those who had slaughtered the innocent Cornishman. Carboni's outrage was justified.

The slight from the moral force man and the sighting of Akehurst were not as traumatic for Carboni, however, as his arrival in Ballarat. His tent had become a gambling den by day and by night a brothel. His stock of brandy had disappeared. He had been robbed of everything worth sixpence: cradle, two tubs, digging tools, cooking utensils, blankets, gold specimens, gold dust and money belt. Fortunately a friend had buried his diary and manuscripts under a tent and Carboni recovered them. He complained to diggers and authorities; some were sympathetic but did not lift a finger, others called him a grouser. When he had first come to Ballarat, he was fit and hopeful. Now he was in poor health and worse spirits. He had been robbed both by the government and fellow diggers. Some of his best mates had been killed in the Stockade, but the memory of that episode was fading. He would not even have known where to doss but for his 'Good Samaritan', Carl Wiesenhavern, who put him up at his Prince Albert Hotel.

Carboni wrote bitterly, freely adapting Horace:

> *The best of friends, by G – in serving you*
> *Takes previous care first to help himself.*
> *Ancestors, learning, talent, what we call*
> *virtue, religion – MONEY beats them all.*

The war to wrest gold continued unabated with a truce in the trenches only on Christmas Day when it was agreed no one would jump claims. The loot was huge; in 1853, the year of nuggets, it had been 319,000 ounces, but in 1855, with less spectacular but steadier finds, it jumped to 769,000. The goldfields population increasingly clustered on the flat. The rich returns financed the diggers to seek basalt-covered rivers of gold.

Ballarat's continuing boom made it ever more cosmopolitan. The Welsh now had an Eisteddfod, the Jews a Synagogue. Apart from diggers from most European countries, with Germans the most numerous non-English speakers, there were miners from Chile, Mauritius and Algeria. Sam Huyghue noted Hindus, Parsees, Kanakas, Zulus, Maoris at the Theatre Royal, and Mongolians, straw-hatted, baggy-trousered, pigtailed. The Chinese, experts at working old ground, had arrived in Ballarat in considerable numbers the previous year. John Aloo, running a restaurant on Main Street, was the official interpreter for the frugal Chinese, who were despised as barbarous homosexual opium-smokers and disease-bearers. At first they lived in an area near the Red Hill red-light district nicknamed Hong Kong, then were put into regimented villages called protectorates.

In 1855 the conjunction of various leads in the basin, the prosperity and the concentration of population made Main Street a thriving thoroughfare. While professional men and banks had their offices in the city proper, shops and stores congregated on this busy diggings street, which was either dusty in baking heat or a quagmire. Many of the stores were tiny, crammed with teetering stacks of goods and lined with canvas and calico, which made them perfect tinder. If they survived fire and flood, they still might have to shift to make way for a shaft, but it was all worthwhile for more than 30,000 potential clients.

Some of the stores were more substantial, wooden with ornamental two-storey façades. There were ever more restaurants and also large, even elegant, hotels, some with attached theatres and concert halls which staged opera and serious plays as well as slapstick and melodrama. The Victoria Theatre could seat 2,500 for concerts and plays, which were followed after 10 p.m. by dancing with expensively-dressed wenches who, according to one connoisseur, had beef-red hands big enough to fell a bullock and were redolent of eau-de-cologne, onions and brandy.

At Mrs Hamner's Adelphi Theatre, Carboni received a good reception from the diggers when he sang, to the tune of the *Standard Bearer*, his song written in prison which began:

> *When Ballarat unfurled the 'Southern Cross',*
> *Of joy a shout ascended in the heavens;*
> *The bearer was Toronto's Captain Ross;*
> *And frightened into fits red-taped ravens*

Chorus:

> *For brave Lalor –*
> *Was found 'all there',*
> *With dauntless dare: …*

On 9 May, the government declared an amnesty for Lalor and other Stockaders, such as Vern, who previously had a price on their heads.

The Gravel Pits mines in front of the Camp where Carboni was working were always damp, but torrential June rain flooded them. Carboni began a poem, written, he noted, during winter at the South Pole, *'Trotta, trotta, finchè la terra scotta'* (Trot, trot until the ground scorches/ straight to a sea of woes). The rain had dampened his spirits, but in the remainder of the year they resurged. Gradually he recovered from the debilitating prison dysentery; as an experienced miner, he probably participated in the bonanza; and, most importantly, he was elected unanimously to the Local Court.

'With clean hands, I go out'

After a carnival-like campaign over the soggy goldfields, on 9 July the diggers assembled near the Charlie Napier Hotel to vote for the Local Court established on the recommendation of the Goldfields Enquiry Commission. Warden W.C. Sherard (who had replaced Robert Rede after his appointment as deputy-sheriff of Geelong) attempted to hold the election from the top of a dray but, as the crowd was too great, postponed it to the following Saturday at Bakery Hill.

On Saturday an estimated 3,000 miners voted for twenty-six candidates. Barriers were erected with openings which permitted passage of one man at a time. He displayed his newly-issued Miners' Right and expressed his vote to a teller.[51] Carboni was one of five elected unanimously; the Chartist Henry Nicholls was one of the other four. Under young Warden James Daly, the Court drafted local regulations, adjudged partnership quarrels and breaches of its laws. Claim disputes, however, were usually decided by wardens of the Court of Petty Sessions.

Election to the Court for a six-month term seemed a tonic for Carboni, who took his mandate very seriously. The first time he went to the Court he stopped outside at the spot where, together with Father Smyth and George lack, he had unsuccessfully tried to persuade Rede to desist from provocative licence hunts. Now he vowed that if he regained his former health and good spirits,

> I would speak out the truth; and, further, during my six months sitting in the Court, I would give right to whom right was due, and smother the knaves, irrespective of nationality, religion, or colour.

At their first sitting, the new magistrates found a huge backlog of disputes. When they cleared them, they faced another tangle of cases caused by the Eureka lead reaching Main Street. They were honorary magistrates but had to pay 25 shillings a day for the substitutes at their shafts. They were working at a loss. On 30 August, Carboni and four others decided they would strike in a fortnight unless Hotham granted them pay. Daly, as Court Chairman, wrote to Hotham warning that the remaining four members would concur. 'As the Court is working well and getting quickly through a multiplicity of cases', Daly recommended His Excellency's immediate attention to the matter.[52] Hotham decided members would each receive 10 shillings a case; they were handling twenty a week. Payment of elected court members was a significant innovation, as parliamentarians were not yet paid.

Confidence deriving from his election seems to have been one spur for Carboni to write *The Eureka Stockade*, which he intended to distribute at the site itself on 1 December next. The Local Court was the best evidence that the diggers had won the right to run their own affairs. The author was living the most tangible consequences of the event he was commemorating. (He was later criticised for using the initials MLC after his name when he was not a Member of the Legislative Council. He may have been merely playing on the identical initials, but perhaps for him it was as proud a title to be Member of the Local Court.)

The man who had spent his Sundays scribbling in his tent to achieve fame in the distant future far away now aimed at a local audience. He listed his motives for writing *The Eureka Stockade*. He wanted to rescue from 'ignoble oblivion' those who had fallen, particularly his mate and bearer of the Southern Cross, the Canadian Lieutenant Ross; he wanted to avoid unjustified accusations when, at 40, he would publish a play on which he had been 'working for the past eighteen years' and join the 'illustrious of Rome'; he wanted to set the record straight because he believed in the 'resurrection of life'. He challenged anyone to disprove his eyewitness account, its facts or deductions from them, and confessed he was not a hero who had set British soldiers to flight. The epigraph to the first chapter, a pastiche of the Psalms, underlined his intention of veracity: 'The lie, like the whirlwind, clears itself a royal road, either in town or country, through the whole face of the earth. The fool in his heart says 'There is no God.' The truth, however slow, step by step, like a little child, someday, at last, finds a footpath to light. Then the righteous shall flourish like a palm tree.'

Carboni was to show there were more irritants than the licence fee leading to the Stockade clash; he was sensitive to political nuances, intuiting the Rede-Hotham relationship (on which Archer may have supplied inside information); and he portrayed Rede convincingly as not bad, but weak and pompous. But although open to complexity, he did not fully recognise the Camp's fear of being overrun.

It was probably about this time that he had his photograph taken. Standing in a three-quarter face pose, he appears solid and farseeing. Not tall, but compact, he wears a long, dark mantle over a suit which is likewise dark. Cuffs gleam whitely beneath the sleeves. The beard is full; a broad-rimmed hat rides upwards to reveal a spacious forehead. One hand rests on a plinth, the other grasps a rolled parchment. He is not a digger, but a man of the written word, be it legal, literary or revolutionary. The cape and beard give him a wild romantic look offset by the classical plinth and the bourgeois, best-suit air of his other garb. Marcus Clarke was to describe Carboni as an Italian conspirator-type, but it could be the photograph of a Founding Father.

Court work and the fight for recognition of its status were onerous, which may explain why, by mid-August, Carboni was at only the sixth chapter, in which he described his return to Ballarat after shepherding near the Loddon at Easter the previous year. On his return to Ballarat after imprisonment, Carboni had been disillusioned by the miners and, later still, was to see with chagrin that diggers kowtowed to mining companies, but at the moment he was full of idealistic enthusiasm: he believed in digger control and digger justice.

On 25 September, he wrote the Colonial Secretary complaining of the failure to endorse the Court's regulations against shepherding or holding claims in reserve by 'men, boys and often children! aye, and even women!!!'[53] At the time, about a quarter of Ballarat's inhabitants were shepherding, that is waiting above a shallow hole to see the gutter's course, before going to the expense of sinking a shaft.

Carboni's letter concluded, 'we have the honour to be'. It suggested he was writing on behalf of all the Court members. But as his signature's comely flourish is followed by 'Member of the Local Court' without mention of others, it could also be the royal plural, which would flow readily from his pen. The reference to the miners as 'the sinews of the Colony, aye even its very life' is authentic Carboni, for he was unabashed by sweeping claims and was surely convinced, after his unanimous election, that he had been chosen, aye, by the colony's chosen people.

The letter showed disillusion with remote Melbourne control and capitalists. At the same time as the government had constituted the Local Courts, it had passed an Act laying legal basis for limited liability mining companies. But initially diggers mainly elected those like Carboni who were opposed to companies, capital and machinery.

The letter also foreshadowed another battle in its reference to the Members of the Bar who 'want to force their eloquence and earning on us for a fee'. With all the Court members but Nicholls, he opposed the government proposal that barristers appear in court as advocates or 'advisers'. In its first ten weeks, the Court had settled 201 disputes, involving some half a million sterling, without any diggers protesting.

All the Court members, except Nicholls, convoked a public meeting at Bakery Hill on Saturday afternoon, 29 September. After hearing two speakers, the diggers called for 'Great Works' (Carboni), who said any Goodenough present should take care not to mislay his notes as had the spy before the Supreme Court trial. Carboni received a rousing affirmative when he asked if he had done his duty to the diggers' satisfaction. He said he was under no obligation to lawyers as his trial services were provided for him as a state prisoner. He recounted that his lawyer had ignored his request for sixpenneth of snuff, then asked permission to take a pinch on the spot and, amid cheers, did so. Admission of lawyers to the Court, he maintained, would lead to endless time- and money-consuming feuds.

> And are you going to allow Ballarat lawyers to fleece you of your hard earnings? Are you fairly represented by us? Don't say yes if you don't mean it, I don't like yabber-yabber.

Of course they roared 'YES'; a volley of cheers came from the diggers. Carboni presented his bill: the diggers should oppose lawyers being enabled to plead in the Court. They did so and on 4 October the Court members sent to Hotham a twelve-point protest against admission of lawyers:

> all are convinced from long Experience that too many of the Members of the said Profession prostitute the high and legitimate functions of their honourable Profession by frequently screening the rascalities of a rogue and bullying the honest suitor for justice. Men whose ignorance of law is only equatted [*sic*] by their impudent audacity; men who are blind to the principles of moral rectitude and deaf to the claims of Justice … as

> plain working men [the Court members] object to have their time wasted in listening to insipid and irrelevant arguments made for the purpose of concealing rather than eliciting truth and frustrating the ends of Justice instead of promoting it.[54]

Despite the protest, the government prevailed on grounds that the Court was handling complicated partnership agreements involving lawyers.

Pride in the people's Court made Carboni as punctilious as any detested Camp official. On 8 October, he objected to Mr Watson, clerk of the magistrates' bench, sitting inside the rail dividing the public from the Court, parties, lawyers and reporters. Evidently Carboni associated Watson with Camp injustice. When the Court chairman, Warden Daley, declined to remove Watson, all members sided with Carboni and left the Court. Next day Carboni tabled a motion excluding all but involved parties and reporters from the inner area, but the chairman reserved the right of enforcement.

Within forty-eight hours, once more cocky and combative, Carboni was sparring in a new paper, the *Star,* with a lawyer who dared point out that, despite their objections to lawyers, Court members themselves pocketed fees. The Court was entitled to its fees, Carboni stated, and

> if Mr Lawyer ... is fond of declamation, a descendant of the Gracchi is just now getting better and better in health, and will give him a good feed, all hot, of the old style Quousque tandem abutere Catilina patientia nostra? – How long will you try our patience Catiline?

Carboni's restored élan was evident not only in fulfilling his vow to smother knaves, but also in more rapid writing. When he interrupted his Eureka Stockade account with a reference to the public meeting convoked by the Court on 29 September, he had written only eight of the 100 chapters and was still providing background. By 10 November, however, he had completed the fiftieth chapter, in which he mentioned the arrival of James McGill at the Stockade. The rhetorical repertoire he had mastered at Urbino's College of Nobles was used to shape his account. To the image of the storm refreshing nature he added those of the phoenix and the mustard seed to suggest subsequent events sprang from the burning of Bentley's Hotel. Similarly he depicted Ross as 'bridegroom of our flag' and compared the diggers affirming solidarity under the Southern Cross to the Crusaders. For Carboni it was a sacred moment, which made Goodenough's spying sacrilegious.

Carboni was using his diary and those letters he could recover. He seems to have realised late that he would need the letters sent to Archer. On 14 October he wrote him a note saying, 'we are collecting positive information …' (about the burning of Bentley's and the 29 November meeting). Did the *we* mean others were collaborating with Carboni – perhaps Seekamp or more likely Carboni's mate Manning? Although Carboni prefaced the account with a note saying he had never mastered English, despite their mistakes his letters suggest he was capable of writing *The Eureka Stockade* without help. And if he had received help with his English, he might have been expected to acknowledge it in the prefatory note or have his collaborator reproach him after publication. His English is idiosyncratic but his letters in Italian are likewise jaunty, trenchant and scatty.

Archer, who wanted to know what use was to be made of the letters, apparently returned only that about the 29 November meeting. Carboni incorporated much of the *Ballarat Times* account of Bentley's burning without acknowledgment, even though, in some respects, his own letter to Archer was more graphic. He also inserted into his account, without acknowledgment, the choice description of the Southern Cross flag from the *Times*: 'silk, blue ground, with a large silver cross, similar to the one in our southern firmament; no device or arms, but all exceedingly chaste and natural'.[55] As well as unacknowledged use of other's material, he quoted letters and documents verbatim to give a documentary effect.

Carboni did not play altogether fair about his Italian background either. His claim to be from an old Roman family is understandable, as it was a legend he shared with his brother. He described him as headmaster of the grammar school in Coriano, which could be misleading as it was a one-teacher school. He included an explanation to be submitted by Antonio to Pope Pius IX without mentioning that his struggles had not been directly against Austrians, as he claimed, but against the Pope. Nor did he mention his run-in with the pontifical police.

He headed chapter 31, in which he reported the speech of Timothy Hayes at the 29 November meeting, with words he put into the mouth of the Mazzinian, Mattia Montecchi, in the Colosseum: 'The slave who wants to end his pains … / Has first of all to break his chains.' These words linked diggers' protests with Italian opposition to oppression. He interrupted chapter 51, on the confusion in the Stockade, with the news:

> This day, Saturday November 10, 1855. A glorious day for Ballarat: PETER LALOR, our late Commander-in-Chief being elected by unanimous acclamation, Member of the Legislative Council for this 'El Dorado'.

Certainly it was a legitimisation of the Stockaders' struggle. Carboni, who dubbed himself Lalor's historian, felt particularly involved, for, with James Oddie and John Campbell, he had nominated Lalor.

On 16 October the new Constitution Act had arrived, but as it was to be more than a year before the first parliament elected under it met, Hotham appointed a ministerial cabinet with, as its Chief Secretary, English-born W.C. Haines, 48, who had been a surgeon then a Geelong farmer. The engineer Captain Pasley, a hardliner at the time of the Stockade, was Minister of Government Works. The goldfields were to have two non-official members. One was Lalor; the other, not mentioned by Carboni, was J.B. Humffray, likewise elected unanimously. Humffray was a truer representative of reform, but either this did not interest Carboni or it was too early to see it, for Lalor was yet to vote for a property qualification for parliamentarians, develop into a goldfields capitalist and claim the Local Court members exercised 'a species of terrorism'.[56]

Carboni's term at the Local Court was coming to an end. He was satisfied that he had kept his word to give right to whom right was due. He announced that he would not sit in the Court after Christmas and wrote his own testimonial: 'with clean hands I came in, with clean hands I go out: that is the testimony of my conscience. I look for no other reward.'

Great Works' greatest work

Carboni had made a proud declaration of incorruptibility which, with time, not all Local Court members could underwrite. Initially, the Ballarat Local Court was knowledgeable and designed suitable regulations for local conditions. Its judgments were speedy and accepted. However, a month after Carboni's resignation, Chairman Daly wrote that he did not 'believe it [the Local Court] possesses the confidence of the public to any great degree'.[57] He maintained there were suspicions about the Court members' impartiality in cases of partnership and company holding.

But Carboni had known the Local Court at its best. Pride in it had encouraged him to record the diggers' battle lest people forgot and the Establishment succeeded in downplaying the Stockade as no saga of solidarity, but a squalid episode. However Carboni had to rush to meet the first-anniversary deadline. Allowing at least a week for printing meant Carboni completed the second half of *The Eureka Stockade* in two weeks. Such breakneck speed explains the use of large slabs of documents and the confusion of the final chapters, which do not reach any conclusion but merely chronicle his battle for his stolen property.

The *Ballarat Times* published a letter Carboni wrote at the Prince Albert Hotel on 12 June. He noted this was the feast of Corpus Christi (the real presence of Christ in the eucharist), which may have had a particular significance for him because the Urbino Corpus Christi confraternity celebrated it solemnly; it had even commissioned, in the mid-16th century, a processional banner painted by Titian which was still used. Carboni may have recalled the spectacular feast but his letter concerned more mundane matters for it was a lengthy complaint about the loss of what he now claimed was £49 and his watertight boots 'so useful in the Antarctic cold and floods' of the 1855 winter. It concluded with the punchy paragraph:

> Were I owned by the stars and stripes, I should not require assistance, of course not; unhappily for the sins of my parents, I was born under the keys which verily open the gate of heaven

and hell; but Great Britain changed the padlocks long ago! Hence the dreaded 'Civis Romanus sum' has dwindled into 'bottomed on mullock'.

The appeal ('Let the restitution come from a Board of Inquiry, a Poor-law Board, a Court-Martial, or any Board except a Board [full] of Petitions. The eternal petitioning looks so Italian to me!') had no effect.

Eventually, after Carboni's letter written from Richmond at the end of March had done the bureaucratic rounds, Assistant Colonial Secretary J. Moore replied on 20 September. Carboni annotated Moore's reply in French:

> In reference to your application of the 31st March last for the restoration of a sum of Thirty pounds, (*Pardon, Monseigneur, y compris mes habillements jusqu'à la chemise, s'il vous plaît, Monseigneur* [I beg your pardon, Sir, it entailed my clothes including my shirt, if you please]) alleged to have been taken from you by police on your arrest at Ballarat on the occasion of the riots there, I am commanded to inform you that the Governor has afforded the subject his consideration and finds that you neither represented the matter to the Magistrate before whom you were brought (*Comment parler de ma propriété devant le magistrat, quand j'avais à me defendré contre un tas de Mouchards qui avaient soif de mon sang!* [How could I talk to the magistrate about my property when I had to defend myself from a pack of police-spies who wanted to drink my blood!]), nor laid your case before the Board appointed to investigate claims arising from the Ballarat riots. (*Mon affaire était entre les mains de Mon. R.W. Archer qui se disait mon ami. C'est à lui la faute, Monseigneur.* [My affairs were in the hands of Mr R.W. Archer, who called himself my friend. It is his fault, Sir.]) It also appears, from your own showing, that you allowed the money to be taken concealed in such a manner as to exclude the care due to valuables. (*On me donna de coups-de-pied si impitoyables que l'on me fourra dans le Cachet presque hors de mes sens, Monseigneur.* [I received such vicious kicks that I arrived in the lock-up almost unconscious, Sir.])
>
> Under these circumstances His Excellency does not consider that the Government would be justified in awarding you

compensation in the absence of clearer evidence of the loss of property. J. Moore A.C.S.

Carboni responded, in French, to Hotham:

> So, Sir, I am nothing but a liar! It is sad for a man whose honour has never been questioned and who has shown his courage, at the age of 40, in exile, unhappy but still one of the judges chosen by his workmates; it is sad, I say, to see oneself forced to reach the conclusion, humiliating for an intelligent and well-educated man, that I am nothing but a liar. Sir: torrents of tears fall from my eyes.

After giving his address at the Gravel Pits on the Ballarat Flat, he added, 'at my hard work with water almost swamping us'.

Hotham, working himself to death trying to manage all the colony's affairs single-handed, sent a memo to Moore:

> Government is compelled to adhere to fixed rules-they by no manner of means doubt the veracity of Mr Rafaello, but that they have a duty to do by the Publick as well as by him & that is never to grant money in compensation except when the clearest evidence is given of the loss & that a personal statement-no matter by whom provided is never accepted as Sufficient testimony.

Moore faithfully relayed the memo to the lachrymose but persistent Italian. It spurred Carboni to improvise doggerel verse for the Magpie perched on the Southern Cross Hotel run by Carl Wiesenhavern's brother at Magpie Gully:

> *No more from MOORE*
> *Too dear his store*
> *Hang the 'Compensation':*
> *Speak of 'RESTITUTION'.*

Carboni next wrote to Police Inspector Henry Foster (Foster had been in charge when Carboni gave the watchhouse-keeper his goods and money). In his response, as Carboni noted, Foster ignored his loss of money and said he did not know what had happened to Carboni's clothes. In fact he knew what had happened but could not trace them. As he had no time to search the prisoners' clothes properly on the morning of the 3rd, he had stacked them in a corner of the room where the prisoners had stripped. A few days later he saw police and soldiers helping themselves to this property which had been thrown out of the room.[58]

If a Briton were robbed in Italy, Carboni claimed, the whole British press would be indignant, but when

> a friendless Italian is ROBBED … oh! that alters the case. What business have foreign beggars to come and dig for gold on British Crown lands? BASTA COSI! [That's enough!] that is, Great Works!

He appealed to the Melbourne press to drag out the 'Toorac small beer' correspondence on this matter between eight officials, for

> it would astonish the natives, teach what emigration is, and I believe the colony at large would benefit by it. There are scores of cases similar to mine, and more important by far, because widows and orphans are concerned in them.

He predicted that, if the press was not vigilant, 'the jackasses in the Australian bush will breed as the locusts in the African desert'.

Archer may have informed him of the revealing correspondence. In fact, in April an official inquiry had ascertained that the watch-house-keeper had bolted with the property taken from the prisoners:

> [they] were searched by Inspector Foster and the proceeds handed to the Watchhousekeeper Robert Dixon (this is the man also referred to as Nixon). It appears that no proper entry of the property and money taken was made in the Watchhouse book. Though this neglect may to some extent be accounted for by the excitement & confusion prevailing at the time, it was most irregular. Inspector Evans, then in charge in Ballarat, stated that he took a rough Memo of the property and gave it to the Watchhousekeeper. Inspector Foster afterwards sent the Watchhousekeeper to Richmond, stating that he was unsuitable to remain at Ballarat, but omitted to take any return or Account whatever,

of the property in his possession. The Watchhousekeeper, on his arrival in Melbourne, absconded and has not since been heard of, so that it is impossible to state with certainty what property was taken from any prisoner, and it will remain with His Excellency to decide how the various claims are to be met.

The Attorney-General and the Solicitor-General later advised that Carboni should be compensated for 'such visible property as was taken from him', provided there was some evidence of it other than his own, but not for the concealed money, 'as it was not possible to give it the care due to valuables.' Police Chief Captain Charles MacMahon sensibly commented that 'probably no claim had been made to the Magistrate as

> [Carboni] presumed that if it [property] was taken from him there would be no difficulty in obtaining it. I have already made every possible inquiry from Inspector Foster & Evans & as they are to blame for their carelessness by which this loss was occasioned I can only suggest that they should pay the Amount between them.'

The Colonial Secretary W.C. Haines thought the government should compensate.

> The fact that it is rendered impossible to ascertain the amount of property taken from Raffaello, by the loss of the memorandum made by the officer of Police, should not prevent the Government from making a reasonable compensation to him. The only question to be settled is this amount, and I confess that I see difficulty in making any deduction from the claim made by Raffaello, unless there is some good reason for believing he is making an unfounded demand.

'Does "Mr Archer" believe the statement of "Raffaello" to be true?' Hotham asked in a note of 10 September. Five days later, Archer replied, 'I do believe it, *in toto*'. Nevertheless, after another five days Moore, on Hotham's instructions, sent Carboni his glacial reply that 'His Excellency does not consider that the Government would be justified in awarding you compensation …'

The focus at the end of Carboni's briefbook on his unsuccessful compensation campaign made an overly personal coda. But it was germane, for, like the events which led to the Stockade clash, it showed authorities deaf to a just claim. Once again, Hotham had fussed as if personally concerned, but his eventual response was that of a blank-faced bureaucrat.

The account of the compensation claim increased the book's disorganisation but added to its immediacy, due mainly to the wide tonal range incisive style preserved by his idiosyncratic, inventive English and his direct address to readers, inviting them, for instance, to light up their pipes as they read. He even dialogues with an imaginary reader who tells him to calm his indignation over the licence fee. He interrupts his narrative to talk of later developments which can be confusing, as when he breaks off a letter to describe events at that moment, then resumes but steps outside the letter to draw the reader's attention to the importance of the letter's next point.

His presence can be obtrusive but is also a major strength, holding the disjointed account together. Other strengths are his exuberance and shrewd profiles of some protagonists when Carboni resists his tendency to exaggerate physiognomy as a clue to character. Oddly, he says little about his mate and Southern Cross flag bearer, the Canadian Captain Ross, although at the beginning he pays him a special tribute for his bravery. The jagged vividness of the account has tended to hide the fact that it is not a chronicle but a history, an interpretation based on hindsight which aimed to determine future readings of the event.

Surprisingly, Carboni's compensation campaign took place at the same time as the procedure for his naturalisation. The quarry, he had decided, could be a home. His earlier pastoral idyll by the Loddon, where on recovering from conjunctivitis he had seen the land as being as beautiful as Italy, amounted to an informal naturalisation, and may have helped convince him to settle as a wine grower. But to acquire land he needed British citizenship. Soon after his trial, he had sent testimonials of his character and education to Hotham. Archer was probably Carboni's sponsor. Hotham had said he was glad to hear Carboni was 'so respectable', and on 29 November granted. Carboni, 'wishful to possess a legal title to real estate and settle for life', all the rights and capacities of a natural-born British subject.[59]

The friendless outcast could become a landed proprietor on the Loddon where earlier he had eased his conjunctivitis-clogged eyes and found respite from the searing northerlies. The dream he had had on Ballarat's Bakery Hill, when he looked beyond the political strife to a bountiful land of plentiful harvest where each would hold 'a tumbler of Victorian wine', seemed about to come true. He could grow vines and crush grapes. Urbino, Rome, Paris, Hanover, London, Melbourne, Ballarat – he had always been a townie and, perhaps in reaction, chose the countryside. Banking, interpreting, mining might not have been the ideal apprenticeship; his shepherding experience hardly promised well either. But resourceful Carboni may have picked up the rudiments of wine production in vineyards near Urbino. True to his vow, on 1 December Carboni distributed his account of the clash between Hotham's forces and Lalor-led diggers which had 'cost [him] immense labour'. His first-ever publication, it was Great Works' greatest work. 'As Peter Lalor's historian', Carboni depicted him as a hero and aimed to give the valorous of Eureka the stature of the British troops fighting in the Crimea: 'to swell them up to the level of Sebastopol'.

The Age, which published extracts from *The Eureka Stockade*, found Carboni's style

> trenchant, vigorous and animated; his language racy, picturesque and graphic; his physiognomical sketches of character acute; and his descriptions of events are vividly dramatic ... It will be read with interest by the writer's contemporaries and with curiosity and wonder by those who come after him.

Although Carboni's book accused the Ballarat correspondent of the *Argus* of 'perverted' reports and the paper of flunkeyism, it published such a puff-par it might have been written by Carboni himself. It called *The Eureka Stockade* 'a work of genius' destined for a 'prominent place in our national literature'.

Describing Carboni as a 'well-educated Italian gentleman who was intimately associated with Garibaldi in the famous movement to secure Italian independence', it praised his account as 'thoroughly characteristic and original'. 'There is no man more generally liked on Ballarat than Raffaello', it claimed, adding that he intended to become a 'landed proprietor, and cultivator of the vine and olive, on the banks of the Loddon'.

In Ballarat, the book's reception was more mixed. The *Geelong Advertiser*'s Ballarat correspondent spoke of the possibility of 'horse-whippings' (of Carboni) by those who considered themselves harshly treated. However the correspondent admitted that Carboni had given a 'pretty correct summing-up' of Frederick Vern, whose own account, with himself as hero, had begun the previous month in the *Melbourne Magazine*. But it had no sequel.

The book exacted revenge on Sub-spy Andrew Peters, who had just married in Ballarat. When passages of *The Eureka Stockade* were read to him, he fled to Geelong where his bride followed him.[60] The *Geelong Advertiser* correspondent said Ballarat was in a great state of excitement, for, in addition to Carboni's book, a fire had destroyed the United States Hotel during race week and news had come the previous day of the fall of Sebastopol. The Melbourne *Argus* called it the greatest day since Waterloo; it was not the time to pursue republicanism and independence.

The Crimea War and the Eureka episode were on a different scale: one was a prolonged grinding of military-political tectonic plates which prefigured the First World War, whereas the other, by comparison, was a brief bushfire. But they were related as two aspects of imperial polity. Carboni, probably influenced by a jingoistic press, claimed those responsible for the massacre at Eureka were as bad as the Russian Czar Nicholas I. What he did not realise was the British commanders in the Crimea sent men into the valley of death as blithely as Nicholas. An Englishman, W.C. Howitt, who was in Victoria at the time of the Stockade, said that similar blunders had been made by inept leaders in both Ballarat and Sebastopol.

Hotham, who had regretted that he was not in the Crimea clash where the Anglo-French naval squadron had bombarded not only Sebastopol but also Odessa, died on 31 December. Some said it was from apoplexy, others from a stomach germ picked up on the African coast; if so, a foreign body finally had the better of him. He had been caught between the diggers' dissatisfaction and an exigent Colonial Office. Perhaps disappointment, stress and overwork triggered his death. The Legislative Council discussed Hotham's burial. John Pascoe Fawkner proposed £500 be devoted to the funeral and £1,000 to a monument. Lalor objected to the £1,000 expense, saying the thirty who died at Ballarat would be 'a standing monument to the memory of Sir Charles Hotham'. James MacPherson Grant, the state trial lawyer, said Hotham's political character could not be inscribed on the monument. Humffray seconded Grant's amendment that the appropriation be for funeral expenses only; the amendment was lost but, for one of the last times, Lalor and Humffray voted together.

Despite his naturalisation, the favourable reception for his book and his landed-proprietor-on-the-Loddon aspirations, on 18 January, a little more than a year after his original planned departure, Carboni sailed from Melbourne. He had enjoyed Angela's friendship in Rome and Anna's in Hanover; did he fear he might have to settle for a lubra on the Loddon? Had the compensation battle convinced him finally that if he was going to be misgoverned it might as well be in his birthplace? Or, in other words, *Basta così* (That's enough). On the Loddon, he would never become one of the 'illustrious of Rome'. Perhaps his brother's appeals to return were a major factor, or restlessness.

Whatever the cause, it was an abrupt change of plans. In Victoria he had achieved much; he had made money amid keen competition in a hard trade; he had been elected to a court by his peers; as a writer he had found a function, for he realised the miners' struggle would fade unless he attempted both to document it and to give it epic stature. Between his 35th and 38th years, the ex-exile had become an author, a public figure and a man of substance. Probably he looked forward to greater achievements in the same vein in Italy, but circumstances would prove different.

He sailed past the Gellibrand lighthouse, the lone passenger on the French *Princess Eugénie* bound for Calcutta, leaving the book which provided a foundation for the history of the Eureka Stockade. It was just over three years since Carboni had arrived. He had gleaned the gold he sought but also gave more than he took.

Left

Urbino was 'like a ship's prow sustained by the waves of hills'

Below

Extract from the parish register recording Carboni's birth

Commemorative plaque on the Urbino house where
Carboni spent some of his first years

The ducal palace of Urbino was one of the first and finest Renaissance buildings

Left

Luigi Vecchiotti, Carbon's music teacher 'if the College of Nobles' rhetorical tradition could be a straitjacket, Vecchiotti was a liberator'

Below

Holy Trinity church and the adjoining pilgrim hostel where Carboni first lived in Rome

Top Left
Pope Pius IX, clutching a tobacco case

Top Right
Monsignor Vincent Eyre gave Carboni English lessons in Rome

Left
Giuseppe Mazzini who influenced Carboni's politics and writing

Guiseppe Spada, Carboni's mentor at the Torlonia bank 'transformed him from a sacristan to a man and a gentleman'

Alfred von Seefeld of Hanover, a friend of Carboni

William Archer, Carboni's influential friend in Melbourne

'Cradling' from a watercolour by S.T. Gill

'The licence hunts seemed a surrogate for a war or riding at hounds'.
A check on a digger's licence.
S.T. Gill, *The Victorian Goldfields during 1852–53*

Left

Sir Charles Hotham, Governor of Victoria 1854–55.
State Library of Victoria

Below

Peter Lalor. 'A prolonged "hurrah" from the waiting diggers greeted the announcement that [he] was Commander'

The troops arriving at the government Camp in Ballarat

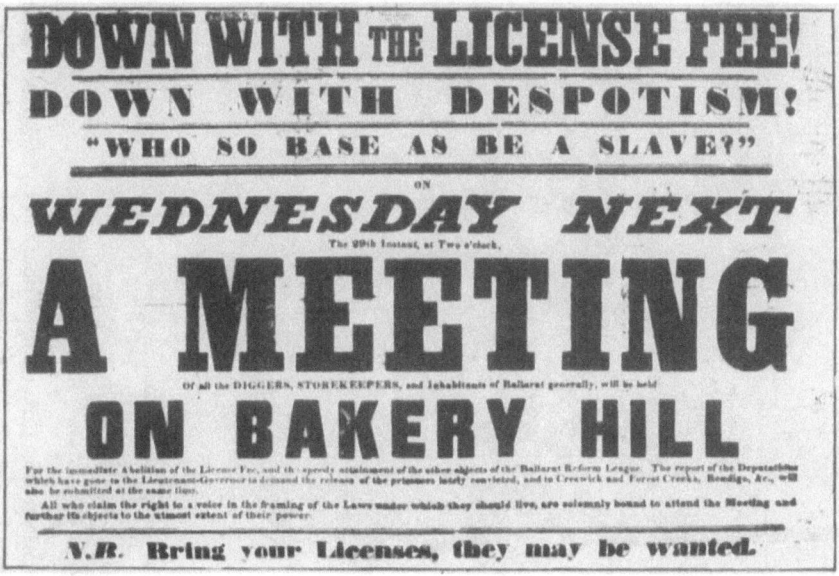

At the Bakery Hill protest meeting, the diggers vowed before the Southern Cross flag to defend their rights

The thirteen Eureka prisoners at their trial: 1 Timothy Hayes, 2 James Campbell, 3 Raffaello Carboni, 4 Jacob Sorenson, 5 John Manning, 6 John Phelan, 7 Thomas Dignam, 8 John Josephs, 9 James Beattie, 10 William Molloy, 11 Jan Vennik, 12 Michael Tuohey, 13 Henry Reed

Raffaello Carboni. Probably this photo was taken after his trial

CERTIFICATE TO NATURALIZE,

Under the Provisions of an Act of the Governor and Council, 11 Victoria, No. 39.

WHEREAS in accordance with the Provisions of an Act of the Governor and Legislative Council of New South Wales, passed in the Eleventh year of the Reign of Her Majesty Queen Victoria, intituled, "An Act to amend the laws relating to "Aliens within the Colony of New South Wales," *Carboni Raffaello* of *Ballarat, in the Colony of Victoria Gold Mines* has presented to me a Memorial in the form and manner prescribed by the said recited Act, praying that he may be naturalized; and whereas, I have enquired into the truth of the circumstances set forth in the said Memorial: Now I, the Lieutenant Governor of the Colony of Victoria, do hereby certify that it has been established to my satisfaction, that *the said Carboni Raffaello* is a native of *Italy thirty eight* years of age, and that having arrived by the *Ship "Prince Albert"* in *the year 1852*, he is now residing in *the said Colony* and *Member of the Local Court Ballarat being desirous to possess a Real title to real estate and settle for life in the said Colony* he desires to obtain the advantages of the said Act; and I do therefore grant to the said *Carboni Raffaello* (upon his taking before one of the Judges of the Supreme Court the oath prescribed by the said recited Act) all the rights and capacities within the said Colony of Victoria, of a Natural born British Subject, except the capacity of being a Member of either of the Executive or Legislative Council.

GIVEN under my Hand and Seal, at *Melbourne* in Victoria aforesaid, this *Twenty Ninth* day of *November* One thousand eight hundred and *fifty five*.

By His Excellency's Command,

C. Hotham L.S.

William C. Haines

Carboni was naturalised, as he intended to buy a property near the Loddon

Left

Angelo Bargoni, colleague and friend of Carboni. The original caption states that Agostino Bertani, another friend of Carboni, is hidden in Bargoni's beard

Left

Ippolito Nievo, a Garibaldian officer, a novelist and friend of Carboni

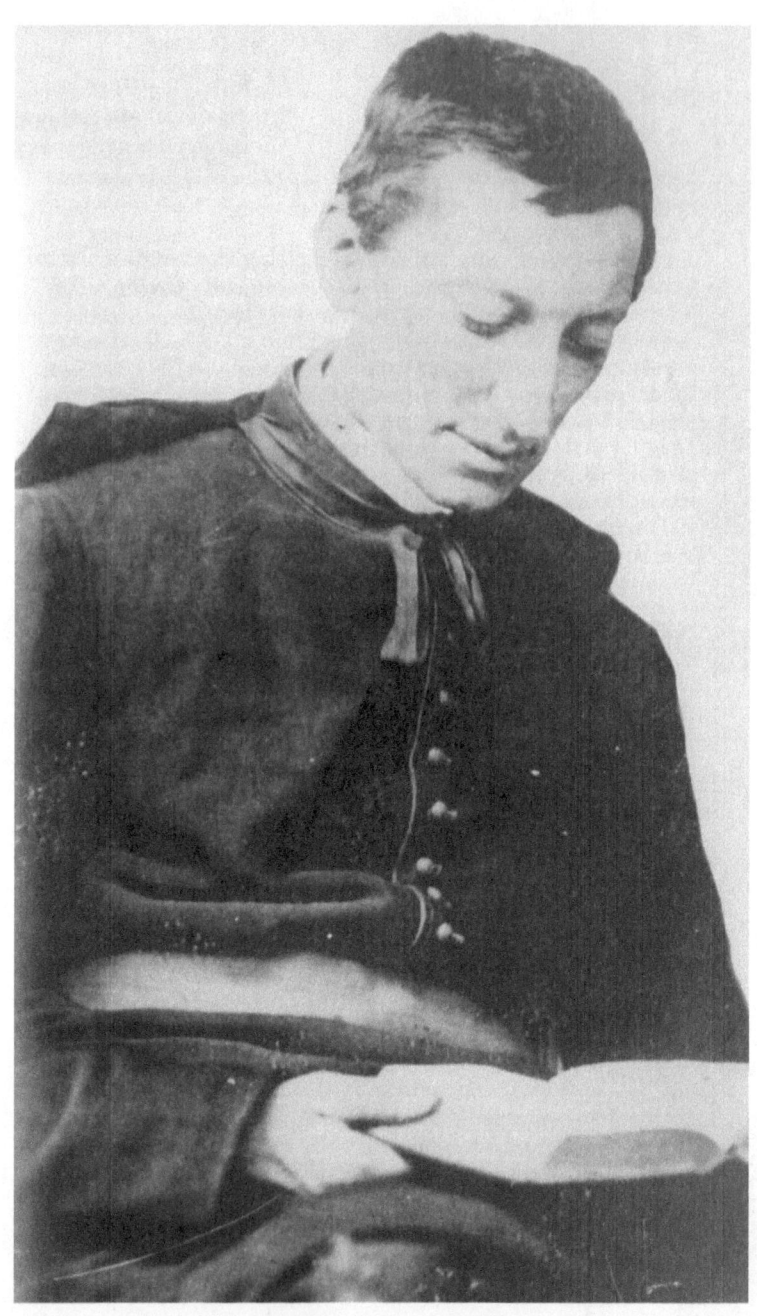

Monsignor Frédéric François Xavier De Mérode 'although Carboni questioned De Mérode's virtue, he was Rome's most edifying prelate'

Mattia Montecchi, Carboni's Giovine Italia companion, in his later years

Left

The title page of Carboni's volume of plays presented to the 'Royal Academy of S. Cecilia from the author' with his signature

Below

Giuseppe Garibaldi at a Rome banquet in his honour in 1875 – it was the first time he was in the city since his defeat in 1849

Homeward Bound

Further lucky strikes

Carboni reached Calcutta when Lord Canning was taking over as Governor-General from Lord Dalhousie. Dalhousie, who had worked as relentlessly as Hotham in Melbourne, was returning to England a dying man at 43, another martyr to the Empire. In eight years, Dalhousie, who described himself as a 'curious compound of despot and radical', had achieved much but had aroused deep hostility. He had annexed the Punjab, completed an ambitious Ganges-fed irrigation scheme, extended roads and ports, introduced the electric telegraph and improved the postal system. On 6 March he left for London confident that the future was unending progress.

Dalhousie's governorship completed the imposition of civil government in what had been a trading empire. The East India Company, which had established British influence throughout India, was purely a commercial enterprise. Gradually, however, the 'glorious sahibs', the Empire builders, established their sway introducing British law, administration and language. In 1813 the East India Company's commercial monopoly was abolished and in 1833 it became a governmental administrative agency. The advantages were obvious; when the aim was to make money, the East India Company's ill-paid employees had been as exploitative as was the Company itself on a larger scale. But there were also disadvantages when the British aimed at something other than profit; there were risks involved in trying to alter the structures, customs and beliefs of Indian society.

The Empire builders were convinced they were introducing a superior civilization. One aspect of this was missionaries who had been kept at arm's length by the East India Company. Many Indians now suspected the government was encouraging missionaries because it intended to impose Christianity. Dalhousie's modernisers had no qualms about destroying Hindu temples when, for instance, they blocked roads. Progress and Christianity both threatened certain Indian traditions.

Moreover, British attitudes had changed as their sway spread over 60 per cent of India, seemingly proving an innate superiority. A long-term resident, Frank Brown, noticed that 'supercilious arrogance' developed, and H. Russell commented that, because the British considered themselves the world's civilisers, they were intolerant. The Indians bore exploitation better than contempt: a year after Dalhousie's departure, British supremacy was contested by a Mutiny.

Originally Calcutta, Bombay and Madras were of roughly equal importance, although Calcutta was the port for most of north India because it was only in 1869, with the opening of the Suez Canal, that Bombay had a much more direct link to London. As British-government power extended, the Calcutta governor's sway was no longer confined to Bengal but covered all British India, of which Calcutta was the capital.

With 360,000 inhabitants, the city sprawled along the Ganges tributary, the hazardous Hooghly, at 120 nautical miles from the Bay of Bengal. It was called a city of palaces. Government House was an imposing three-storeyed neo-classical building with a colonnaded verandah. The colonnaded Writers' Building, seat of the East India Company until it was abolished in 1858, was also monumental and, on Carboni's arrival, a university modelled on London University was being planned. The scale of Calcutta's buildings reflected the volume of India's trade. It had brisk commerce with the Australian colonies, but the bulk of its trade was with Great Britain: in the previous twenty years this trade had trebled. It suggested a major source of the abundance Carboni had witnessed at the Crystal Palace, but increasingly the wealth was Britain's, the poverty India's: the grandiloquent buildings of Calcutta were surrounded by slums.

India, as one observer remarked, was a 'system of outdoor relief for the British upper classes'. It provided a career for younger sons of leading families who, in the homeland, may not have found positions. A bachelor might have as many as fourteen servants. Some servants' occupation was wiping the damp from writing tables, books, clothes, shoes and hat-lining to prevent instant mould.

It was not Devon. The damp heat was enervating and oppressive. An acquaintance of Lord Canning complained of *'nuotando nel sudore'* (swimming in sweat). At 7.30 a.m. Lady Canning closed Government House and windows were covered against a flood of heat until 5 p.m. when there was a chance of a sea breeze. The British created replicas of London, but beyond were excesses in poverty, climate, asceticism and eroticism. After colonial service, some retired to Australia to escape the enervating Bengal heat, but also bleak Britain.

After his long sea trip Carboni, the successful goldminer, made another lucky strike in Calcutta, for he found someone after his own heart: François (Babu) Saint Yves who became his friend. Saint Yves lived and ran a shop in Cossitholla (Butcher's) Street, leading to the temple of Kali south of the city centre. Saint Yves was a jack-of-all-trades to rival Carboni. He advertised as:

> artiste Mechanician; repairer of musical boxes, bird boxes, clocks, carcel, moderateur and other lamps; copper plate, seal and gem engraver; manufacturer of indigo stamps, bronze and Plaster of Paris figures, wood and metal frames; recanveser, cleaner, restorer and varnisher of oil paintings; and French polisher.[1]

If this were not enough, he also sold books: at Saint Yves' shop Carboni found the long-sought *Legend of the Sibyl of Mount Peterlato* which rose opposite Urbino. It may have brought a gust of Urbino mountain air into the Ganges' delta heat.

The discovery inspired Carboni to write a poem about a boy finding the first spring violet.[2] A blonde girl comes running at his cry of pleasure and takes the violet. The boy, claiming it is his, promises forgiveness if she kisses him. 'Kisses are neither demanded nor given on command', is her response. Nevertheless he kisses her. Memories of an Urbino boyhood? It is in line with his sexual initiative at Holy Trinity. It showed he was in buoyant spirits writing 'on the Ganges' banks' in the rainy season, which began late in April and was worse than Ballarat, for chariot-like cockroaches appeared, bats abounded, lizards invaded houses and wine glasses had to be covered against insects.

Carboni had another good strike shopping in central Durumthiola Street.

He purchased yellow idols similar to those on the Thames junk which had caused protests when he was in London, setting his 'Voltairean bile' flowing and provoking him to write a farce, *Spiantacore*. On publishing it, he specified that the idols, bought in Calcutta with Ballarat gold, were available for any theatrical producer. At the same time he bought the Hindu holy books, the Shastras, which he called the 'Bible of the Brahmas'. It was only a few months since, at Eureka, he had had the gratification of publication. The Shastras inspired him to write once again as if they were legends as evocative for him as those of the Peterlato Sibyl. He began *Rita,* a five-act 'oriental' drama with some scenes in Cossitholla and Durumthiola Streets. It included a 'mystical ballet' based on the Hindu king of demons, Ravana, and was probably inspired by a temple morality play. Carboni transcribed temple music and sent it to Luigi Vecchiotti, the musician who had been his mentor in Urbino. Since 1841, Vecchiotti had been the Loreto cathedral choirmaster and that is where Carboni addressed his transcription, in March 1856, 'with grateful memories'.

Did Carboni, now a gentleman of leisure, feel a pull to go native? If he did, he resisted succumbing to a culture which preached the vanity of action in a world of illusion. After all, Carboni subscribed to the belief that Italy could be united through action and words. He was heading home with gold, a book already published, and poems and plays fermenting in his brain, racing from his pen.

Urbino Once More

You can't go home again

Carboni did not rush the remainder of the return journey, which was sensible, as he was unlikely to pass that way again. In any case, he probably had mixed feelings about his reunion with his brother Antonio. And he could write just as well in Egypt as in Italy. In mid-August 1856 he worked 'in the shade of the Pyramids' on the poem-riddle 'Cherry-earrings', which he had begun at Bryant's Ranges in 1853.

Then, well-equipped by his familiarity with the Bible, he visited the Holy Land. He had compared the Ballarat diggers pledging solidarity to 'Crusaders in Palestine'. Now that he was in Palestine he prepared to write a narrative poem, 'The Holy Cross in Jerusalem'; in Nazareth on 1 September he wrote a poem for the Virgin Mary ('by a disciple of her Son'); he visited what was thought to be St Joseph's tomb in Naplosa, and also Lake Galilee. He claimed to have been in Jerusalem on New Year's Eve 1856 and also to have visited Lebanon, the Euphrates, Mount Sinai, Mount Carmel, the Red Sea and Bethlehem.

Eventually he berthed in Trieste, Vienna's port, part of the detested Austrian Empire. He would have seen Austrians, perhaps for the first time. They emerged from rhetoric into reality. In Rome patriots had berated Austria for blocking national unity, but the fight had been against the French who defended the pope. Of course, for Carboni, Trieste was Italy, even if Italian was not even taught in the schools. He would stay there only as part of an army of liberation. He moved on to Venice, which was also under Austrian sovereignty. Lounging in a gondola under a full May moon, he dreamt up a play, *La Benedetta*. He headed down the coast to Rimini:[1] no Austrians, and Antonio was close by in Coriano. Only the year before, Antonio had received a pension after teaching for a decade in the administrative-agricultural centre.

The background to the Carboni brothers reunion is a long letter Antonio sent to Raffaello on 8 January 1856 which, of course, reached Melbourne after his departure.[2] Written over a five-month period, it responds to Raffaello's letters from Victoria and reveals Antonio's excitement at Raffaello's gold finds. The gold which, in August 1854, Raffaello had announced was on its way had not arrived. Antonio, believing Raffaello had entrusted it in Melbourne to a certain unreliable Montefiore, had been almost out of his mind: 'How much worry brother!' he wrote,

> How much uncertainty! How much agitation! What fears! What anxieties! How many different tracks you've made me follow, dear brother! How many letters, how many attempts to find what happened! What huge postal expenses!

Finally, alleluia, the gold had arrived: 'Happy days-the gold is in Rome!' Antonio realised the delay was because it had been despatched months after the date Raffaello had first announced. All Coriano, Antonio advised, would stage a feast for returning Raffaello; the chickens, cheese and wine were all ready.

Antonio quizzed Raffaello on his financial situation because he needed help to achieve independence. He gave details of his earnings from the municipal school (proving himself Raffaello's brother, he complained of 'persecution') and Mass offerings. He had accumulated more than 300 lire in the Rimini savings bank which he intended to invest in a small farm for retirement. But now he hoped Raffaello would enable him to retire earlier because of his health and an 'unfortunate physique' (he admitted to becoming fat). As in another letter, the elder brother was appealing to Raffaello as if he had taken the place of their father. This could be suffocating. Antonio complained that Raffaello's response to an earlier query as to whether he was prepared to help him 'change his fate' had been an unsatisfactory, tight-lipped *'Bon'*.

But even apart from that unsought responsibility, the remainder of the letter shows the brothers' intense relationship. Antonio complains that, as always, headstrong Raffaello wanted to go it alone: 'rather than tell your brother your needs, you prefer to lead a difficult existence, to face risks and dangers which threaten your life, honour and health'. Antonio says Raffaello's failure to confess his needs had greatly disappointed him: 'I wrote that you should not doubt my heart. But this has always been your system, a very cruel system for your brother'.

For his part, the footloose, unpredictable Raffaello seems to have his guard up against his brother's emotional (as well as financial) demands. Antonio's fussy concern for his younger brother suggests he is taking the role of a mother while expecting Raffaello to take that of a father. Not only did Raffaello not tell Antonio his problems until they were finished, he kept his brother completely in the dark about his political involvement and also his spell in Melbourne Gaol. Raffaello had called Antonio 'donkey' for a letter 'full of errors and worse Italian'.

'Thank you brother, I willingly receive everything from you', replied Antonio, turning the other cheek, but he later claimed Raffaello's letters in French had helped 'bastardise' his Italian. Antonio's profession of limitless affection, his reference to their descent from Roman consuls go together with commiseration about their 'adverse fate'. Brotherly love is mixed with giving and receiving hurt and a conviction that they are both destined to be victims. Given their age difference and their separation for more than fifteen years, it remained a remarkably hothouse relationship.

Just as striking in the letters between the brothers is the picture provided by Antonio of home-sweet-home. Antonio refers to Metheldina, perhaps a step-sister, 'all wrinkled', and to the bone 'which emerged from her foot' which can occur with diabetes. Thinking that the sick girl was improving, their father Biagio had been overjoyed, but the doctor told him she would die all the same. Biagio had then gone to his shop, had an apoplectic fit and died. It was 8 January 1853. It is not known what happened to Metheldina. With his second wife Geltrude, Biagio had fathered three step-brothers and two step-sisters for Raffaello. Geltrude was not tired of marriage. Within what Antonio considered an indecently short period after his father's death, Geltrude had married a young good-for-nothing, Luigi Mini ('a servant, gambler, brawler'), and was spending hard and fast, setting up a 'superb house', opening a second-hand shop and putting everything in her new husband's name.

On becoming a priest Antonio had renounced his part of the Carboni inheritance. Now it was entirely Raffaello's. When Antonio saw Geltrude had stripped their father's house, he challenged her with squandering Raffaello's inheritance. She produced a letter, signed by Biagio, specifying the dowry she had brought and also the objects due to her because she had settled his debts. However Antonio claimed she brought 'only her blouse' to his father's house.

Antonio blamed Geltrude for his father's death. He claimed she forced him to sign the dowry document and 'finally our poor father broke down because she never left him in peace'. Antonio called Geltrude 'usurper, ungrateful, imprudent, reckless, restless, malicious'.

Home life was as strongly tinted as any 19th-century melodrama with ghastly deaths, a wicked stepmother and a vanishing inheritance. The whole catastrophic story would have broken over Carboni's head on his return: father proved a fool by the woman now living with a young man; inheritance gone and elder brother pleading help. He would have been reminded why he had wandered so far.

Presumably he heard the bitter story of Antonio's ten-year stint in Coriano's one-teacher municipal school. When Antonio's biennial contract was renewed for the second time in 1852, parents complained to the Town Council about his shortcomings. By 1856 he was criticised for 'beastly' disciplinary methods, including hitting students, vindictively pulling their hair, making them stand for hours without even permission to go to the toilet, vulgar language and laziness, for allegedly he arrived at school towards midday but left shortly after.

These criticisms may have been the 'persecution' Antonio lamented. Apparently he achieved quite good academic results. In 1856 he was given a further chance on condition he be less harsh, but immediately he became worse than before. Evidently Antonio was irremediably crotchety and at certain moments saw his students as enemies. His correspondence shows he was excitable and emotive; he admitted to being sick. He agreed to resign provided he was given a pension. The Town Council granted only a third of the pension he requested.

It was a cautionary tale revealing the misery of stay-at-homes. There were other examples in Urbino itself: the moneylenders Cavioli and Concini, after squeezing the peasants dry, had gone bankrupt and fled to a friary; Foglietta had a steady income from his salt and tobacco shop but his wife had died;

Ugolini had ended his days mad in a Perugia hospice; X was dead, as were Y and Z ... Carboni, successful goldminer, world traveller, was not to be trapped in the quicksands of the past. The small hilltop town could not hold him; Geltrude alone may have provided sufficient reason for him to leave.

Milan

Make war not love

In mid-1858 Carboni fell hopelessly in love with Adelaide Ristori, the most famous actress of the period, whose performance in Giacometti's *Elizabeth of England* inspired him to improvise an acrostic sonnet based on her name.[1] It was 19 July 1858 at the Covent Garden Theatre, London, which, after destruction by fire, had been recently reopened, gleaming from its huge chandelier to the gilt decorations. Ristori, Carboni's sonnet said, showed powers similar to the woman who crushed the head of the Father of Lies; her great merit, it added, was to inspire English admiration for Italian dramatic genius. It would be hard to say whether Carboni was infatuated with Ristori or with the idea that she could make London rafters ring for an Italian playwright such as he aspired to be. Later comments imply that in London Ristori, who shared Carboni's nationalist passion, asked him to make translations. But there was no hint that she reciprocated his feelings.

The successful goldminer could be man about town in London and Paris, but for the first time since 1848–49, the fight for Italian unity was resuming on a large scale. In April 1859 Austria, which ruled Lombardy, presented an ultimatum to Piedmont against enrolment of Lombard exiles in its army. When Austrian troops advanced towards Turin, combined Piedmontese and French forces not only repulsed them but liberated Lombardy. At the same time there were successful uprisings against foreign rule in Florence, Parma, Modena and Emilia Romagna. The Società Nazionale, founded in 1857 by the Sicilian Giuseppe La Farina and others, played an important role in fomenting these uprisings.

United geographically and religiously, Italy had long been chronically divided politically, but now the combined effects of the Mazzinian belief that nothing was impossible, Garibaldi's military prowess and Cavour's shrewd assessment of possibilities made feasible the unity which, after 1849, had seemed a mere mirage. In Milan exciting events followed in quick succession. On 7 June the French victor over the Austrians, Marshall MacMahon, passed through the city; the following day, Napoleon III and Vittorio Emanuele II entered it to an enthusiastic welcome. A Te Deum for the victory was celebrated in the cathedral. The Piedmontese Prime Minister Cavour, who had astutely provoked Austria's ill-judged invasion, arrived on the morning of 9 June, followed that afternoon by Garibaldi, whose *Cacciatori delle Alpi* (Alpine Hunters) had driven the Austrians from Varese. La Scala Opera House staged a gala performance in honour of the victors. News of the death of the Austrian statesman Metternich on 11 June added to the jubilation; it was said his dying words were that only one diplomat would now be left – Cavour. Count Camillo Benso di Cavour, an innovative agriculturalist before becoming a politician, had gained international support for the kingdom of Sardinia, which included Piedmont. He had outmanoeuvred Austria by sending 15,000 troops to fight alongside the French and British in the Crimean War which enabled him to participate in the peace negotiations.

The presence in Milan of Napoleon III and more French than Piedmontese troops recalled Napoleon Bonaparte who had made the city capital of his Italian kingdom. Reverberations of his descent into Italy were probably young Carboni's first hint of a possible new order. Learning French from the Parisian monsignor at Holy Trinity had pitched him into prison and politics, but now he used his knowledge of the language to advance the cause of unity. From June he was employed by the Milan Town Council as interpreter for the French army's hospital services and ambulance corps. His French employers praised him as 'intelligent and zealous'.[2]

However in July, worried by the rapid progress towards Italian unity, Napoleon III negotiated at Villafranca an armistice with Austria. Italian nationalists felt betrayed. But a lawyer, Francesco Crispi, who after the 1848 Sicilian uprising had eked out a living in Malta, Lisbon, London and Paris, was convinced the battle for unity could resume on his native soil. On a false American passport, he returned to Sicily to organise uprisings against the Bourbon regime.

After the French troops' departure from Milan, Carboni continued to work with 'zeal and intelligence'[3] as interpreter in the city's military hospitals. He was still employed by the Town Council, which had changed few personnel, for the Austrian administration had been competent. In the years preceding the French–Piedmont victory, public services had improved and building boomed in a city whose population rose to over 210,000. The square before La Scala was enlarged, a Leonardo da Vinci monument built and restoration of his Last Supper begun, an arcade from the cathedral to San Fedele square was planned and work commenced on the central railway station. Austrian Milan had been a city of canals and a gay social life centred around La Scala, which had charmed Stendahl. Nevertheless walls had been plastered with signs *'Viva V. E. R. D. I.'*, which referred both to the patriotic composer and also to the Piedmontese sovereign under his future title Vittorio Emanuele Re d'Italia (Vittorio Emanuele King of Italy).

Liberated Milan's literary idol was Alessandro Manzoni who had refused to receive the Austrian emperor's brother Maximilian, Governor of the Veneto region and Lombardy. Carboni had unbounded admiration for Manzoni, but thought he could aid the patriotic cause in the literary field himself. In November 1859, he submitted *La Santola* to the Milan Philo-Dramatic Commission. He suggested this play, based on his experience of Rome as 'the emporium of bastardy', was suitable for independent Italy's national theatre and requested that he be allowed to give a reading of this fruit of '18 years' work'. It was a proud pitch but, as Carboni complained the following Easter, it brought no response: 'zero, nought, nothing and vice versa'. He published also (in Turin) *Rita,* the 'Oriental drama' inspired by his Calcutta sojourn, but local episodes, rather than the exotic, were now priming him.

A crass Milanese play *El Cervel del Carabui* moved him to write a saner one on the same theme of marriage. In *El Cervel* an innocent servant girl, Virginia, dreams she cannot respond to her parish priest's questions about matrimony. She seeks illumination from a delicatessen owner. 'You get the gift of the child Jesus.' 'Give it to me or I'll be sent away from the Church', she pleads. His response is to show her the swollen salami dangling from his belt. Such crudity, in Carboni's opinion, was a disgrace to liberated Milan: the revolution implied a more rigorous morality, an edifying art as an alternative, Carboni proposed *Nazzareno Schiantapalmi* (the name Nazarene Palmcrusher may hint he is a Christ-figure), which seems to hew close to his experience.

Not only has the protagonist returned to Italy from goldmining in Ballarat, but the writing is more vivid than in his other stage works where conventions and polemics tend to choke out the ripple of life.

Nazzareno, who first appears in gold diggers' garb, is a guest at the Milan home of Count Vittorio of Roccaspaldi, his school mate and companion-in-arms during the 1849 defence of Rome. Nazzareno's story, remarks Vittorio, is that of many patriots: 'those not killed set out for foreign countries like a school of dog-fish in search of bait devoured at home, with the blessing of Christ's vicar, by loathsome strangers'. Vittorio suggests to Nazzareno that in London's fog, at the South Pole, in Egypt he has 'lost the poetry of life.'

However Nazzareno feels reborn in the company of Vittorio, his wife Countess Dantelina, the orphan Olimpia, who has been adopted by Vittorio sister and her young aristocratic girlfriends. Generous Nazzareno, who had 'more gold rings and watches than a Jew', has sent his nephew Benedetto to his goldfields companion Pastorello (the name used also for the Carboni figure in *La Santola*) in Paris. Pastorello is to give Benedetto 100,000 lire plus a ring of Ballarat gold in case he spots a Parisian suitable as a wife.

Nazzareno, delighted with the female company, struck by Vittorio's domestic content, asks his help in finding a wife. A friend of the family, the bigoted widow Marchioness Margherita of Torrestorta (Bent Tower-perhaps meaning she is from Pisa), has designs on Nazzareno, but he spots in her what he considers the signs of a priest-ridden woman: corrugated forehead, staring eyes, ruined teeth.

Described by one of the young aristocratic women as 'nearly as handsome as he is good', Nazzareno is persuaded to demonstrate the latest Parisian fashion which he picked up in Saint Germain. He enacts the 'Gallican greeting', showing how Parisians give assignations when meeting on the Champs Elysees. In the course of the demonstration, he declares his love to Olimpia, who is perturbed, as she thinks of him only as 'uncle Nazzareno'.

Marchioness Margherita asks Nazzareno about the women he has known in his travels. Women are marvellous, Nazzareno tells her, unless priests turn them into jealous vipers. As a young man, he confesses, 'I could not decide in which of my thousand and one castles in the air I should live and who I should bring to the nest'. In London,

> I was seized by the Satanic desire to make gold so I'd be adored by all! ... and loved by no one. After having worn out my soul to cover my body with gold; look (he touches his hair) soon there'll also be silver! It comes by itself but decent unmarried girls abhor snow on the mountain ...

Margherita suggests he marry a widow. Nazzareno replies that not all his castles in the air have crashed, adding that widows always lament their first husbands. Presumably to scandalise Margherita, Nazzareno mentions that Australian native women go nude. Vittorio says they would arouse interest performing a ballet at La Scala. Australian natives, Nazzareno tells Margherita, 'see and enjoy each other day and night in the woods'. 'They have no religion!' she gasps. 'They haven't Milan cathedral', Vittorio remarks dryly.

The scene shifts to Vittorio's villa at Monza, outside Milan, where a young aristocratic couple and two of Vittorio's servants are to be married at the same time. Margherita, piqued by Nazzareno spurning her and ridiculing the Church, tells Vittorio his rich friend is trying to seduce Countess Dantelina.

Her lie is uncovered. Next the aristocratic bridegroom, who is racing to the Monza villa with Nazzareno's nephew Benedetto, falls from his horse, damaging his foot. Nazzareno has a panacea: Eureka balsam! One drop on the tongue, accompanied by 'Yes' from a female, cures all ills. Nazzareno is told similar balsams can be derived from Italian plants but he does not have the knack; his beloved Olimpia, he finds, is to marry Benedetto. Ultimately it is Nazzareno's gold which has put Benedetto in a condition to marry her. The young couple invite Nazzareno to visit them; their affection is sincere but he is to remain an outsider to conjugal life.

The play suggests that the ex-goldminer who had long lived in a predominantly male community rejoiced in exchanges of affection, the expression of 'emotion for emotion's sake', and young female company. His young women are. vivacious, noisy, prone to sweet nothings. Carboni wanted to enter the play's chichi world but it may not have satisfied one who, in Ballarat and elsewhere, had wrestled with Beelzebub. The lines on his disillusionment in love, his search for gold and discovery of silver seem to have the truth of experience: he had found the Eureka balsam of gold but no suitable female who would say 'Si'.

The play used aboriginal women for titillation but Carboni returned to them more seriously in his second work set in Australia which he was yet to publish, Gilburnia. It takes place among the Tarrang tribe in the Loddon valley with whom he had spent some time. This gave him a sympathetic outlook not widespread when he wrote what he called a 'pantomime in eight scenes.' Two aboriginal suitors fight over Gilburnia, the beautiful daughter of the tribal elder. She shows her independence by rejecting the winner in favour of the loser, called Rang, but goldminders arrive and take Gilburnia for their leader Gruno. However Gilburnia escapes into the forest with Gruno in vain pursuit.

Some aborigines, unaware that Gilburnia has managed to flee, set out after the goldminers but are killed by them. Gruno finds Gilburnia's father and is about to kill him when Rang kills Gruno.

The Protector of the Aborigines arrives and, acting as a Prosecutor, imprisons some aborigines charging them with murder. However a hurricane destroys their prison, freeing them. Gilburnia and Rang, presumably, live happily ever after.

The storm is providential, providing a justice superior to the human. In The Eureka Stockade, Carboni devoted a chapter to the beneficial effect of storms as if to show that a clash within nature can lead to refound harmony. During Redmond Bary's summary at Carboni's trial, there had been a clap of thunder which spurred him to remind the jury of divine justice. The Age and the Argus took Barry to task for this but Carboni probably agreed with him, although he did not mention it in his account. He saw his release as human justice in line with divine justice. Somehow he linked this with nature.

Tony Palgiaro, who brought attention to Gilburnia by translation and commentary, claimed that its hidden intent was identification with the Stockade rebellion and the subsequent trial. Carboni does refer to them in Gilburnia but, if that was his intention, it conflicts with the text where miners are wholly loathsome and the aborigines nature's children. It is difficult to see those tried after Eureka as the colony's white aborigines, particularly as Carboni admitted to sharing the diabolical lust for gold.

Gilburnia goes against Carboni's experience of British justice which he mentions in the text. The play took shape while he was in cell 33 of the Melbourne prison, quaking at his possible sentence, but he had years in which to modify the text after his just release. As he did not do so, the text implies that British justice, although admirable in his case, did not apply to aborigines.

Gilburnia showed Carboni could be more serious about aborigines than in

Nazzareno Schiantapalmi which reflected a heart still young but frustrated. He was soon to find that, unlike Olimpia, the god of war accepts even silver-haired devotees.

Crispi's mission to Sicily was producing results. An uprising was planned in Palermo on 4 April 1860. However the insurgents, led by the tinsmith Francesco Riso, were betrayed. Trapped in the Gancia convent, thirteen were killed.

Thirteen victims! The same number as the state prisoners after the Eureka clash. Carboni read everything available on the uprising and planned a play to give the insurgents mythic stature.

A few days after suppression of the Gancia insurgents, Rosalino Pila, with a small force, reached Messina from Genoa to foment peasant unrest. Although reports were confusing, Crispi convinced Garibaldi that Pila had received a promising welcome. On 5 May, Garibaldi with just over 1,000 volunteers set out from Quarto, near Genoa, to challenge the Bourbon kingdom defended by 100,000 troops. Five days later they landed in Marsala. On 11 June, 20,000 Bourbon troops surrendered in Palermo to the redshirts.

As a majority of the 'Mille' were Lombards, Milanese were intensely interested in news from Sicily. One of Carboni's few remaining castles in the air was becoming a reality. Garibaldi was putting the enemy to flight again, as in Rome, but this time it looked as if he would chase them into the sea. Carboni's blood must have raced at the news. He had to be there.

On 20 June Francesco Crippa, administrator of the Milanese military hospitals, certified that Carboni, during a year's employment, had shown 'efficient zeal, notable intelligence and outstanding energy'. The mayor, Antonio Beretta, likewise testified to Carboni's 'exquisite skill and notable intelligence'; he added that the Town Council thanked Carboni for his zeal, energy, and conscientiousness not only as translator-interpreter, but in 'various and difficult administrative tasks'.[4] If these recommendations were not enough, Carboni bore also others from a Milan pharmacist and a doctor to the head of the Garibaldi Aid organisation in Genoa, Agostino Bertani, who had directed the Roman Republic's medical services. On 27 June Carboni began to work for Bertani as translator from French and English, but only ten days later set out for Palermo, donating his Genoa salary for the cause.[5] He was to work with the Medical Corps. As he sailed from Genoa to participate in a great adventure, the personal problems reflected in *Nazzareno Schiantapalmi* were left in the wake.

Palermo

Living a novel

'Really, to be so fortunate, is like [living] a ... novel.' Carboni, who had arrived in Palermo on 24 June 1860, was working with the provisional government's Secretary-General Francesco Crispi. He was doing what he had long desired, forging Italy and, what is more, was gleaning material for his plays. 'As in your office', he wrote to Agostino Bertani, 'I am working as protocol officer and translator.'

He had seen 'our General' in superlative health, 'looking 12 years younger than when he was in Rome in 1848'. Garibaldi, he continued, 'is in his element now and God help him plant the sacred Tricolour on the Campidoglio again'.[1] Later Carboni claimed Garibaldi had ensured his position as administrative officer with Crispi.[2]

General Giacomo Medici had arrived with 3,000 reinforcements and 8,000 Enfield rifles. Alexandre Dumas had also arrived on his yacht *Emma*, together with a nymphet dressed as a sailor, to offer himself as Garibaldi's ambassador. Stirring days; Carboni's snuff consumption must have soared. Garibaldi, who occupied three small rooms in the Palace of the Norman Kings, went daily to the seafront Italic Forum (which until his arrival had been called the Bourbon Forum) to review troops embarking for the Milazzo front. And on 15 July, in poncho and red shirt with unsheathed sword, seated on a throne in the cathedral, the Freemason had a tribute of incense from the archbishop who called him a 'defender of the Faith and the Church'. It was the Mass for Saint Rosalia, the patron of Palermo, and the ceremonial required the bearded warrior to kiss her relics. Saint Rosalia and

Giuseppe Garibaldi – Palermitans were in ecstasy.

On Garibaldi's entry to Palermo, sixteen days after landing in Marsala, a quarter of the city had been flattened or burnt by a two-hour bombardment from the Bourbon fort and fleet. The Sicilian capital of nearly 200,000 inhabitants seemed devastated by an earthquake but the rubble was quickly cleared. The redshirts had been dirty, dusty and ragged on arrival, but Captain Nino Bixio, who had convalesced at Holy Trinity with Goffredo Mameli in 1849, immediately requisitioned brothels for them. Soon the officers were smartly dressed, wore gloves and were invited to patrician palaces. Palermo entertained the redshirts in scintillating style. Nightly they had theatre boxes and afterwards promenaded on the seafront. The intersecting main thoroughfares, Maqueda and Cassero, were once again open-air salons. The victors enjoyed exotic local products such as melon, cinnamon, prickly-pear, rose ice cream and fried, ground-chickpea patties. To the novelist-officer Ippolito Nievo, Palermo seemed a baroque 16th-century city, both rough and refined.

News from the battlefront fuelled Palermitan festivities. On the 18th Garibaldi had sailed from Palermo on the *City of Aberdeen*. At 10 p.m. two days later, an army relay rider brought word that immediately after Garibaldi's arrival, Milazzo had been taken. Church bells rang and thousands thronged via Toledo shouting *'Viva Garibaldi, viva Italia, viva Vittorio Emanuele!'* Young men improvised a band to add to the noise; lamps were lit throughout the central city; red, white and green flags waved. To applause like gunshots, the National Guard arrived playing *The Tricolour Flag*. Carboni's eardrums, he wrote to Bertani, had never been subjected to such piercing expressions of enthusiasm, particularly by the women.

Euphoria was followed, however, by consternation when the Milazzo losses were learnt. It was almost a week before Carboni heard the grisly details, including a grave injury to the Neapolitan Captain Montemajor who had preceded him in Bertani's office. In all, he wrote to Bertani, there were 239 wounded in the Milazzo military hospital, another 201 in private homes and 600 dead. 'Civil war is, perhaps, God's most terrible curse', Carboni commented, but he argued it must continue until independence, or 'our children would curse us'.[3]

There was not even adequate medical assistance. Crispi sent Carboni to General Guiseppe Sirtori, a former priest, to obtain some improvement.

However, as Carboni informed the Garibaldi Aid Organisation in Genoa, even ten days after the battle he could not obtain a complete list of the wounded and injured. Perhaps this was why Bertani reproved Ippolito Nievo, who was second-in-charge in the Military Inspectorate: 'Your administration is discredited by not having a list of the dead and wounded'.

In Carboni's estimate, Palermitan public administration had fallen into the hands of 'cosmopolitan crooks'; he feared the revolution would suffer as in Rome in 1849.[4] In fact, the Garibaldians were in greater danger from maladministration than from Bourbon troops. A political war was being fought in Palermo with Cavour's agents discrediting Francesco Crispi who, with the formation of a provisional government, became Minister for the Interior of Garibaldi's administration in Sicily.

The novel Carboni was living was an epic with many heroes. Garibaldi was the Man of Providence, Divine Messenger, Hero of the Two Worlds or, simply, 'The Man'. Crispi, whose receding hairline emphasised his high forehead, was 'The Brain'. He had convinced hesitant Garibaldi to lead the expedition to Sicily, for he considered him 'the greatest of all condottieri'. But he also considered Garibaldi 'incapable of running a village' and, in diplomatic negotiations, 'as weak as a woman'. Crispi himself was a craggy negotiator. Later he formed a mutual admiration society with Bismarck. The Prussian said Crispi was a greater man than himself. Bismarck was certainly the more successful politician.

From a family of distant Albanian origin, Crispi was grandson of a Sicilian Greek Orthodox priest. In years spent conspiring against the Bourbon regime in Sicily, there are hints that he engaged in terrorist activities. Energetic, vain and abrasive, now that the Bourbons had been defeated, he shaped the provisional government's political and administrative decisions from his office in the stately 15th-century Palermo Senate building. Carboni claimed to have translated secret correspondence between Crispi and Gideon S. Lang, agent for Palmerston's Foreign Minister, Lord John Russell.[5] (Presumably Carboni was unaware that six years before, while presiding over the Colonial Office, Russell had reproved Hotham for lodging the wrong charge against him and the others brought from Ballarat for trial in Melbourne.) Carboni would have been one of the older officials; half the original redshirts were students under 28, while Crispi himself, at 40, was two years younger than Carboni.

If there were heroes there were also villains – two Sicilian ex-Mazzinians,

Giuseppe La Farina and Filippo Cordova. Now they were both Piedmontese agents and, to Ballarat-trained eyes, must have appeared little better than Spy Goodenough and Sub-Spy Peters. La Farina, who had been an impassioned Republican during the 1848 Palermo uprising, had arrived on 7 June with a commission from Cavour to hasten Sicilian annexation by Piedmont. Tall, ceremonious La Farina quickly found entry into patrician palaces and high-class clubs, although at the same time organising 'spontaneous' pro-annexation demonstrations. On 7 July Garibaldi ordered La Farina's expulsion, together with two men accused of plotting to assassinate the Dictator (Garibaldi). 'The three men', said the Official Gazette, which made no distinction between the two assassins and Cavour's emissary, 'were in Palermo plotting against the present government.' But La Farina returned and ordered Crispi's arrest which he avoided by diving out of his office window. Crispi's newspaper *Il Precursore*, recalling that La Farina had persecuted the hero of the 1848 anti-Bourbon uprising, Rosalino Pila, called him 'despite the gold patina, fetid slime.'

Carboni had to stay afloat in a choppy political sea subject to sudden squalls and insidious currents. From the north the tensions of a fractured political movement had been imported to Palermo. For Cavour schemes for Italian unity in the short term were 'silly nonsense'. He wanted to unify Italy north of the Papal States, which could not be touched because of possible international complications. He did not intend to challenge the Bourbon kingdom south of the Papal States. Surprised by the success of Garibaldi's invasion of Sicily, he set about harnessing it to his cause. Some of those who wrested Sicily from the Bourbons believed Garibaldi should push on to Rome and proclaim Italian unity from the eternal city. Cavour knew Garibaldi respected King Vittorio Emanuele, but feared that, if he reached Rome, this could be exploited for a takeover by 'red republicans and socialist demagogues'. Cavour wanted to rein in Garibaldi and immediately hold a plebiscite in Sicily to endorse Piedmontese annexation, even though in many ways Piedmont was closer to Paris than to Palermo. This bit-by-bit extension of the Piedmontese sway was called the 'artichoke policy' in contrast to creation of a new Italy with Rome as capital.

Carboni was involved in fierce infighting between pro-Piedmont and pro-Garibaldi factions. Moreover there were tensions between Garibaldi and Mazzini, aggravated by the fact that many former Mazzinians were now saying that Italy could not be united against King Vittorio Emanuele, that, in a phrase coined later, republicanism divided but the monarchy united. Mazzini believed in people power, Cavour could work with a parliament, Garibaldi wanted benign dictatorship rather than democracy. Carboni was in for years of living confusedly.

On 18 July Cavour had written that Garibaldi was surrounding himself with ever more Mazzinians (Mazzini had returned temporarily from London to Genoa where he was hunted by Piedmontese police) and concentrating his authority in 'the hands of Bertani, our declared enemy'. Crispi now considered King Vittorio Emanuele essential for Italian unification; but he wanted this proclaimed from Rome, after liberation of that city and the Veneto region. He had founded *Il Precursore,* whose motto was 'Independent from all Strangers', to counter Cavour-inspired press attacks. Ignoring difficulties facing the Garibaldian administration and exaggerating its defects, this press campaign implied only immediate union with Piedmont could forestall financial and social anarchy.

On 21 July Agostino Depretis, became Pro-Dictator but lasted only a few months because he clashed with Crispi. Carboni sent Depretis a query regarding volunteers who, after reaching Palermo, had not been accepted for Garibaldi's forces and were requesting payment of their return trip. Carboni could not read the crabbed handwriting of Depretis's reply. Breezily he upbraided his superior: 'thank God, I can read twelve languages but not that which you write, especially in the note on the piece of paper attached herewith'. Depretis scribbled that the volunteers should be sent home the following Friday and classified his cheeky clerk's note 'private'.[6]

Like Garibaldi, Mazzini, Crispi and other prominent figures of the movement for unity, Depretis was a Freemason. Carboni worked with many of them and shared their anti-clericalism and fervent nationalism. If he had become a full member of the Giovine Italia movement in his Roman years, he may have been initiated into the Freemasons although Mattia Cattabeni, who had interested him in the movement, did not become a Freemason himself for another 30 years. If Carboni did become a Freemasoni he did not explain how he reconciled this with his proclaimed Catholicism when they were considered incompatible – but not by the archbishop of Palermo to judge by his tribute to Garibaldi.

An incident in eastern Sicily that hot August undermined the Garibaldian revolution. Carboni probably heard of it from the protagonists, for early in August he planned a trip to Garibaldi in Messina,[7] which, with the exception of the fort, had been occupied. They were the days in which peasants at Bronte, on Etna's slopes, seized the *latifundia* they worked. The main proprietors were descendants of Lord Nelson. Perhaps during these days Jane, the daughter of the Duchess of Bronte, was present. Carboni would have recognised her, for when he was in Ballarat she had been Charles Hotham's wife and was now married, for the third time, to yet another naval captain, William Armytage. She outlived him also and survived until 1907.

The peasants at Bronte believed Garibaldi's arrival meant a social revolution as suggested by his first decrees, such as abolition of the hated grain tax. King Vittorio Emanuele and Italy were distant concepts, but the peasants understood the fight against the Bourbons and wanted land. Although Garibaldi recognised that peasants had provided valuable support, land seizure, especially that of the English who were potential allies, could inspire fear of anarchy. From Catania, Nino Bixio led troops to butcher the Bronte peasants; social justice could wait until Italy was united.

Carboni, shot at in Ballarat, was now part of an army shooting the land-hungry; Sicily was the antipodes of Ballarat. Of course, it was all for a threatened cause but it showed that a successful revolution were not a panacea. Cavour was controlling the flow of money to the provisional government to ensure Piedmontese annexation of Sicily. At the same time, he encouraged a Neapolitan anti-Bourbon uprising to steal Garibaldi's thunder because the 'Liberator', the 'Hero of the Two Worlds' was now racing through Calabria as if headed for his native Nizza or, as it had become since Cavour had traded it off to France, Nice.

If Garibaldi enters Naples, Cavour wrote to his Minister there, *'c'est lui et non Victor Emmanuel qui sera le véritable Roi d'Italie'* ('he will be the real king of Italy, rather than Vittorio Emanuele').[8] On 7 September, having conquered half Italy in four months, Garibaldi did enter Naples but with less éclat than in Palermo; he came by train from Salerno and was welcomed by Liborio Romano, the former Bourbon police chief, and a crowd organised by the Camorra (underworld) bosses. Shortly afterwards, Depretis went to ask the Dictator's approval for immediate Sicilian annexation. In protest, Crispi resigned and also went to Naples, avowing he would not return unless Cavour's agents, particularly Filippo Cordova, were expelled from Palermo. Garibaldi refused immediate annexation and expelled Cavour's agents. Crispi had won a little time for Garibaldi to reach Rome and seize the initiative from Cavour. But Crispi himself had become unpopular in Palermo.

Crispi's man there, Carboni, who detested spying, did a little or at least gathered political intelligence for the cause. On 16 September he wrote to Crispi that he had gone to the departing *Panther* to confirm that Cordova, whom he called a Jesuit, was on board in fulfilment of the expulsion order. He reported also that some conservatives wanted to proclaim the Duke of Genoa, Vittorio Emanuele's brother, King of Sicily.

Three days later, Garibaldi paid a lightning visit to Palermo. He arrived on the Florio company steamship *Elettrico* at 2.00 and left again at 9.00. He brought with him Agostino Bertani, who was now his Secretary-General in Naples, and the new Pro-Dictator Antonio Mordini, who had visited London's Pentonville prison about the time Carboni interpreted there. To the crowd which gathered in front of the Royal Palace, he said self-interest inspired those who wanted immediate union with Piedmont: 'We will proclaim Italian unity', he promised, 'in Rome'. It seemed he had routed the immediate-annexation lobby.

In a high-spirited letter to Crispi, who had remained in Naples, Carboni said on 4 October that nothing (*'niente, rien,* nothing, *nada, nichts'*) of Crispi's policies had been changed.[9] Carboni reported that the Pro-Dictator (Mordini) had complimented him, presumably for his translations, on behalf of the journalist Count Charles de la Varenne, whom Garibaldi had made his public relations man. He added that Giorgio Tamajo, head of the police, did not even have time to put on his underpants before receiving requests for help. He revealed he had not forgotten what it was to be needy: 'When will the government show the Revolution was for the benefit also of the proletariat?' 'Apart from kindergartens', he continued, 'nothing has been done although it is said everything has been provided for'.

Carboni's life could have changed if he had had the courage of this assessment. Perhaps the thought tugged at him that some of the thirteen victims he was commemorating in *La Campana della Gancia* were likewise from the Palermo proletariat. His Ballarat experience should have sharpened his sensibility; at times he acknowledged the treatment of the underprivileged was the criterion of a revolution but he did not hew consistently to this insight.

A perambulating Pasquin

On 18 October Carboni adopted, in Ballarat terms, 'gold and silver lace'. he was promoted sub-commissar of war, Grade 1, the equivalent of a captain.[10] He now went on the army payroll and welcomed the recognition with an advertisement in *Il Precursore* which praised his 'energetic temperament and honest heart'. He was making a rapid career. Before he had occasionally been bumptious, and now he may have become officious. On a windy mid-winter night with high seas, he waited in the bay for the arrival of the steamship *Ercole* because he was to take receipt of government despatches. When, about midnight, the ship approached, Carboni noticed sailors throwing sacks of green, waxed canvas to rowboats and concluded they were smuggling tobacco. Armed with his new authority as captain, he ordered that the sacks be returned to the *Ercole,* but there was no response from the ship. The quarantine launch came to his aid and the official on it tried to scale the ship's ladder. But, perhaps with a little help from the crew, it gave way: with the descending passengers, the customs official fell into the bay. The *Ercole* skipper told Carboni he knew nothing of the sacks. The following day Carboni, the poacher turned gamekeeper, recounted the episode in a letter to the Minister for the Navy, adding that both passengers and cargo had been released before health officials gave approval.

But for all the zeal of officers such as Carboni, Garibaldi's administration would have a short life unless annexation could be postponed by elections for Sicilian and Neapolitan assemblies, followed, perhaps, by a Constituent Assembly on Italian unity.

Although the new Pro-Dictator Antonio Mordini began as a Republican, anti-Piedmontese revolutionary, since the mid-1850s he had become increasingly critical of Mazzini and was a Tuscan representative in the Piedmontese parliament. Energetic but also conciliatory, black-bearded, wide-faced Mordini initiated several administrative reforms. One measure which must have pleased Carboni was state assumption of all the debts of Francesco Riso, a rebel against the Bourbons, and confiscation of the possessions of the 'public enemy', the former police chief Salvatore Maniscalco. Maniscalco was the villain, Riso one of the protagonists of Carboni's almost-completed play *La Campana della Gancia* ('The Gancia Bell').

Cavour had his way and an annexation plebiscite was scheduled for 21 October. In Palermo it was preceded by three days of special illumination, a forest of green, red and white flags, military bands playing patriotic tunes and processions bearing busts of Vittorio Emanuele. On the eve of the vote, Cavour raised the number of Piedmontese troops in Palermo to 5,000, heavily outnumbering the remaining Garibaldians. All males over 21 were entitled to vote. In Sicily, with a population of 2,392,414, only 432,700 voted, a mere 677 of them against annexation.

Immediately after the plebiscite, Giovanni Acerbi, head of the Military Commissariat, wrote from Naples to his deputy Ippolito Nievo warning that it was impossible to expect justice, let alone benevolence, from the new government. He advised Nievo to prepare an exact account of his administration. The Piedmontese who had discredited the Garibaldian administration were likely to double the dose now they had to decide the fate of Garibaldi's army. In fact, a parliamentary inquiry into the Commissariat was initiated.

Cavour was delighted that, with his help, Garibaldi's international reputation was declining: the London *Times* was beginning to see him as a threat to law and order. Even some Garibaldi supporters were half-inclined to believe hostile press reports but in a letter to Federigo Bellazzi, of the Garibaldian Aid Organisation in Genoa, Carboni reassured him that the General was still popular.

In the same letter Carboni gave news of a mutual friend, Benedetto Cairoli, one of Garibaldi's captains, who had not recovered from a wound received during the battle for Palermo. Cairoli lay in the Royal Palace and it may have been there that Carboni met the talented young writer Ippolito Nievo who, when bored by the polkas, decolletes and cassatas of Palace receptions, often called on his bedridden fellow officer. Carboni said he conceived a poem while enjoying the breeze on the terrace of the Royal Palace.

For the Mordini administration, the five post-plebiscite weeks were a strange twilight period because, as *Il Precursore* complained, there were two parallel governments.

A multitude of functionaries from Turin who are not responsible to Mordini flatter, praise, promise jobs and recruit for those who are to govern. There are two bodies of militarised police, two armies, one responsible to Sicilian authorities, one to Turin. There are two police – one, visible, born with the revolution has maintained order amid the emergence of popular forces – the other, secret, tries to destroy all order, plots to create clashes, to throw the country into anarchy so the Turin government's semi-official newspapers can show Europe they are not lying when they calumniate us ...

In this twilight period, Carboni transferred to the Pro-Dictatorate where he worked in the accounting section under his friend, the sturdy, bearded Secretary-General Angelo Bargoni. Summoned in July by Depretis, Bargoni had remained when Mordini took over. Bargoni had committed himself to Italian unity since sent from his native Cremona to study in Pavia. Under investigation for his student political activities, he had sought refuge in Genoa where he had become friendly with Mordini, Rosalino Pilo and other Mazzinians. A legal consultant in Italy for Gresham, an English insurance company, and with a family to support, he nevertheless offered himself for service in Sicily.

On 2 December Mordini handed over to the King's Lieutenant-Governor Marchese Massimo Cordero di Montezemolo. Mordini, along with Benedetto Cairoli and many Garibaldians, left for the mainland. Montezemolo's adviser was Giuseppe La Farina, who had been expelled less than five months earlier.

On 1 January La Farina ordered Crispi's arrest, but Crispi escaped and took legal action against his enemy. The following day the police chief prohibited public meetings and threatened use of the Riot Act. Shades of Robert Rede! Carboni, once more, could feel he was against the government.

But towards the end of January, Carboni was reconciled with the world. He received 386.[10] lire back pay and asked Bargoni, who had returned to Turin, to invest 100 gold Napoleons for him.[11] He wanted to provide for his old age but also for printing his Dramatic Novena, nine plays for Garibaldi, on his return to Rome, which he considered imminent.[12] In a midwinter which was more like a delicious prolonged autumn he felt fit and, for only the second time in Italy, was to vote; the candidates were the pro-Piedmontese Marchese

Torrearsa and Crispi to whom he was less attached than the previous year. His mood swung yet again, for, on 22 February, he wrote to Bargoni:

> We're headed for disaster faster than ever. Scrawny hen vultures *ôte toi que je m'y mette* [make way for me], because of snow or indigestion from chestnuts, were forced from the north to the south hopeful of stuffing themselves in Palermo with milk and honey, little suspecting that three months after the red-shirts departure they will be stoned by this rare race of Etna holy devils!
>
> Montezemolo and company held a great ball in the Hall of the Ram to enjoy themselves with ladies who feel the need to sweat under their aristocratic crinolines for the benefit of these noble police who know what they're after: but the Palermitans did not in the least appreciate that apart from Bartolomei, Colonel without a regiment and two other *aides de rien,* the red shirts were not allowed entry. Five days ago, the Lieutenant did everything possible to show his affectionate subjects his wife's arrival: the decorated porters [presumably Piedmontese army officers] let it be known that Her Ladyship was a filthy rich Russian and that she brought her deserving husband a 4 million roubles dowry: but, as she did not bring it to Palermo, it was impossible to understand how much a rouble is worth: so much so that when, with regal pomp, their Excellencies went in the morning by carriage to thank their God in the cathedral, they were confused not, as they perhaps expected, by the cheers of youngsters but by the solitary whine of the canons who, as is custom, sang the 'Te Deum': not a soul accompanied them from the palace to the cathedral: consequently, ever since, the decorated porters have busily whispered that H.E. Montezemolo has been promoted to a very high post and is preparing his trunks to return home. He can go wherever he wants and is able to with the thought that he has inspired so much love among the Palermitans for the Gentleman King that openly he is already called 'the Bourbon without a rod'.
>
> Things have deteriorated to this extent! I write you with aching heart: unfortunately I have to recognise that I have written the truth. The black tempest gathering over Palermo will be fatal

for the unity of our beloved fatherland: the Piedmontese have already sickened the Palermitans with the benefits of united Italy: gambling houses and brothels have been the result so far. Who doesn't believe it should come and see. What an affliction we're preparing for Garibaldi's great heart.[13]

Carboni suggested he might leave Palermo the following month (most of Garibaldi's army had already been recalled to Turin) and conveyed to Bargoni the greetings of Ippolito Nievo who had just returned from Naples. At Nievo's request, Carboni had been sent at the end of 1860 from the Pro-Dictator's office to the Inspectorate; once more, as when with Crispi and Mordini, he was at the point where Piedmontese pressure was most intense. Carboni worked again with Major Luigi Salviati who had been his commanding officer in Rome in 1849. Carboni shared Nievo's literary interests, including knowledge of German literature while Nievo would have valued Carboni's experience with the Torlonia bank as well as his work capacity.

Pallidly handsome, with fine features, thin moustache and brushed-back hair, Nievo was often melancholy and reserved. But at the Inspectorate he became irascible; he described himself as a cannibal-director who spent most of his day shouting, a 'rabid Cerebus' defending the Treasury. As well as fighting, and at least twice risking his life, he had escorted the strong box containing funds for Garibaldi's forces from Marsala to Palermo and once, when it fell, gathered the coins one by one. When for the first time he had to organise a government, Garibaldi had immediately made the Army Inspectorate the State Treasury. He had abolished the unpopular grain tax while introducing administrative and social measures which required huge expenses, but the Inspectorate-Treasury coffers were empty.

Apart from Alessandro Manzoni, idealistic Nievo was probably Italy's most talented novelist. However, he had no preparation for financial administration and would have preferred to follow Garibaldi. Despite the post-Bourbon confusion, Nievo administered scrupulously, instituting rigorous controls over assignment of army supply contracts which aroused hostility from those anticipating substantial profits. There were charges that the bloodless Garibaldian occupation of Palermo had been facilitated by a deal between the two armies to help themselves to the Bourbon coffers.

Aware of enemies in both Sicily and Piedmont, Nievo was anxious that the Inspectorate be vindicated. He ensured thorough accounting before departing, in mid-December, for a North Italy vacation. It was a relief to leave the Sicilian capital where he was both overworked and so bored that he bit his fingernails.

It was 23 degrees when Nievo returned on 17 February, but he was in no mood to enjoy the weather, for he had to gather documentation to take to Turin. As soon as the trunks were sealed, he booked the first available vessel, the *Ercole,* which was sailing for Naples on Monday, 4 March.

One of the Inspectorate officials accompanying Nievo, Achille Majolini, told Carboni he was loath to sail on the slow, unsafe *Ercole.* Built as a sailing ship in England in 1832, the *Ercole* had been adapted for steam, but at times the engines shook the frame violently. Carboni's immediate superior, Luigi Salviati, was also diffident: he wanted to leave five days later on a regular postal steamer but could not convince Nievo. Accusations against a senior Garibaldian, Cenni, of having sold the Royal Palace's furniture were, in Carboni's opinion, a factor in Nievo's pig-headedness.[14] Presumably they convinced him that, as those determined to discredit the Garibaldians would stop at nothing, it was urgent to give them the lie.

At the port, realising something had been forgotten, Majolini sent a message to Carboni, working at Holy Trinity barracks, to bring it. Carboni reached the port at midday. It was busy: the American *Fran Star,* with a sulphur cargo, was leaving for New York, and the Dutch schooner *Pamorze* for Vlaardingen. Two fruit-laden cargo ships were sailing for Naples, as well as the passenger vessel *Pompei,* which, however, did not carry military personnel.

Carboni took a rowboat and approached the *Ercole* just as, at 12.30 with over fifty passengers and eighteen crew, it was turning to leave the port. Nievo and the Inspectorate's third-ranking officer Salvatore Seretta, Major Majolini, Major Salviati and another official came to the prow to greet Carboni, who delivered what Majolini had requested. Nievo reassured Carboni that he would soon go, on his behalf, to Pavia to clarify a misunderstanding with their mutual friend Benedetto Cairoli. The *Ercole* was headed now for Naples, and Carboni, arms extended towards his colleagues and friends, matched their cries of *'Addio'.* It should have been *'arrivederci'* ('see you again'), for he too was soon to sail for the mainland. Dark clouds above the mountains framing Palermo threatened rain but not the awesome storm which broke at 8 p.m.

Five days later, the Florio company, owner of the *Ercole,* told Nievo's anxious friends that the ship seemed to have sought refuge from the storm at Sarpi. On the 14th, rumours circulated that the *Ercole* had sunk near Lipari or Capri. Carboni, upset by these rumours, was 'profoundly sad'.[15] However, hope survived in the absence of shipwreck evidence, but only a little longer. It was said that an explosion destroyed the *Ercole:* it is still being debated whether a time bomb was put on board to prevent Nievo reaching Turin.

The sadness at the loss of the *Ercole* and all aboard could have been attenuated by celebrations for Garibaldi's name-day, 19 March, the feast of St Joseph. A procession was planned along the path Garibaldi and his conquering redshirts had taken across Palermo, from the Termini Gate to the Royal Palace, concluding in the three rooms he had occupied. But another tragedy thwarted the plan. On the 17th Lieutenant-Governor Montezemolo's 15-year-old daughter died from typhus, and her body was put on display in the Royal Palace room which had been Cairoli's.

That day a huge advertisement, three columns wide and seven-eighths the depth of the broadsheet *Il Precursore,* advised readers they could subscribe for Professor Raffaello Carbone's [sic] *La Campana della Gancia,* which he announced, had been written with the help of Syracuse Moscato and Marsala wine. The advertisement gave 4 April as the play's publication date, was repeated on 31 March. (Proceeds from the play were to go to a kindergarten run by a priest in Albergia, a central Palermo slum.)

The publication date was the first anniversary of the suppression of the Gancia uprising which was one of the main inspirations for the Garibaldi expedition. The insurgents took refuge in the Gancia monastery, whose bells they rang. The year-after publication formula, developed in Victoria, was being repeated, just as Carboni's approach suggests he saw parallels between the Ballarat uprising and the Sicilian. There were basic differences, however, between *The Eureka Stockade* and *La Campana della Gancia. The Eureka Stockade* was a prose narrative which allowed Carboni to freely recount events. *La Campana* was a stage work in which the convention favoured rhetoric and stereotypes. As in *The Eureka Stockade,* there was a documentary intent, as shown by quotations from a history of the uprising and reproduction of a commemorative plaque at the Gancia church, but these contradicted the theatrical form. A fundamental difference, of course, was that Carboni had been a participant at Eureka and conveyed his experience, whereas in La Campana he was commemorating an event he did not know at first hand.

Differences in the events themselves may also have affected the two works. *The Eureka Stockade* celebrated a battle against maladministration which led to social advances. *La Campana* celebrated the overthrow of tyranny which, however, was followed by the Bronte slaughter, then the arrival of the Piedmontese. This may account for *La Campana*'s over-emphatic tone; it was accompanied by several acrostic sonnets, including one to Vittorio Emanuele, the 'first soldier of Italy'. Was it an attempt to curry favour?

Piedmontese officers and bureaucrats came from Turin to replace Nievo and the other *Ercole* victims. Carboni took it as an example of the 'justice' of the 'thin, envious locusts' who, he claimed, 'persecuted to death the unfortunate Garibaldians'.[16] Piedmontese small beer was no more palatable than that of Toorak. Carboni gagged at his friends' enemies taking their place, but may also have considered himself entitled to the vacant positions; rank was important when it was said that the Piedmontese planned to demote all Garibaldians.

Carboni was consoled that Palermo elected Mordini ('we've won, thank God')[17] to the Turin parliament despite Piedmontese accusations that he had robbed the city. Another satisfaction was Agostino Bertani's election as representative for Milazzo after Carboni had campaigned for him. (Carboni informed Bargoni that the arrogance of Crispi had unfortunate electoral consequences: 'he fosters the mess of which he remains a victim'.)[18]

For Carboni, the electoral success of Mordini and Bertani confirmed Sicilians still supported Garibaldi. He had welcomed the success of Verdi's *The Sicilian Vespers* at the Bellini Theatre, attributing the popularity of its evocation of the Palermo anti-French revolt in 1282 to hostility towards the French-allied Piedmontese and the 'puerile Palermitan aristocrats'.[19] The officers of the King's first and second Regiments, Carboni considered, were French in body and soul, and Italian only for gain. His anti-Piedmontese obsession recalled a character in *La Campana della Gancia* who walked the seafront listening to anti-Bourbon complaints. 'Palermo's perambulating Pasquin' was Carboni's alliterative description, derived from the Rome statue to which satiric pasquinades were attached, but it applied also to himself once the Piedmontese assumed control. He no longer asked whether the revolution had failed the poor, for once again he had an enemy to whom all shortcomings could be attributed.

The word was, he told Bargoni, that Sicilians would soon link with the English. Anyone, he implied, would be preferable to the Piedmontese: 'Italian unity is wrecked'. He underlined the Palmeritans indifference to the second Lieutenant-Governor, General Alessandro Della Rovere, who arrived at 9.20 a.m. on 17 April:

> His Excellency ordered the garrison take arms and the National Guard was called out. Meanwhile the cannon reverberating through our mountains advised the servants that they would not remain without a master while the decorated porters, for the greater glory of the Alps, criss-crossed via Toledo, bumping into one another as they waited with longing. Few of the national guards turned up. Finally, at 2.00, His Excellency, in court carriage with the Colonel of the Carabinieri beside him, passed through the Quattro Cantoni. During the trip from the quay to the Royal Palace there was not one shout 'Long live the king' nor 'Long live Italy'. All Palermitans are disgusted by the breakdown in polity – almost no one uncovered their heads at the sight of this second boss who, when he reached the Royal Palace and came out on the balcony, saw the National Guard file past in Vittoria Square but did not hear one 'long live'; the sun burnt the ground but all hearts remained frozen. I am telling you what I saw with my own eyes and without spectacles. Not one tricolour flag, not a single lamp were put outside windows in the whole Toledo zone.[20]

Carboni added that Palermitans were uneasy because Montezemolo had abolished the Town Council and Alessandro Della Rovere the Lieutenant-Governor's Council. 'The Piedmontese officers have refurbished the Croats' arrogance: their preferred hobby is to despise Garibaldians.'

He may have written in this tenor for *Il Diritto*, a Garibaldian daily of Turin which Angelo Bargoni was editing. At Bargoni's request, Carboni found distributors for it in Palermo. He also sent Bargoni unsigned anti-Piedmontese articles from *Il Precursore* which may have been written by Carboni himself. They compared the Piedmontese with the Bourbons, pointing out that Piedmontese now had the best positions, just as the Neapolitans under the previous regime, and that the traffic was all one-way-Sicilians did not obtain positions in Piedmont. Carboni may have written an anti-Piedmont article for *Il Diritto,* for he was very concerned when it did not reach Bargoni:

> In my 19 April letter I wrote somewhat in the form of an article for *Il Diritto* on the political situation ... it would be a worry if you have not received it ... because I wrote freely on the causes of the distressing dissatisfaction that prevails throughout Sicily and, although the Piedmontese do not see it, gathers menacingly like a hurricane above Palermo.[21]

Had it been intercepted by government agents? It would have boded ill because the red-haired captain, who perambulated Palermo mulling over anti-Piedmontese polemics, was headed for the Piedmontese capital. By April he was one of the few remaining Garibaldians and they were not even allowed to wear their colourful red shirts, blue jackets and soft caps. He noted that the period in which Garibaldians could be paid off had been prolonged but, rather than accept, most were leaving for Turin: 'they insist on drinking the wine of the vines they planted'.[22]

The attempted Garibaldian revolution had been absorbed. Cavour had turned Garibaldi's success to his advantage by using the anti-clericals' victories as an excuse to annex part of the Papal States ('the aim has been holy', he averred). Garibaldi, who was courageous with brilliant guerrilla skills but little political ambition, shrank from instigating a civil war. After occupying Naples, on 2 October 1860 he met Vittorio Emanuele and acknowledged him as King of Italy, not solely of Sardinia-Piedmont. The two warriors, Garibaldi and Vittorio Emanuele, found an accord which was beyond Cavour and Mazzini.

It was followed by one of those moments when, 'tired of the civilisation of priests and police', Garibaldi was inclined to recall his arrival, as captain of a cargo ship, at Three Hummock Island in Bass Strait between Melbourne and Tasmania, where partridges took flight and he found a limpid stream.[23] Three Hummock was too far away, but Caprera Island, between Sardinia and Corsica, was at hand. Taking seeds, coffee, sugar, macaroni and dried cod, he went there. He placed his bed where he could look across the sea towards his birthplace, Nizza, now Nice, which he hoped to recover for Italy. Other heroes, sponsors and colleagues of Carboni were likewise far away by now. Bargoni and Cairoli, two close friends, were in north Italy. Nievo he would never see again.

There was little left for Carboni in Palermo. And Piedmont promised little more. Carboni told Bargoni that he did not know where he would lay his head. The uncertainties may have seemed more insidious than the sea when, like Nievo, on 28 May 1861 he boarded a ship to begin his journey to Turin.

Turin

A captain first, then crowned a poet: Soon the whole wide world must know it

Within three weeks of Carboni's arrival in Turin, Camillo Benso, Count of Cavour, died after a brief illness. It was 7 a.m. on 6 June; Cavour was only 51. Even opponents recognised his consummate political skills used to gain French support against Austria but also English support against France. Carboni, who had worked on a lament for Rosolino Pilo in Palermo, applied the same words to Cavour: his poem was an all-purpose funeral wreath.

In Turin he could see Piedmontese qualities as well as the defects which exasperated him in Palermo. Carboni lodged in the handsome wood-shuttered five-storey Hotel Feder near the Portici Po (Po Colonnade), which led to the river and sheltered the city's liveliest cafes. Under their delicately stuccoed ceilings, Lombard, Venetian and Roman exiles discussed the new Italy with Piedmontese. Some exiles affected a Piedmontese accent, for Piedmont had been a path-blazer when it was the only Italian state with a constitution and a parliament, enlightened legislation, an honest administration and an army without mercenaries. In Ballarat Carboni had looked forward to the publication of *The Eureka Stockade* in Turin: its leadership in the independence struggle had enabled it to rival Florence as an intellectual centre. Carboni had reasons to appreciate Piedmont apart from his liking for its Barbera wine.

As the unity movement gathered momentum, the influx of exiles in Turin diminished provincialism. Moreover, although Piedmont had sacrificed some of its territories to France, it had gained influence elsewhere: it had lost

Savoyards but gained Sicilians; it had replaced Nizza with Naples. A new railway station, railway tracks to the Swiss, French and Austrian borders, and a tunnel through Mount Cenis to bring Paris within a day's journey, showed a determination to modernise. Industrial development and canal building gave foreign banks a stake in Piedmont's future. With slightly fewer inhabitants than Palermo, Turin was becoming one of Europe's major cities.

Young Vittorio Emanuele II, whom parliament had just decreed King of Italy, was loved for his bluff simplicity. Countless stories, such as that of him helping a carter straighten his overturned cart, circulated about the humanity of 'Togu', as he was nicknamed by his admirers; for his critics he was 'King Polenta'.

The solid buildings and grid-patterned streets of Turin bespoke a powerful central authority. Built on what had been a Roman encampment, it had a marked military character. The King was a warrior, usually in military uniform and surrounded by army officers. The Court was somewhat like a military headquarters and the heir to the throne was educated with martial discipline. A military career was the most prestigious and, in moments of crisis, army commanders were ready to take over the government. Turin could seem a huge barracks; Piedmont was Italy's Prussia.

It was hardly the city to welcome a victorious, irregular army. Hierarchy, discipline and obedience were threatened by Garibaldi's troops. The politicians closest to the regular army wanted Garibaldi's soldiers paid off. If the Garibaldians were patriots, they argued, now that the Kingdom of Italy was proclaimed they should return to their previous occupations. For them the Garibaldians were not serious soldiers but anarchic adventurers.

'Why accept the southern provinces', asked Garibaldi, who had come from Caprera wearing his trademark red shirt and poncho, which disconcerted the other, frock-coated parliamentarians he addressed, 'if you don't accept the troops who did so much to liberate them?' But Garibaldi had sold the pass himself when, outside Naples, he meekly handed over to King Vittorio Emanuele without obtaining guarantees for his army. Militia of annexed states, such as Tuscany and Emilia, and even ex-Bourbon soldiers, were more readily accepted than Garibaldians whose unforgivable sin may have been their spectacular victories. The political debate daunted Garibaldians to such a degree that, in November 1860, almost 30,000 accepted six months' pay and left the army. At that stage there were 7,343 officers.

But when, in March 1862, Urbano Ratazzi, the successor to Cavour, fused the remaining Garibaldians with the regular army, only 1,740 Garibaldian officers entered it. Those who satisfied a commission of their qualifications were accepted, but compared to regular army officers they were still disadvantaged in several ways.[1]

Carboni knew that the hostility of the Piedmontese in Palermo had precipitated Ippolito Nievo's injudicious departure, and he had been chagrined to see them take all the positions vacant after the death of Nievo and his colleagues. The government had not expressed gratitude to the Garibaldians. What is more, despite appeals by Verdi and others, Mazzini was still under a death sentence.

Carboni had a year in Turin to reflect that an honest administration could still be curmudgeonly and that non-professional soldiers were unfairly judged by their lack of military schooling rather than by their victories. Finally, on 21 April 1862, he was accepted in the administrative branch of the regular army as under-commissioner of war of the first class.[2] It corresponded to captain among the combat forces. He had the same rank as in the Garibaldian army and was once again in the Inspectorate. His uniform was turquoise flannel with gold braid on collar and cuffs and a trouser stripe. If only Captain Thomas could see him now.

Difficulties, however, did not end with this acceptance; regular officers remained hostile and the disciplinary commissions were extremely severe with ex-Garibaldians. It was hardly the setting for impetuous Carboni. Genova Thaon de Revel, one of the heads of the Scrutiny Commission, predicted that even those Garibaldians who survived the severe examination and entered the regular army would be eliminated: 'the dross which clings to the army will be removed by the Disciplinary Commission'. Perhaps Carboni fell foul of the Commission or could not bear his colleagues' hostility: on 29 June, after nine weeks as an Italian army officer, he resigned. Once again, as in Victoria where he had been naturalised, he abruptly changed his course. Later he complained that the envy of the Piedmontese had 'deprived him of the bread Garibaldi had given him'.

In his demobilisation papers, Captain Carboni told several lies: as he had done elsewhere, he lowered his age by three years and gave Rome as his birthplace.[3] He also stated that he had sailed with the Bertani Committee from Genoa on the *Veloce* on 18 June 1860 when, in fact, he was still in Milan; and that he began to work with Crispi in Palermo on 27 June when, instead, he had begun to work in Genoa with Bertani. Harder still to understand was the June 1861 date given for his return to Turin, as the correct record was surely available to the regular army. Either the lies had been necessary previously to receive his commission or he was showing his real vocation was inventing stories.

The month after Captain Carboni arrived in Turin, with the highest hopes he had forwarded his play *La Santola,* which concerned Roman personages, to the Valle Theatre in Rome. There was no response, which he attributed to ecclesiastical censorship; but there was no such censorship in Turin, where he published it at the end of 1861. In a prefatory note he said many had expected him to produce another patriotic play like *La Campana della Gancia.* But today, he added, the mission of our literature is to convince our people that 'they are not sheep ready for shearing'.

Carboni threw himself into a series of poems set to music and yet another play likewise based on his Roman experience, *Mérode,* for which he claimed to have had the collaboration of the renowned actor Gustavo Modena. He also gave a thought to Australian friends and benefactors; he may have heard that a memorial sword of Victorian gold had been sent by Australian admirers, through Turin, to Garibaldi on Caprera. Or, perhaps, a three-month prison sentence and a fine for the managing editor of *Il Diritto* on 7 November made him recall his Australian experience. The next day he sent two copies of *La Santola* to Melbourne. One went to Peter Lalor, who, like several of Carboni's Italian colleagues, was pursuing a parliamentary career, with the dedication

> God bless my old commander-in-chief of the armed diggers on the extra-memorable Sunday December 3, 1854; Ballarat Massacre Hill, Eureka. A very, very hearty farewell from Carboni Raffaello Garibaldi's Captain now confirmed by Royal Decree for the Italian Army.

The other copy was for his trial judge, Mr Justice Barry, and W.C. Haines the Colonial Secretary. In this case, Carboni's message was simply 'Gentlemen God bless you both. Respectful remembrance from Carboni Raffaello'. But he did not mange to publish in Turin a 'proper' editon of *The Eureka Stockade,* meaning in Italian, as he had promised when he had brought it out in Ballarat.

Presumably he did not know that his trial judge Redmond Barry had come to Rome that year to admire ancient statuary and visit artists' studios. In one he saw a bust of W.C. Wentworth, who he described as 'the NSW patriot to whom we are indebted for responsible government'.

On 6 April 1861 a withering attack on *La Campana della Gancia* had appeared in the Milan 'critical-humouristic' periodical *L'Uomo di Pietra* ('The Stone Man'). It invited readers to sit back and laugh at extracts from the published play with a 'incomprehensible plot'. It derided the poetry and accused Carboni of an incapacity to write simply, even in prose, because, believing himself a poet, 'he wants always to be original'. It advised readers that, although the whole thing might seem a jape, Carboni was serious about it. Sardonically it added that, for those who did not believe there could be poetry so original and profound, the text was available. Antonio Ghislanzoni, librettist for Verdi's *Aida*, had links with the periodical but it is not known if he wrote the put-down signed *'Sorcio'* ('Mouse'). Nor is it known if the periodical's hostility to Garibaldians and Mazzinians affected the judgement.

Carboni was still on the outer of the theatrical world, but an unsurpassed opportunity to make his mark there occurred when Adelaide Ristori, who he claimed had requested him to make translations in London, arrived to perform at the Carignano Theatre. In December 1860 Ristori, a convinced monarchist and patriot, had carried out a diplomatic mission for Cavour while performing in St Petersburg. Carboni hoped she might perform an artistic mission for him.

He was now living in a narrower street (via Barbou 5) and in less prepossessing accommodation than when at the Hotel Feder. From here he wrote to Ristori that his play *Nazzareno Schiantapalmi*, the product of thirteen years' work, was ready and that she was the type to play Countess Dantelina, and still more, he continued, Francesca in his *Mérode* and Tassolena in *Misererio*:

> Both tragedies, the result of 20 years extremely difficult work, are nearly ready. You know from experience, Signora, how bitter, tedious, revolting it is for an Italian litterateur to take the first step; I have not the presumption to bother you, but I trust in your protection.[4]

Adelaide Ristori had not experienced such difficulties because she had been a star from the age of 14. Carboni wrote once, he wrote twice, he wrote four times, but Adelaide, as if she believed herself Queen Elizabeth of England whom she impersonated, did not deign to respond. Carboni could ask what had become of her passion for Italy and the Italian theatre. What was the point in being beautiful, elegant, regal, the toast of Turin, if she could not help a former quasi-colleague take his first steps in the theatrical world with a foot ulcerous because he had defended Rome?

Carboni was caught between the haughtiness of Ristori and the envy of the Piedmontese establishment, symbolised for him by the Knights of Maurizio and Lazzaro or, as he impishly called them, 'Mallow and Lettuce'. The year 1862 closed like a tomb stone. He might have flipped back three decades: '32, about to begin university; '42, installed in the Torlonia bank; '52, about to land in Melbourne, all widening horizons. Now, his military career abandoned, his former colleagues launched in public life, the silence was deepening around him as if Turin fogs, as well as entering his aching bones, blotted him out.

In these circumstances, the evening of 6 February 1863 must have been immensely gratifying.[5] In a sense it was his final curtain, his farewell to Turin, for he was headed again for London, leaving without regret Piedmont to the Piedmontese. In another sense, it was an adult Academy similar to those of the Urbino College of Nobles but this time before the nobles of a new Italy who could ensure Carboni a future dux's prize. The Honourable Giovanni Civinini had invited him to the home of Carboni's friend from the Palermo period, Benedetto Cairoli, who was acquiring a reputation as an able parliamentarian. Other parliamentarians present were the former Pro-Dictator Antonio Mordini, Angelo Bargoni and Giorgio Asproni. It was a gathering of Garibaldians with assured political futures but included the only one attempting to scale the slippery slopes of Parnassus.

They asked Captain Carboni, self-proclaimed inventor of the Garibaldian stanza, to recite passages from his farce *Spiantacore*. Their applause encouraged him to recite the fourth act of *Misererio*, then to perform the poem begun at Eureka: *Trotta, trotta finchè la terra scotta / Dritto al mare dei guai*.

It was a triumph in that small theatre of distinguished friends. And to cap it all, as exhausted but satisfied Carboni acknowledged their applause, Emilia Bargoni placed the Poet's Crown of dark-green laurel on his bushfire hair.

What a vindication in the city where he had been treated like dross! Carboni took it as a prefiguration of the day when he would come into his glory on the Campidoglio. That day, he may have foreseen, they would be with him in paradise, Cairoli on his right hand, Bargoni on his left, while he was crowned Poet by Adelaide Ristori.

To commemorate the evening at Cairoli's, a sonnet was published, addressed to Professor Carboni Raffaello, hailed as:

> *expert in travels, arms and languages,*
> *inventor of the Garibaldian stanza*
> *restorer of Italian drama*
> *when he was solemnly crowned poet, augury*
> *Ah! too obscure and weak*
> *of the splendid incoronation*
> *that Italy is preparing for him*
> *on freed Rome's Campidoglio.*

The sonnet, surprisingly not an acrostic on Carboni Raffaello, was as fulsome as the salutation which accompanied it. Italy, the Ganges, Albion, Etna and Vesuvius admired Carboni, it asserted, and Australia prepared laurels for him. Rome crowned him, it continued, for his 'new style'; his fame echoed from Calcutta and Melbourne to Italy.

It was signed 'Carboni's friends stupefied with admiration', but the author was probably was none other than the Poet himself.

Naples

Tread lightly

The Poet headed north once more. On his way to London he stopped in Paris where, accompanied by a fawning acrostic poem on the name Clothilde, he offered *La Santola* and *La Ceciliana,* his album of poems set to music for voice and piano, to Princess Maria Clotilde, Vittorio Emanuele's daughter, who had married the emperor's cousin Gerolamo Bonaparte.[1] Four days later, their Royal Highnesses' chamberlain returned them to Monsieur Carboni at the Hotel des Genes with a note which meant thanks, but no thanks.[2]

His plays, in any case, were addressed primarily to Italians and one of their aims was to replace decadent French drama. Moreover his open, 1849 leg wound needed a kindly climate. Palermo would be suitable but Naples was nearer Rome, which parliament had already decreed would be Italy's capital. The Italian tenor and patriot Mario, star of the Covent Garden Italian Opera, paid Carboni's fare from London to Naples. Carboni expressed his gratitude in acrostic verse;[3] Mattia Montecchi, who had brought Carboni to the Giovine Italia movement, may have introduced him to Mario as he had been the tenor's secretary. But Carboni had his own contacts in the Italian theatrical world in London who had assured him that his stage works would be well received in Naples, which, with 450,000 inhabitants, was Europe's fifth largest city. Neapolitan theatrical acclaim would guarantee a triumphal return to Rome but, as the papal city might fall at any moment, Carboni neeeded swift success. In London he had met some of the Neapolitan Fondo theatre management and also Amina Boschetti who had asked him to translate articles from French papers.[4] She was now the San Carlo opera's leading ballerina, admired for her ability and praised for her generosity.

On arrival in Naples, Carboni's creative vein seemed richer than anything he had struck in Ballarat. A pilgrimage to Virgil's presumed tomb at Posillipo on 7 September 1864 inspired a poem 'Masianello a Marco' (Masianello to Marco), which he also set to music. That same day, on Mergellina beach, he completed his poem 'La Concordia' arguing the need for Italian concord despite the curses of pope, foreigner and, a new bogey, municipalism. By moonlight, still on the beach, perhaps inspired by local samples, he wrote an homage to Italian wines called 'The cases [in a grammatical sense] of Bacchus'.

Carboni lodged in the central Chiaia zone on the third floor at 27 via della Vittoria (now Arceoli). At the end of the street were public gardens; isolated on the hill above was the colonnaded 17th-century San Martino convent, while in front the bay, dominated by Capri's serrated silhouette, curved from Castel dell'Ovo to Mergellina. Carboni's 'volcanic head' evidently found the inhabitants of the city nestling by Vesuvius's broken cone congenial. He shared the Neapolitans' vivid histrionic instinct.

Although Carboni received a small emigrant's allowance, he did not have sufficient funds to print his works. In April 1865 he applied for commemorative medals for the 1849, '59 and '60 campaigns. The medals gave pension rights but he could not wait on the bureaucracy for funds to publish when he was in full creative flood. On 19 May he pawned two medals and a silver ring (130 grams) for 21 lire.[5] He also pawned a watch which, he claimed, Garibaldi had given him in Palermo. But weren't his plays a further phase in the Garibaldian-Mazzinian project? For Carboni there were many stages in the revolution.

Eleven days later he wrote to Angelo Bargoni that Amina Boschetti was 'almost passionately' interested in his play *Raffaello d'Urbino*, which was based on a German study of the Renaissance painter.[6] His Giovine Italia friend from Roman days, Giovanni Battista Cattabeni, who like Carboni had gone to Australia but returned in 1860, had interceded for him with Boschetti. Cattabeni, now a colonel, had been one of Garibaldi's most valorous officers. He had become a hero in the battle of Caiazzo, north of Naples: he had led two others in putting a Bourbon cannon out of action before being shot in the arm and bayoneted in the stomach.

In the same letter to Bargoni, Carboni wrote that a Catanian musician, Salvatore Pappalardo, predicted his *Raffaele d'Urbino* would be a worldwide success. Carboni asked Bargoni to subscribe for *La Ceciliana*; he explained that in order to retain copyright he needed the 'mere bagatelle' of 800 lire for the fifty-four linotype plates. He suggested that Bargoni was being asked to back a winner, then added that fleas were very active under Naples' beautiful sky. His reference to himself as 'Scalds-or-Stains' may have been unwise when requesting money from Bargoni, whose forehead was scarred from a childhood fall on smouldering embers. Once scalded, twice shy; nevertheless, Bargoni subscribed.

At least, his name appeared in the subscribers' list when, the following Sunday, anniversary of the Statute granted by King Carlo Alberto in 1848, Carboni published an edition of *La Ceciliana*, which he claimed was exactly as he had conceived it as a young hopeful in the Colosseum in Rome. The subscribers' list included the heir to the throne, Prince Umberto of Savoy; the Naples prefect and police chief; Giuseppe Garibaldi and Mazzini; former colleagues who were now deputies in the national parliament (Crispi, Mordini, Cairoli, Bargoni, Bellazzi, Depretis); Adelina Patti and six other members of the Royal Italian Opera Covent Garden; Agostino Bertani; the editors of the newspapers *Il Precursore* (Palermo), *Il Diritto* (Turin) and *Il Popolo d'Italia* (Naples); Giovanni Battista Cattabeni; friends in France, England, Germany, India (François Saint Yves) and Australia. Whether they had all really subscribed is open to question; it could have been largely a list of people Carboni had known or would have liked to know. Among the Australians were Father Patrick Smyth; Samuel Irwin, the *Geelong Advertiser* correspondent at the time of the Stockade; Peter Lalor; James Basson Humffray; Timothy Hayes; and Carboni's trial lawyers, James MacPherson Grant, Richard Ireland and Butler Cole Aspinall.

The title *La Ceciliana* did not derive from Santa Cecilia, the patron of music, but, Carboni claimed, from the Arabo-Chaldean '*See Scil*', meaning reed whistle. After underlining its perfect unity of words and music, Carboni added that *La Ceciliana* 'had been conceived in 1848 at the Colosseum where he had learnt the "conspiratorial art"'.

'God's name be praised', exclaimed Carboni when promised the National Guards would perform in the municipal villa the *La Campana della Gancia* music from *La Ceciliana*. He confessed it set his heart racing, as did a certain Priscilla in Rome when she said 'Si'. It was an intriguing comment, as the Priscilla in *Misererio* was the sister of the Carboni-figure protagonist. His thanksgiving was premature. On 9 July he wrote to the Prince of San Teodoro and Duke of Arpino asking him to provide eight bells for the National Guard's performance. The prince-duke, aide-de-camp of the King, returned Carboni's letter with the enclosed poems, music ... and three lire. Carboni sent the money straight back. The eight bells, he wrote, would perhaps be ready to ring with that of Rome's Campidoglio the evening before the Last Judgement in the Josephat valley.[7]

Hadn't he been crowned Poet in Turin? He did not know that his host on that occasion, Benedetto Cairoli, talking about Carboni's subsequent behavior in a letter to Bargoni, had described him as 'a real clown'. In any case he was confident that the four plays he had just submitted to the Fondo Theatre would speak for him.

One was the matrimonial comedy *Nazzareno Schiantapalmi,* which he claimed to have completed on the roof of Milan Cathedral. Another was the farce *Spiantacore,* an allegory which begins in the pagoda Pi-Ho in Peking but eventually transports characters to Paris in the recently invented Goddard balloon. The grit for the third offering, the five-act tragedy *Misererio,* was losing his mother's pearl ring after pawning it at Bishopsgate, London; recent recourse to Neapolitan pawnbrokers may have revived these London memories. 'Pawnbrokers', he wrote, corresponded to the Italian 'Monte di Pietà', but with a bilingual pun he added that in England it meant Mount Calvary. The play's pawnbrokers solve their financial problems by stealing the pawned objects, burning their shop and skipping the country.

Carboni specified that *Misererio*'s protagonist Tassolena, first ballerina of the Italian opera in London, was written with Adelaide Ristori in mind. She had loved young Gesualdo, but, believing she preferred richer men, he left her. She lives with the retired ballerina Boschetti-Puttiferi-Incisa (presumably based on Amina Boschetti) and hires a domestic Priscilla, not realising that this daughter of a poor widow is Gesualdo's sister. Gesualdo pawns his painting of Priscilla at the Jewish pawnbrokers, Gnorgnasalmi (Psalmwhiner), where they choke on his name Gesu-aldo (Jesus-aldo). As a playwright, anti-Semitism was perhaps the only characteristic Carboni shared with Shakespeare. Misererio Gnorgnasalmi and the pawnbrokers trick Gesualdo into forging promissory notes for a Russian Viscount Pascovia who is courting Tassolena. When Gesualdo's forgery is discovered, Tassolena proves her love by aiding him, but, mistaken for Pascovia, he is killed. In revenge, Tassolena kills Misererio. The play is a museum of 19th-century theatrical kitsch.

The fourth play Carboni submitted to the Fondo Theatre was *Mérode*. Carboni claimed his second prison spell, in 1843, resulted from exposing an attempt to declare venerable a prelate who had strangled a rich English convert while hearing her confession. He mentioned this macabre story, which has some relation to the play, in its preface but, said it was first conceived during his initial prison spell three years earlier.

The protagonist is based on a well-known Roman figure. Carboni's Agostino Mérode is a soldier of Pius IX's forces who, after becoming a priest, has a rapid career culminating in his appointment as governor of Rome. The real Frédéric Francois Xavier De Mérode, a Belgian aristocrat, had been an officer in the Belgian army and with French forces in North Africa. He was ordained in 1848 and Pius IX made him his Army Minister in 1860. He claimed the Papal States could be saved by enrolling foreign volunteers, but in September 1860, at Castelfidardo near Ancona, the papal army, which included foreign volunteers, suffered a crushing defeat from Piedmontese troops.

A French contemporary Francis Wey described De Mérode at a diplomatic reception:

> A long, angular body is closed in a tight soutane ... long, thin, pointed nose; dry lips turn up at the comers; lower jaw juts; pointed chin; flattened ears; hard hair with rebellious tufts. Add, under eyebrows which fly towards the temples, cross eyes whose pupils are too small and you have a face of lively temperament, and almost diabolic willpower.

De Mérode, continued Wey, kept a long hand near his breast and punctuated his conversation with jerky movements in which his fingers worked like those of a violinist. His 'scornful gentleness' was accompanied by bursts of silent laughter; when the French ambassador beat a retreat De Mérode pursued him, 'buzzing around his head like a hornet'.

After the papal forces' defeat at Castelfidardo, De Mérode became papal almoner. He reformed the prison system and organised medical help for the needy but also devoted himself to urban transformation as if foreseeing the fall of papal Rome and the rise in land values. He could well have been called Monsignor 600 per cent, for in the post-unity building boom the price of the land he acquired eventually skyrocketed to that extent. Although Carboni questioned

De Mérode's virtue, he was Rome's most edifying prelate.

About the time Carboni was completing the play, Henry d'Ideville of the French embassy met De Mérode outside Santa Maria degli Angeli church opposite via Mérode. De Mérode had bought all the land to piazza Santi Apostoli two kilometres away and was levelling it. D'Ideville wrote:

> This morning I saw him [De Mérode] give orders to the workmen with that ardour, vivacity and commitment he puts into all things. We were together for an hour and I can well understand the new proprietor's pleasure in seeing the displacement of that earth from which every now and again a fragment of precious marble or a bronze was removed. Under our very eyes the workmen discovered an arch whose existence was not even imagined. 'Well, do you understand this passion?' said De Mérode.[8]

In his play, Carboni pilloried the Belgian prelate for the lurid sin of smothering a penitent, but perhaps he should have accused him of pioneering destructive inner-city development. Some praised De Mérode's vision; at least his plans were on a scale appropriate to the occasion. He was in touch with his time, whereas Carboni's imagination seemed stuck in the past. He was engaged in stale polemics so evident in his harsh portrait of De Mérode, whom many praised for introducing prison reform, for his asceticism and for courage shown during a cholera epidemic.

The play is tightly plotted at the expense of characterisation and plausibility. Carboni attempts to attribute Mérode's villainy to thwarted love but he still remains a Simon Legree. It is a melodramatic revenge play, the revenge being that of the author for what he had suffered in Rome. Once again, the Carboni figure meets obstacles in his attempt to marry an aristocrat.

Carboni claimed *Misererio,* which he considered captured 19th-century European life, 'was proof of his genius', but by the same token *Mérode* aimed to rip the lid off Roman corruption. Combined with the lighter *Schiantapalmi* and *Nazzareno Spiantacore,* they must have seemed an irresistible quartet, especially as he was submitting them to the Fondo Theatre people he knew from London.

One of the more imaginative elements of Carboni's works were the title pages of these musical-ballet-dramas; he noted where they were conceived, developed, finished and given the last touches. The elaborate packaging was designed to show he had worked at least a decade on the product and in all corners of the world. For instance he said that *Misererio* was conceived among London fogs in June 1850, then worked on in the ghettos and synagogues in Hamburg, Hanover, Amsterdam, Calcutta, Jerusalem, Constantinople, Frankfurt, Berlin, Trieste, Genoa, Turin, Paris and, once again in 1858, London. It was completed, he concluded, in Naples under the most beautiful sky of Italy by Santa Lucia's sulphur springs in 1865.

There were lies in these self-advertisements, such as Carboni's claim that he worked eighteen years on *Nazzareno Schiantapalmi* for evidently it was based on experience in Milan a few years before the play was completed. The lies and the geographical frenzy revealed the title page's meaning: this is my life, tread lightly.

Sciochezze! Dummes Zeug! Nonsense!

It was chilling that the Fondo Theatre management remained indifferent to Carboni's four plays. Indeed it did not even deign to return them; Carboni had to collect them himself. Perhaps the fact that the management knew him from London was anything but an advantage. He took them to the Fiorentini Theatre, doubtless hoping clamorous success there would mortify the Fondo management. He even obtained a recommendation from the influential Police Chief Nicola d'Amore. Another hammer blow! Rejected again. He sought a more exalted angel. When he presented his *Raffaello d'Urbino* at San Carlo he had the backing of his former employer, Prince Alessandro Torlonia. The only reaction from San Carlo management was shrugged shoulders. Carboni claimed to be indignant at the slight to the Prince but probably was more upset at the snub to the Poet.

Was the San Carlo management adversely influenced by Amina Boschetti? Despite Carboni's translation of French newspaper articles for her in London, despite her earlier enthusiasm for *Raffaello d'Urbino,* Boschetti withdrew her support. Carboni took legal measures to recover the 27 lire publishing subscription she had failed to pay and then complained he had to pay 12 lire in expenses. Carboni noted that, although Boschetti owed him money, she could afford to renovate her villa at Portici, and that theatrical journalists, confirming his suspicion of their servility, praised her generosity in paying for the funeral of a dancing master.[9]

Women! In the epilogue to *Spiantacore*, Carboni warned Neapolitan women that Piedmontese were providing a diet of French comedies advocating adultery, as they wanted to seduce them. At the same time he suggested they read more and act out of respect for God rather than from fear of hell. He was fighting on two fronts: against Piedmont and against priests. Adelaide Ristori, who could be his salvation, gave no sign that she recognised his existence: five times Carboni tried to give her *Misererio* when she lodged at the nearby Washington hotel, but the porter refused him admission.

However, Benedetto Cairoli's mother Adelaide sent him a 10-lire subscription which, Carboni told her, fell 'like parmesan [cheese] on macaroni', while her accompanying letter was 'a raft for a sailor in a tempestuous sea of woes'. In return he sent her his poem 'The Patriot's Fate' in which he compared the patriotic emigrant's fate to crucifixion or imprisonment. He told her it had been inspired by the knockbacks from the San Carlo, Fondo and Fiorentini management.

The 'tempestuous sea of woes' was his debts. If the Neapolitans were too obtuse to stage his plays, he was nevertheless printing them. Indeed no less than forty etchers and printers were preparing a two-volume compendium of his stage works and a fuller edition of *La Ceciliana*. He considered himself representative of the Italian genius which embraced poetry, music and dance. Total theatre by a total genius, but where was the money for the printers? His subscribers covered only half the cost of *La Ceciliana*.

Amid these worries Carboni managed a trip to Florence where, at long last, he completed the poem 'Trotta, trotta ...' He described it as a twin to 'The Patriot's Fate'; the depressed tone of the first couplet echoes equally well that dirge and the mood induced by Ballarat's winter rain: 'Trot, trot until the earth scorches, straight to a sea of woes'. In 1865 Florence had become the Italian capital and Carboni may have visited former colleagues now making political careers, including Agostino Depretis. From Florence, on 20 October 1866, Depretis wrote to the Prefect of Naples advising that the Ministry of the Interior had decided Carboni's subsidy as a migrant would continue.[10] But unless he found 200 lire quickly, the printers would stop work. No wonder he slashed wildly with his Bowie knife when a death-masked fellow approached him in the Fosso trattoria in via Cavallerizza. Overwrought reaction to a carnival jape? A premonition of death stalking him? The incident followed a discussion in which Carboni had opposed Neapolitans who claimed things were better before Garibaldi's arrival.

The more time passed since the Bourbons were ousted, the greater seemed their merits. Not only had they introduced in Italy the first trains and steamships, the first telegraph service and iron bridges, but they exacted only light taxes. With unification Naples was no longer the capital of a kingdom of 8 million, but merely one city in a kingdom of 22 million. Many public services, building contracts and employment possibilities disappeared with the royal court. Rigid Piedmontese centralisation, on a society which considered northerners inferior aliens, aroused resentment. 'Northern Italy is united', had said Cavour, who never set eyes on Naples. 'No longer are we Lombards, Piedmontese, Tuscans, Romagnans, we're all Italians. But there's still the Neapolitans ...'

To many southerners the benefits of much-vaunted Italy seemed higher prices and heavier taxes. In September 1866 an uprising in Palermo was suppressed. South of Naples, banditry, by those nostalgic for the older order or defrauded by the new, became endemic. Was newly minted Italy in danger of a war between the north and south like that bloodying the United States? 'A painful necessity' was General Alfonso La Marmora's explanation of the killings by the 120,000 soldiers who repressed the peasant revolt. The seal of national unity was Italian soldiers shedding Italian peasants' blood.

Carboni was too involved in his music and plays, convinced of their bite and brilliance and busily raising money for their publication, to concern himself with these broader issues which could have made his writing more arresting. The plays were part disguised biography, part polemical journalism without achieving an autonomous interest, but he had banked everything on them.

Early in 1867 a German visitor sparked high hopes: a gymnastic teacher Auguste Teyssedze, on hearing the waltz Carboni had begun when an assistant sacristan in Rome, said it was just the thing for Ernest Renz's celebrated equestrian schools in Berlin and Vienna. Carboni wrote enthusiastically to Alfred von Seefeld, the friend he had made in Hanover, who had since established a prosperous bookshop (where *The Eureka Stockade* was on sale) and become the United States' honorary consul, asking him to interest Renz in his polka 'Trotta, trotta ...' and other *La Ceciliana* compositions. He offered to orchestrate them for Renz's band. Carboni needed outside help; the Neapolitan nobility, he told von Seefeld, was not patriotic but interested solely in women, horses and gambling.[11]

A well-placed friend told him that the Prefecture's secretary, Davide Silvagni, would help financially. A last chance. Carboni, whose hair and beard were now discoloured, hobbled up the Prefecture stairs not once but eight times without obtaining an audience with Silvagni. Finally, anxious but hoping against hope, on 22 January 1867 he wrote to Silvagni, including the available proofs of *La Ceciliana*.

For the ninth time he climbed the Prefecture's stairs. This was it: if Silvagni recognised his achievement, his woes were ended. Carboni was ushered into the secretary's presence. Silvagni pushed Carboni's letter back at him and 'with the tone of a Doctor Squartamorti' ('Corpse-splitter'), called *La Ceciliana 'sciocchezze'*.

Sciocchezze! Dummes Zeug! Nonsense! The polyglot pyrotechnics were triggered by the shock which could have sent Carboni toppling down the stairs. To reject his plays was to kill his hopes-him. He saw himself dead in hospital like another Roman emigrant, Giacomo Valeriani ... How could Silvagni call *La Ceciliana 'sciocchezze'*? They resented his talent, that was it or, as he put it, 'Italians envied even each other's lice'. He felt like another poet, Torquato Tasso, condemned to madness by lack of sympathy, who had huddled in the winter garden at Chiaia so he would no longer have to pay his rent. For Carboni, Naples' beauty, fleas and indifference were too much.

He was not dead yet but could not have survived the blow, he said, without support from Ferdinando and the brilliant 22-year-old pianist Beniamino Cesi. In a letter to von Seefeld in Hanover, to illustrate his thesis that 'in Italy people don't love but hate', he recounted his misadventures with Boschetti and with the Prince of San Teodoro and Duke of Arpino over the bells for the *La Campana della Gancia*.

The searing letter, which appeared in the epilogue to *Nazzareno Schiantapalmi*, could scald and stain. Even though it set teeth on edge, he said it was devoured at the club of Prince of San Teodoro in Chiaia. The 'Torquemadas' tore it to pieces and sent it to be pulped, according to the 'In a nutshell' appendix to *Misererio*. In this play, evidently to even the score with Don Tomasso Salvini of the Fondo Theatre, Carboni added his name to that of the governor of Newgate Prison which appeared as Salvini Stagnacore (Shrivel-heart) while he gave his comeuppance to the Prefecture secretary by making the Newgate head guard Silvagni Squartamorti (Corpse-splitter). Carboni claimed to have found a scrap of the savaged *Nazzareno Schiantapalmi* text on which was written, significantly, *Buffi e Buffoni,* a derisive epithet which Carboni now applied to the 'magnificent management' of the Fiorentini Theatre; the 'magnaminous' Fondo Theatre and the San Carlo 'magnates'.

Did Carboni, as he said really pick up a scrap of his play as he roamed the outskirts of the club of the Prince of Sann Teodro, gloating at the turmoil he had caused inside? The discovery of the scrap, and perhaps the turmoil also, were probably a Carboni fantasy, but he had achieved satisfaction by somehow managing to print his plays in which he denounced part of the

Neapolitan establishment. He did not speak, however, for needy Neapolitans. Supporters of the Russian anarchist Mikhail Bakhunin, who spent two years in Naples at this period, claimed Garibaldians were indifferent to the Neapolitans' economic plight. In Palermo Carboni had been alert to the populace's problems, but here he remained besotted by an unresponsive theatrical muse. The city must have begun to pall, he would surely have exchanged places willingly with the Bourbons who had fled to the Farnese Palace in Rome almost alongside Holy Trinity.

'A writer has to be a banker or a money changer', Carboni complained, 'otherwise he is a victim of a wordy patriotism while the Camorra [the underworld] milks him dry leaving him fit only for the gibbet.'

He advertised his one-act farce *Squartamorti* but at the same time attacked the actor Antonio Papadopoli for being, like Ristori, prepared to see a writer 'languish in misery'. He warned that *Squartamorti* should be staged before the 'abused author dies embittered in hospital'.

To hasten their return home, Roman emigrants attempted to foment an insurrection in the papal city. Organiser of these efforts was Carboni's friend and mentor from his Roman years, Mattia Montecchi. Montecchi, stouter than when he had watched from St Peter's dome the French advance on Rome, had returned to Italy after a long spell in London. He came to Naples to contact Roman emigrants and presumably had a reunion with Carboni and Cattabeni.

However, the insurrection plans were abandoned when, late in the summer of 1867, Garibaldi's volunteers gathered along the Papal States' border. Mazzini cautioned Garibaldi that Prime Minister Urbano Rattazzi would disown the volunteers if they failed and exploit them if they won. Nevertheless, Garibaldi attacked. Rattazzi resigned. The anticipated Roman uprising did not occur and Napoleon III sent the French army to the pope's defence. Vittorio Emanuele then ordered his troops to march against Garibaldi. But the papal forces, organised by Monsignor De Mérode, and French did not want or need this help in defeating Garibaldi at Mentana 15 miles north-east of Rome. Once more there was double-dealing, confusion and bad blood between the Piedmontese and Garibaldians, but also between Garibaldi and Mazzini because Garibaldi believed Mazzini had undermined him. The clash between his two heroes would have distressed Carboni.

Garibaldi had been humiliated by arrest after the defeat. He had vainly attempted to avoid arrest by proclaiming that he was a general of the Roman Republic, an Italian parliamentarian and a United States citizen. Carboni did not join Garibaldi in this venture nor in his other aborted attempt to recapture revolutionary élan in Calabria five years earlier. Then Carboni had been a regular army officer; now his only skirmishes were with theatrical managements, but he must have been dismayed by the Mentana debacle: a victory of papal forces over Garibaldi seemed against the course of nature. Could the pope hold Rome indefinitely? Carboni was becalmed, bothered and bewildered. He did not want to see only Naples and die.

His sense of déjà-vu must have been acute when, towards the end of 1867, the former Lieutenant-Governor of Sicily, Marchese Massimo Cordero di Montezemolo, was made Governor of Naples. One of his tasks was to keep an eye on Garibaldians in case they again organised to attack the Papal States.

Finally, on 26 March 1868 Carboni's right to medals (and pension) for the 1849 and 1860 campaigns was recognised, but not for the 1859 campaign because he had worked as translator for French forces.[12] He announced that from 15 September his address would be care of the Spada, Flamini Bank in Rome; Alessandro Torlonia had sold part of his bank to his former employee Giuseppe Spada.

Still more patience was needed, however, for Carboni was to spend another two long years in Naples during which he added to *La Ceciliana* and worked on other plays, sticking to his last as if there were rewards for persistence. When the breeze turned and brought the sea's salt to the city, it could have reminded him of his voyage to Australia. Then there had been fear of never arriving and it was much the same now; he seemed cruelly adrift. He did not know how many years he would have to survive before he could travel the 135 miles to Rome where bishops from all over the world, including Australia, gathered in 1870 to proclaim Pius IX's infallibility. Still the same pope he had seen flee the city! The pope had become infallible while he had become infirm. Had he been to the end of the world and back without Rome changing? Would the Argentina or Valle Theatres stage his spurned plays? In Rome he could see Raphael's tomb again, visit Tivoli where he had written a poem, perhaps search for Angela ...

Mere daydreams until, taking advantage of the withdrawal of French forces from Rome to fight Prussia, Vittorio Emanuele's army attacked the Papal States which, only six years before, the king had sworn to defend. Despite use of secret service funds, there was no uprising in Rome before troops under General Raffaele Cadorna breached Porta Pia and occupied the city with the loss of forty-nine men against nineteen papalists. Some nationalists felt guilty and defrauded; the struggle for unity against foreigners had been completed because of Prussia's victory at Sedan. Carboni's exile was over after twenty one years which had changed him from an eager young man to a hobbling veteran. The ex-miner was shifting his pegs for the last time.

Rome 3

Lolly water laced with rum

Carboni hobbled up the easy grades of the long staircase to the Campidoglio like a man completing a vow. His leg was gammy but his spirit must have soared. At last he reached Michelangelo's geometrically patterned pavement before the Town Hall which he called the 'light house of the universe'.[1] He was not to receive there, as Petrarch, the Poet's laurel crown. Nor was there a performance of the *Hymn of Garibaldian Volunteers* with a chorus of the orphans of patriots, which he had composed in Naples for performance on the Campidoglio. But his presence was still a source of satisfaction; 'my words', he wrote, 'have become fact'. The pope was confined to the Vatican, while he was acclaimed in the city he had fled in 1849. In a sense, he had achieved his ambition to become one of the illustrious of Rome,[2] now capital of united Italy which endorsed the principles of the Roman Republic which had been his ideal in 1849.

It was 2 October 1870. From early morning people had gathered in twelve squares to deposit in large urns their votes on the proposed annexation of Rome. At 11 a.m. they assembled at piazza del Popolo to accompany the urns along the Corso to the Carnpidoglio. Flags hung from windows, there were banners, bands and *brio*.

Scientists headed the plebiscite procession, for it was argued that Galileo, Darwin and their ilk had decisively undermined papal power. Next came literary gentlemen, artists and, more numerous than expected, emigrants – some well-dressed, others scruffy, some youngsters exiled only since

1867, others 'bent and bald' Forty-Niners who doffed their hats to the onlookers' applause. Army officers followed, then artisans, clerks and, last but far from least, inhabitants of the Città Leonina (the area near St Peter's) behind a 'Città Leonina SI' banner. This was designed to counter suggestions that the Città Leonina be recognised as part of an extra-territorial pontifical zone. Eleven urns were oak but that of the Città Leonina was crystal. And when the urns were opened in the Campidoglio, the Città Leonina vote was the fairest of them all. Of some 200,000 Romans, 45,000 males had voting rights; 40,875 had voted affirmatively and only 46 opposed annexation. But of the 1567 Città Leonina votes, not one was negative. It was a fairy tale result. The government immediately announced that there would be no further discussion of the status of the Città Leonina. *Vox populi* was law.

Carboni recorded proudly that he voted. Survival was a cool joy: he had been wounded on the Janiculum, duped in Bishopsgate, fired at in Ballarat, tried in Melbourne, scorned in Turin, spurned in Naples but, as he had been saying since Eureka, he was not dead yet.

His old enemy Pius IX had been replaced in the Quirinale by the royal family, even though the Secretary of State had refused to hand over the palace keys; cardinals' carriages, formerly richly decorated, became anonymous; priests were scarce in the streets where hawkers did a brisk trade in books previously forbidden by the Index; during carnival, caricatures of Pius IX, Jesuits and Mérode appeared. Carboni's former mentor Giuseppe Spada, who had taken over the Torlonia bank, was verbally flayed by anti-clerical journalists as a toady of the Vatican-linked aristocracy.

Pius IX celebrated the Easter ceremonies within the Vatican without even giving the traditional blessing to the city and the world. His supporters said that he was a prisoner of the Vatican. Others observed that Jesus had hidden when they wanted to make him king, but if Pius IX could not be king, he hid. Jesuits were expelled from the Collegio Romano founded by Ignatius Loyola, nuns were turned out of convents, government Ministries were installed in monasteries. The rout of the clericals, long invoked by Carboni, seemed complete.

On 9 April a huge crowd followed Mattia Montecchi's funeral, including Adelaide Ristori who had known him in London. Part of Carboni's past died with Montecchi. With Giovanni Battista Cattabeni, Montecchi had given Carboni his first political awareness; their idealism had fired his imagination, convincing him that Rome and Italy had a future as well as a past. But an episode involving Montecchi the previous September should have made Carboni reflect.[3] Montecchi, who directed the Salviati glass factory in Venice, arrived in Rome the day after the breach of Porta Pia. The ex-triumvir, mindful of General Raffaele Cadorna's promise that Romans would elect their own representatives, on 21 September presided over a meeting of 10,000 in the Colosseum, where he had taught Carboni the 'conspiratorial art'. Montecchi was one of the forty-four-member broadly based provisional City Council elected by the meeting but, on reaching the Campidoglio, the Councillors-elect found the military had occupied it. Bersaglieri brusquely repulsed them; *vox populi*, in this case, was less powerful than General Cadorna's orders.

On 9 June Goffredo Mameli's remains were transferred from piazza delle Stimmate near the Campidoglio to the new city cemetery at Campo Verano.[4] There was a grisly identification of the corpse of the soldier-poet who had written what was to become the national anthem-a few hairs on the skull, only one leg, for the other had been removed at Holy Trinity without preventing his death from gangrene. Forty-Niners followed the coffin through the streets and, at Raphael's burial place, the Pantheon, heard Agostino Bertani deliver a funeral oration. For a moment, Raphael and Mameli, two poles of Carboni's aspirations, were united.

The unity struggle had been so prolonged that the victors were old men commemorating its young martyrs. But old men died too. On 10 March 1872 a 67-year old Dr Brown died in Pisa. Dr Brown had diagnosed Italy's ills, prescribed a cure and goaded some into applying it. He was Giuseppe Mazzini, who used a false name because still under a death sentence for organising an ill-fated Genoa uprising in 1857. He had been Carboni's first hero and had a lasting influence. Later Carboni became a fan and follower of Garibaldi but he still showed interest in the Società Operaie, the workers' mutual benefit societies founded by Mazzini, which he wanted to use as a defence against Marxist-influenced movements.

A week after Mazzini's death people began to gather at 8.30 a.m. in Rome's piazza de] Popolo to commemorate him. The first group was that of returned servicemen, including Garibaldi's son Ricciotti and the troops he had led effectively in the Franco–Prussian conflict. There were also workers, parliamentary deputies gathered around a green Freemason banner, artisans and university students. A horse-drawn carriage, where Italy was represented crowning a bust of 'Mazzini the Apostle of Unity', bore an empty coffin covered by black velvet. Three bands and twenty-five men, carrying banners with the names of martyrs such as Mameli, Ciceruacchio and Luciano Manara, accompanied the carriage. The silent crowd in the Corso and those watching from windows threw flowers on the coffin.

Authorities tolerated commemoration of the Republican outlaw but no flags flew at the Campidoglio and no bells rang. The embarrassment was palpable: most of the Council, including Acting Mayor Francesco Crispigni, were absent when the cortège arrived, but one councillor admitted that Mazzini too had worked for Italian unity. Mazzini's bust was placed on the Campidoglio between those of Christopher Columbus and Michelangelo Buonarotti while Benedetto Cairoli reminded the crowd that another tribune of the people, Cola di Rienzo, had died on the same spot. Although Italy had been unified, bitter political divisions and enmities remained intact. As the Founding Fathers had feuded, it was important while celebrating unity to cover contentious aspects with luxurious rhetoric.

In his last years Mazzini had moments of depression: 'Is the Italy I dreamt of', he asked, 'only a phantasm? A parody?' He lamented that he had meant to evoke the soul of Italy but all he had before him was its corpse. He adjudged the new nation rotten with materialism and egoism. Did he intuit his idealistic nationalism harboured the germ of something nastier? As only 500,000 of a population of 22 million had a right to vote, he realised that the national revolution had not become a social revolution.

Carboni was trying to keep the spirit of national unity alive in his plays and scraped together money to continue their publication, which had begun in Naples; theatres were indifferent but a note in a bottle might survive in the vast sea of print. He called the two volumes *Lo Scotta-o-Tinge* ('It Scalds-or-Stains'), a phrase he had first used to describe Mazzini's prose, but which he applied more recently to himself as well as to his plays. Evidently Carboni, who had been scorched by Mazzini's writing, intended to make an indelible impression. Punning on his surname, he explained that *Scotta-o-Tinge* meant 'charcoal which, if lit, scalds but, if doused, stains whatever it touches'. It may be a variation on the Roman saying '*er carbone o tinge or scotta*' (coal either stains or scalds).

The first volume (*Scalds*), which appeared towards the end of 1872, comprised *La Campana della Gancia*; *Rita,* with the interlude *Durga*; *La Santola*; *Gilburnia,* his mime set in Victoria amid the Tarrang tribe which he declared had been devised and worked upon in the Melbourne Gaol, completed among the flying fish of the Bay of Bengal in 1856 and revised, corrected and perfected in Rome in 1871–2; the play *Raffaello d'Urbino* and a libretto for an opera of the same title. The second volume (*Stains*) published a year later, listed on the title page the 'Antartic bitter-sweet' *Eureka Stockade,* but the text was not included because Carboni's 'pocket was empty'. However he included a poem from chapter 83 of *The Eureka Stockade* in which he changed Shakespeare's famous phrase to 'To be or not to have been'. *Stains* contained the quartet which had been ignored by Neapolitan theatres – *Mérode, Nazzareno Schiantapalmi, Spiantacore* and *Misereio* – plus two plays completed in Rome. One was his comic opera *Il Sartore di Parigi* ('The Parisian Tailor') set in the era of Empress Eugénie (1857–70). Gambara, a Parisian tailor and widower, wants to marry off his daughter Priscilla, which is one of the recurring personal names in Carboni's plays, just as Roccaspaldi and Torrestorta are recurring place names. Marcello, Gambara's chief assistant, loves her. The rich Count Bettino of Roccaspaldi aims to marry Dantella, an orphan who is heiress to the Torrestorta barony. Dantella dresses as an army officer to spy on Bettino. Aware of it, he arouses her jealousy by his relations with Priscilla. They are on the point of marrying when, dressed once more as a female, Dantella arrives. She marries Bettino. Of course Priscilla and Marcello then find they love one another. All ends happily and improbably. The barely sketched, inconsistent characters are unconvincing.

The other play completed in Rome, *Buffi e Buffoni,* set in Carboni's Giovine-Italia period, concludes when wounded Goffredo Mameli is carried from the Janiculum towards Holy Trinity. Carboni vouched for the play's accuracy, particularly for the fourth act which he claims is based on 'contemporary documents and personal memories.' However, he has Giovanni Battista Cattabeni participating in the defence of Rome when, in fact, he was defending Venice, and he has Mameli praising his (Carboni's) songs before the Genoese poet arrived in Rome. It reads plausibly, however, as an imaginative recreation of Carboni's experience. He took the occasion to even scores with Adelaide Ristori in the personage of the Sacred Heart Convent Superior Arpia (Harpy) Ristory, who, with a reference to his Naples *bête noire,* is called Marchioness of San Teodoro and Arpino. She instigates with Jesuits the anti-papal insurrection so it can easily be crushed. For Carboni the playwright, conspiracy is the key to history. Interestingly a Sacred Heart sister who is young in spirit, sides with her patriotic students and even accompanies them to the Falcone trattoria, is called Fleurdevant (the French equivalent of Fioravanti, the surname of Carboni's mother).

Towards the end of *Buffi e Buffoni,* as the Garibaldians drill on the Janiculum, Carboni interrupts to ask indignantly if their sacrifices were simply for the benefit of profiteers in post-1870 Rome. It is a jolting jump: one minute he mentions Ferdinand de Lesseps, the French minister who negotiated with the Rome Republic triumvirate, and the next moment it is twenty-three years later. Lesseps has built the Suez Canal, Rome is the capital of the Kingdom of Italy and Carboni is asking where is justice if the Vatican-linked Torlonia, Borghese, Massimo, Fiano, Grazioli, Antonelli and De Mérode families, who can charge exorbitant rents, are those who have benefitted. He rails:

> Those who did nothing [for unity] are in power while Redshirts, for that very fact, are embittered, abused and neglected. Bloodsuckers ... charge a million a year rent. Is this the Italy Garibaldi's volunteers and Mazzini's disciples proposed? God no! Where is justice? It's better to be dead!

But as he repeated like a mantra in his writing, Carboni was not dead yet. He lodged on the first floor at 64 via Leccosa, which led to the roccoco Ripetta port where upriver traffic docked.[5] While onlookers lounged in the sun, sacks of coal and other goods were loaded onto mules. Carboni may have thought his rent exorbitant and blamed Vatican-linked landlords for it. His anger at the consequences of the unity struggle was understandable but he could have modified his vehemence against Alessandro Torlonia. He had successfully sought Torlonia's recommendation when submitting *Raffaello d'Urbino* to the San Carlo management in Naples. And his former employer had suffered a domestic tragedy comparable to that of Montezemolo in Palermo, which had inspired Carboni's compassion.

Giovanni Torlonia had predicted a brilliant future for his son Alessandro while chatting with Stendahl, but now Alessandro was a white-haired old man with a mad wife. 'She is a classical statue', Alessandro Torlonia had said when he asked Prince Colonna for the hand of his daughter Teresa, 'and I have a golden pedestal for her'. But Teresa had become deranged, which, in 1862, made Torlonia close his palace and cede his bank to Carboni's mentor Giuseppe Spada. The French Ambassador Henry d'Ideville wrote:

> Nothing is sadder than the sight of the two carriages of Rome's richest princely family: in one princess Teresa with a lady-in-waiting, in the other her only daughter with two nurses. The princess ... is still very beautiful but her strange smile, her large stupefied and sullen eyes show all that the unhappy woman is mad ... Prince Torlonia has infinite wealth but his home is not happy. His palace is the only one in Rome closed to the public; his art gallery, perhaps the city's most precious, is also closed.[6]

The Piedmontese had maintained that, if true patriots, Garibaldians should return to their normal occupations once Italy was united. But what was Carboni's normal occupation? Before joining Garibaldi's forces in Palermo he had been a beringed 'rich Turk' recently returned 'from the South Pole'. He was an experienced miner but could hardly sink a shaft in Rome, for he would not strike 'yellow boy' but layer after layer of city. Writing was to have become his normal occupation but it was more like a devouring obsession. Did he have to regress to his papal Rome occupations of bank clerk, translator, interpreter? As theatre managements continued to ignore him, there were few alternatives.

He worked as interpreter for the Italo-German bank on central via Cesarini. Alfred von Seefeld may have met him there when he visited Rome in 1872. Von Seefeld's bookshop in Hanover had prospered. They both had spanking new nations and, writing to von Seefeld, Carboni engaged in the patriotic guff which eventually was to lead to patriotic gore.

A Florentine financier Giacomo Servadio had established the short-lived Italo-German bank to cash in on Rome's post-unity boom; he was one of those who had honed techniques for profiting from such occasions when, in 1864, the capital had transferred from Turin to Florence. Nevertheless, Carboni did not mention Servadio among the Unity profiteers he denounced. Rather, in *Buffi e Buffoni* he included a sonnet in honour of Servadio.

Perhaps Carboni hoped that Servadio would contribute to the expense of the 588-page first volume of his plays and the more than 850 pages of the second; or maybe Servadio had in fact done so, just as Rothschild aided Rossini. Carboni may have appealed unsuccessfully for money to Angelo Bargoni and Antonio Mordini, because he called them 'Senators who were once friends'.

Mordini was now prefect of Naples, Bargoni of Pavia. Carboni claimed it was 'almost their duty' to come to his aid to show that his coronation at Benedetto Cairoli's house in Turin had 'been neither 'cruel joke nor clever derision'. Was he assailed by terrible suspicions that it had been one or the other, or even both? The sad fact was that he was no longer their colleague, but someone who begged (or demanded). The gates had closed with former colleagues such as Cairoli, Depretis and Arrivabene, who were now parliamentarians, on the inside while Carboni was left out.

He was heartily sick of writing begging letters. During his pleas from Ballarat for restitution of his seized property, he had commented, 'the eternal petitioning looks so "Italian" to me'. But he had come back for more of it. Aging Mr Foxy may have asked himself if he should have been, instead, Mr Hedgehog rooted in one spot rather than dashing around the world to little profit.

He confessed to exhaustion from thirty years writing plays, then trying to raise publication money. Harmonious development, he prescribed, requires a healthy body, a good nervous system, education, favourable circumstances, succulent food and fine drinks, whereas 'lolly water laced with rum produces only farts'. He maintained that even genius needs appropriate instruments, comparing himself with Paganini and the piano virtuoso Thalberg. 'What would Thalberg be', he asked, 'if for piano he had a bed warmer?'

After correcting forty typographical errors in the first volume of his plays and twenty-nine in the second, he listed no more, although he noted a hundred. His eyes and hands, he wrote, were too tired. He had already spent forty days in San Giacomo degli Incurabili (St James of the Incurables) hospital on the Corso, perhaps for his ulcerated foot wound, and had discovered also how thick-skinned was united Italy's bureaucracy. He had submitted to the Ministry of War a medical certificate from Doctor Gaetano Bencivenga, authenticated by the mayor, with a request for financial assistance. There had not even been an acknowledgment. It may have been why, in the first volume of plays, he described himself as an honorary member of the Santa Cecilia Musical Academy, for it looked after poor and sick musicians. Evidently there were objections, for in the second volume Carboni admitted that he had merely applied for Santa Cecilia membership.

Carboni, who had returned to Rome as if expecting twenty years' back pay, now had a presentiment that he would receive the 'prize for his patriotism … in hospital'. He was embittered like Mazzini, as he recognised that a change of heart and not merely a change of regime was needed. But if his plays were not staged, he was rendered mute.

Their assessment is difficult because often they entail music and dance; it is hard to envisage how they would perform.[7] The texts by themselves, with their creaky plots, make a woeful impression, but as Carboni was prompt and resourceful, his theatrical writing may have improved greatly if he had seen one or two of his plays staged. However, he makes no mention of actual performance amid a threnody of complaints about indifference.

Verdi was too much for him. Carboni evoked the name as if inviting a comparison or at least proposing himself as a successor.[8] But Verdi, who had become the rallying cry of nationalists, enjoyed unchallengeable popularity. For Carboni the novel could have been a more congenial genre; as its conventions were less constricting than those of opera, he may have adhered closer to his experience. However, Verdi had pre-empted this ground too, for there was little audience for novels when opera supplied the national epic.

Carboni was campaigning for a new theatre when Verdi had already created it. Carboni did not have the genius to embody the novelty he proclaimed. Caustic and vivid, he could have excelled as a journalist but, although fifteen dailies and 100 periodicals were founded immediately after the occupation of Rome, he did not emerge in this field.

In Palermo Carboni had felt the pressure of the Piedmontese; in Rome, now that Italy was united, troubles could be attributed also to the Tuscans, the Lombards, the Neapolitans. As Carboni wrote, 'Italy is tired of priests and free of foreigners but lacks Italians …' The German Ferdinand Gregorovius, who had come to Rome in 1852, rejoiced that he had just completed his history of mediaeval Rome and could depart, for he considered the arrival of the Italians had killed his Rome. He described what some called a 'liberation' as 'an invasion of charlatans'. The occupation of Rome had occurred without glory, because achieved thanks to the departure of its French defenders, and many inhabitants had submitted to it without enthusiasm.

The patriot's reward – *basta così*

With the arrival of what the Romans called the 'Piedmontese' or the 'Italians', business and bustle began to stir the once-somnolent city. Wasn't this the livelier Italy Carboni had invoked a quarter of a century before? But he did not like it. It would be hard to say, however, whether it was because it contained too much of the old or too much of the callow new. Carboni inveighed against Mammon, against the 'Iscariot National' bank and buccaneering financiers such as Piero Bastogi, a competitor of his employer Servadio. Industrial fairs, distant reflections of the Crystal Palace exhibition, were planned. Educational opportunities increased. Barracks were built throughout the city as if for an occupying army, and for the first time military service was introduced.

Tall pines and other vegetation were ripped from the Colosseum tiers leaving it bare as a skull; some sandy-stoned palaces were painted white as sepulchres; grazing animals were driven from the Forum where excavations began. Within a few years, taxes doubled. Romans asked what had happened to the income from seized ecclesiastical property and were told it had gone to defray a mounting state debt. United Italy was forging its own traditions.

Although there was new building to accommodate the influx of businessmen and government clerks, most development was in the already-existing city. A law court was opened in the oratory of the San Filippo Neri church, the fire brigade was stationed in the Franciscan Aracoeli friary, while a former convent became the site of the Ministry of War. A Ministry Row was constructed along via XX Settembre to outshine papal palaces but merely outweighed them. Most new buildings were heavy-handed copies of Renaissance models.

After 20 September some of the 'black' (Vatican-linked) aristocracy, such as the Lancellotti, in protest permanently closed their palace doors. Some preachers continued to hurl anathemas against Vittorio Emanuele as the Attila who had seized the sacred city. Some former papal soldiers continued to fight against Italian troops in taverns. Police clashed with pro-papal demonstrators. Catholic papers sprang up in polemical reaction to anti-clerical journals. Particularly in the educational sphere there were parallel State and Church institutions. State and Church competed even over feast days.

But continuance of the Church-State clash was not the whole story. The city council decided to continue Mérode's road project, calling it via Nazionale. Many Vatican-linked aristocrats did not allow political opposition to the Piedmontese regime stand in the way of shared business interests once Rome became capital of Italy as well as of Catholicism. And the Catholic King of Italy, having taken the pope's land, wanted a rapprochement. Carboni, irritated that civil authorities were 'kissing the hand of priests', regretted that parliament seemed to have the same aim. At the Campidoglio (Town Hall), he complained, nearly all are beetles; at the Quirinale (Royal Palace) nearly all are cockroaches; at the Vatican all are scorpions and, worst of all, he concluded, parliament wants to put them together in an Ark.

Carboni seemed to seek refuge from his disillusion in daydreams. The title page of *La Benedetta* explained that the four-act play had been planned in a gondola on the Venetian lagoon in 1857; in June 1865 it was divided into scenes as he sat shaded from the sun in the Florentine Cascine gardens; it was put in order in Genoa on a July morning and in Turin, on the slopes of Superga, in August 1866; then completed in Naples and staged at the 'Capitale Theatre Rome [the former San Carlo church] in October 18??'.

However, San Carlo church had not been converted into a theatre. And the text of *La Benedetta* was not included in *Lo Scotta-o-Tinge,* for Carboni said he would have to be mad to publish it. Apart from his conviction that a literary man 'had to be a crook to win success' by adopting such expedients as slipping 'banknotes in the copies of his work which reach critics', Carboni wanted to see first the reaction to *Buffi e Buffoni*. He was wary of both the Vatican and the Quirinale.

Carboni had also invented a dream topography,[9] melding, for example, in his stage settings the Pantheon with Michelangelo's Santa Maria degli Angeli church as if, dissatisfied with reality, he was composing an imaginary city with imaginary theatres staging his imaginary plays to imaginary audiences … a Rome unchanged from his early years but transformed to make him the toast of the town rather than Adelaide Ristori, whose via Monterone residence was like a court from which she descended to receive tribute at the nearby Valle and Argentina Theatres. (He may have considered the Argentina would be better employed. staging, as he had promised, his most successful theatrical effect when, in the Melbourne court, production of his goldmining licence had confounded Commissioner Webster.) Carboni tried to shame Ristori by inserting in *Nazzareno Schiantapalmi* a comment: 'like Adelaide Ristori searching for young poets who can write in Turkish. For united Italy! ... and then letting the Italian writer die of hardship and hunger'.

Carboni still enjoyed parts of the real Rome, for instance the Janiculum hill and the 'adorable' Pincio gardens looking across the domes of the city to St Peter's. The Pincio was part of fashionable Rome, as different from the new city being grafted clumsily onto the old as from the labyrinthine, odorous Rome of Carboni's Holy Trinity years.

Despite all his embittered comments, towards the end of *Lo Scotta-o-Tinge* Carboni affirmed that the Turin prefiguration of his coronation on the Campidoglio could not have been a leg-pull, that his hour would come. Great Works! Moreover, he asserted that although his body was worn out, his spirit was sprightly, fresh and free as a fish in the Tiber. He could look forward to the resurrection in which he had often reaffirmed his faith.

He dated the preface to *Spiantacore* at Mentana 3 November 1872, the fifth anniversary of Garibaldi's defeat there by papal forces, adding an imaginary feast day 'St John [the Baptist] in the desert'. If the meaning was that Carboni was John the Baptist crying in the wilderness, his Messiah Garibaldi had again crossed the wider Jordan which separated Caprera from the mainland. Elected by Romans as a parliamentary deputy, he returned to the city for the first time since June 1849 when, at the head of his mauled troops, he had ridden away from the Lateran Gate. In January 1875, on his arrival at Termini railway station, a festive crowd welcomed the small, white-haired old man and accompanied him, as he rode in a carriage, slowly to minimise his arthritic pains, to his hotel. Garibaldi evidently recalled that this enthusiasm had been remarkable for its absence when, overpowered by papal forces at Mentana, he needed it. Wearing red shirt and poncho, he appeared at the hotel balcony to make his briefest speech: 'Romans, be serious!'

Both Garibaldi and Carboni had come from a wider world and their very diverse contributions to the unity struggle had been welcome. But now that unity had been achieved, they were no longer needed. They sought other employment in civilian life. Garibaldi had refused a government grant but had considered opening, on Caprera, granite quarries to supply his son Menotti who wanted to build the new Bank of Italy; evidently he recognised builders, not condottieri, were the new conquerors. Unlike Carboni, Garibaldi was having some success as a writer, which was a longstanding ambition. He was offered 30,000 lire for his first novel *Celia or the Government of Priests*, which described a curial cardinal's illicit love for a Trasteverine beauty. In his second novel, with the shrewd title *I Mille* ('The Thousand'), a Mérode-like Monsignor Corvo (crow) has designs on a virgin. She is saved by a generous, patriotic bandit, then, dressed as a soldier, follows the Mille to Sicily. Only a third of the 12,000 'prominent Italians' who were asked to subscribe for the novel did so.

Garibaldi writing soft porn was as if Che Guevara had survived to run a blue-movie cinema in downtown Havana. But Garibaldi had other things in mind as well. He opposed the military who planned to surround Rome with useless fortifications. Instead he wanted to divert the Tiber to avoid Roman floods such as that of 26 December 1870, which some had seen as a sign of God's wrath against the Piedmontese; he proposed to drain the nearby marshes, which caused malaria, making Rome a capital in a desert;[10] and at Fiumicino he wanted to create a port for the city. He needed the backing of major banks and met Alessandro Torlonia. The Garibaldi-Torlonia meeting was yet another indication that unity had merely added new powers to the old – there had been no guillotine. Torlonia had prudently avoided taking sides in the papal–Italy conflict, but he had been the Holy See's banker and his servant's livery had been changed to avoid confusion with that of the opprobrious royal household.

Loss of temporal power had increased the pope's spiritual sway because his universal mission became clearer. And the Catholic character of Rome was hardly dented by construction, for the first time, of Protestant churches or even by Catholic–Protestant debates on whether St Peter had ever been in the city. Despite the seizure of convents, there were still more than 300 Catholic churches and countless other religious institutions.

In 1870 few foreigners had visited Rome, but the following year foreign Catholics began to rally to the pope's support, both through the worldwide 'Peter's Pence' collection of funds for the pope and through visits. In April the Duke of Norfolk led an English delegation bringing a gift of 2 million lire. In June Pius IX began the twenty-fifth year of his pontificate. He celebrated the occasion by refusing to receive General Bertoli who brought the King's congratulations.[11] He implied the papacy would long outlast Europe's oldest royal family, the Savoy, and would never forget the wrong suffered. His strength lay in his adversary situation and in having an ideal which had not been achieved.

Because of the Italian attack on Rome, the first Vatican Council had been suspended, but only after proclaiming papal infallibility. Pius IX was 83; had he become eternal as well as infallible? In 1875 pilgrims in large numbers returned to Rome, even though the Holy Year, customarily held each twenty-five years, was not officially proclaimed. The Holy Trinity hostel, closed by government decree, was no longer able to receive them, but pilgrims made Rome seem an appendage to St Peter's. There were Irish-Americans with faith as firm as Father Patrick Smyth's. There were French, Belgians, Germans, Croatians, Canadians, Spaniards, New Zealanders. Pius blessed Catholic Italy, then Italy without any adjective.

Even though Catholic polemicists claimed Pius 'slept on straw' as a 'prisoner of the Vatican', as a prison it was the world's most palatial: it had more to do with dudgeon than dungeon. Carboni could well have asked why Pius was commiserated worldwide while a man could ruin his health in a Melbourne Gaol with barely a visitor. The Carboni family was without heirs but it was said Pius had a son. Worried by hostile Freemasonic attitudes in the national unity movement and developments elsewhere, Pius condemned many aspects of the modern world in a document *Syllabus of Errors*. It was trenchantly criticised but at least it was discussed, whereas *Lo Scotta-o-Tinge* was virtually a clandestine publication.

Pius was Supreme Pontiff but in Rome was also reputed to possess the evil eye. His soutane had more snuff stains than Carboni's jacket. And Pius had a diploma (no. 33960) from Santa Cecilia,[12] whereas the author of *La Ceciliana* had not even been admitted as an honorary member. Where was justice? Pius was supposed to be a loser, but there were losers too among the winners.

Carboni had prefaced *Buffi e Buffoni* with a discussion of the humours. He advised those who wanted a quiet life to give the choleric a wide berth. He described the choleric humour as 'a fire which burns where it touches and devours without ever warming'. Carboni was a choleric-sanguine who had devoured himself without creating much warmth for his later years. His self pity, which prompted the description of himself in Ballarat as a 'friendless exile', at times now could have made him feel a childless orphan.

The self-pity went with an incapacity for self-criticism, which enabled him to advertise Adelaide Ristori's snubs without suspecting they showed him as an importunate nobody. These shortcomings had been offset by abundant vitality, which, however, was now in decline. His 'fizzing' red hair was bleached and his spirit fizzed ever more intermittently. He had more reasons for choler but diminishing vitality to sustain it. Whereas in Naples he had been litigious and aggressive, now his anger was more diffuse as if mixed with resignation. It was not a ballerina or a theatre manager who were at fault, but the new nation. Italy, he complained, had always been a stepmother to her children. On stepmothers, he was an expert – Geltrude! What was a stepmother but a mother parodied? He could endorse the judgement of Mazzini that united Italy was a parody. It went shrewdly about affairs, vain and avid as Geltrude. Carboni recommended that, like salt cod, Italy should be softened 'by soaking at 400 feet under the Mediterranean for at least forty days and nights'. To use one of *The Eureka Stockade's* chapter headings, he was speaking in the bitterness of his soul. Trapped by time and tribulations, he nevertheless repeated, with desperate vitality, that he was not dead yet, which was more than could be said for the hated Monsignor De Mérode who had died on 11 July 1874.

In 1875 old Mr Foxy found a new lair at the foot of the Quirinale in via Nuova among tradespeople and Polish migrants. It was only a few steps from the Trevi Fountain, a coursing inland sea which provided a cooler on hot nights. He may have sat there seeing himself by the Loddon, perhaps with Peter Lalor, sipping a tumbler of his own wine in a country where his writing had received attention and he was a popular public figure ... For all his travels, for all his talent, the polyglot world-devourer had achieved little which now consoled him. The future he had worked for was already past; the world he aimed to change had changed him; his ideals had been buried under the scree of events. His dire words, 'Civis Romanus sum seems to have dwindled into bottomed on mullock', had become fact, one more fact in what he called 'the stubborn-things store', which was now so crowded that he had little room to manoeuvre. Bottomed on mullock in Rome, a duffer, indeed, *rien, niente,* zero, nought, nothing and vice versa. He may have begun a new activity for, in *Lo Scotta-o-Tinge,* the Poet described himself not only as interpreter-translator, but also as professor of Italian and foreign literature but in October he was once more in San Giacomo hospital. Its title 'for Incurables' was depressing, and, moreover, from 20 October almost incessant rain fell, as bad as Ballarat in winter. Carboni had foreseen that he would receive the patriot's reward in hospital; that's enough – *basta così.* Perhaps he recognised he should have extended what seemed a mere entr'acte in Victoria, or that in Palermo he should have had the courage of his insight that political change had failed to benefit the needy. Although he would prefer to die in Rome than anywhere else, wasn't 57 years old too early to join his abbess – aunt Veronica who had promised to await him in Paradise? If only he could be anointed by Father Smyth – with Eureka balsam he might still rip the mask from Death stalking him. He had survived a previous spell in San Giacomo; he could do it again. Towards 8 a.m. on Sunday, 24 October, a new day beginning, he could still believe his hour would come and affirm, but for the last time, that he was not dead yet.[13]

Acknowledgements

Weston Bate, author of *Lucky City*, opened his own research files, pointed me in the direction of the Carboni compensation-claim correspondence, provided encouragement for the biography and criticism as it took shape. Fausta Samaritani unearthed documents about Carboni in Palermo and Rome. Romano Ugolini of the University of Perugia was unfailingly patient with my queries. Jennifer Lorche supplied advice and microfilms of documents found during her fundamental research on Carboni. Antonio Pagliaro of Latrobe University gave me access to his copy of *Lo Scotta-o-Tinge*, Volume I, and responded to several queries. Gaetano Rando of Wollongong University provided a copy of his annotations to *The Eureka Stockade*, informed me of the results of his research in Urbino and helped in other ways. Richard Divall provided an assessment of Carboni's music.

Encouragement and help came from many others including Claudio Gorlier who obtained many documents; Bernard Hickey; Geoff Serle; Donald Dignan; Bruce Bennett; Vivian Smith; Elizabeth Webby; Lucy Gordan Rastelli; Gaither Stewart; M-C Hubert; Mark Coleridge; George Damborg; Bernard Smith; Gerald O'Collins; Franco Cavarra; Jan Whiteside, Research Officer at Sovereign Hill, Ballarat; William Johnston for military history; T.J. Linane, editor of *Footprints*; Barry Breen; John Emanuel; John C. Orr; Barret Reid; T.J. O'Neill; Margaret Baker-Genovesi; Bruce Grant; Father Giovanni Azuenda; Giuseppina Restivo; Wilma Guatterini; Rosetta Borchia; Afrodite Oikonomidou; Tommaso Stojnic; Edmund Campion; Robert Murray; Kevin Hilferty for pursuing Lady Jane and answering countless queries; and my brother Lance.

Assistance for the Naples chapter came from Michele Prisco; for Calcutta from L. Hardy SJ; for Rome from Giorgio Marincola; for Palermo from

Caterina Mandal and Lucio Zinna, who provided ideas and documents; for Hanover from Martin Schmorl, Anthony Mann, Eric B. Kusch and Uli Schmelzer for translations; for Urbino from Maria Vecchiotti-Antaldi, Monsignor Negroni and Don Gino Severini.

Among the librarians and archivists who gave invaluable help were: Judith Keene, Curator Australiana, Baillieu Library, University of Melbourne; Cecily Close, Senior Archivist, University of Melbourne; Susan Bray, Learning Resources Services, University of Melbourne; Mary Coghlan, Information Division, University of Melbourne; John Thompson, Australian National Library, Canberra; Jack Chisholm, Ballarat Municipal Library; Katrine A. Kelly, Research Librarian, Central Highlands Regional Library Service; Norman Houghton, Archivist, Geelong Historical Records Centre; the Latrobe Library staff; Melbourne Diocesan Historical Commission; Isabella Ricci, the State Archives, Turin; Paolo Zaghini, Biblioteca Communale Coriano; Dott. Sangiorgi, Urbino University archives; Father Placido Benzi, Biblioteca Scolopica, Rome; the staffs of the Santa Cecilia Conservatorium of Music library, Rome; the Biblioteca di Storia Modema e Contemporanea, Rome; and the State Archives, Rome.

The author and publisher thank copyright holders and providers of illustrative material. Sources are: author photo by Christopher Warde-Jones; Urbino, courtesy Assessorato alla Cultura e Turismo, Urbino; Urbino ducal palace from Italy Down Under; Carboni's birth certificate from Cathedral Archives, Urbino; Urbino plaque by Desmond O'Grady: Luigi Vecchiotti courtesy Maria Vecchiotti-Antaldi; pope Pius IX, Alessandro Torlonia and daughter; Giuseppe Spada, Monsignor De Mérode, Garibaldiin Rome 1875 from Nuovo Album Romano, Neri Pozza; Vincent Eyre, courtesy Venerable English College, Rome; Alfred von Seefeld, courtesy von Seefeld family; Naturalisation certificate, courtesy National Archives of Australia; William Archer, courtesy of Melbourne University Archives; Peter Lalor, courtesy National Archives of Austrlaia; Charles Hotham, courtesy State Library of Victoria; S.T. Gill material from his The Victorian Goldfields 1852–53; Courtroom sketch of the Eureka 13 from The Age 10 March 1855; Ippolito Nievo courtesy Stanislao Nievo; Angelo Bargoni cartoon from Strenna del Pasquino, 1862, Biblioteca de Storia Modema e Contemporanea, Rome; Lo Scotta-o-Tinge title page, courtesy Library of the Conservatorium of Santa Cecilia, Rome.

Notes and Sources

Naples 1868
1. This scene is based on an episode recounted in a footnote to R. Carboni, *Buffi e Buffoni, Lo Scotta-o-Tinge*, vol. II, 1873, Santa Cecilia Conservatorium Library, Rome (S-o-T II).

Urbino 1
1. San Sergio parish records. The early years of Carboni in Urbino are hazy. A plaque on a house in via Santa Margherita states it was his birthplace, but Monsignor Negroni, part-time archivist of the cathedral, after recent research says the family moved into this house shortly after Carboni's birth, which took place farther up the street where its name changes to via dei Maceri.
2. Gaetano Rando located a notarial act in which Biagio Carboni witnessed a signature.
3. Fleurdevant (Fioravanti) in Carboni, *Buffi e Buffoni*, S-o-T II.
4. Gaetano Rando found records of a tax-collector named Fioravanti.
5. Miscellanea Letteraria, vol. Unico FIX 6 Biblioteca Scolopica, S. Pantaleo, Rome.
6. G. Jacoletti, footnote to *Rita*, S-o-T I, *De Aloisia Vecchiotto commentarium*, Urbino, 1863. L. Vecchiotti, *Pensieri intomo all'arte e musica*, Tipografia della Capella, 1876.
7. The university of Urbino archives confirm Carboni's university enrolment. He later produced printed copies of two slightly different documents, of the same date, allegedly recording his academic successes. One is reproduced in the preface to S-o-T II; the other is in Mazza 431, Archivio Militare di Sicilia, State Archives Turin (AMS–SAT).
8. In a letter from Antonio Carboni to Raffaello, 8 January 1856, Australian Reference Section, Australian National Library (A.C.–R.C., ANL).
9. Carboni claimed to be a descendant of the family 'de Carbonari Carbonis which give two proconsuls under the Roman Empire'. (Letter to William Archer, 29 June 1854, ANL). At times both Raffaello and Antonio signed as Carbonis. Perhaps Raffaello had in mind Gnaeus Papirius Carbo, one of the leaders of the popular movement led by Mario (85, 84 and 82 BC). (In a letter to Angelo Bargoni from Palermo on 19 April 1861, Carboni referred to the

'odious period of Sulla and Mario'.) A proud, if unlikely, lineage which did not augur well. Gnaeus Papirius Carbo, who did not have children, was put to death. Cicero (Ad Familiares: IX, 21, 3) said the unfortunate family was mainly on the side of the people in the political struggles from the time of the Gracchi to Sulla and many of its members had a miserable death. The Carboni brothers may have found this further confirmation of their links with the family, for they tended to see themselves as victims.

Rome 1

1. Documents of the Arciconfraternità di S. Trinità dei Pellegrini in the State Archives Rome (Busta 995, Filza di Giustificazioni del Libro Maestro).
2. R. Carboni, *La Ceciliana*, Naples, 1867, Santa Cecilia Conservatorium Library, Rome.
3. For instance, on the death of Leo XII in 1829:

   > Some blame the surgeon
   > For the death of Leon;
   > However Rome sustained
   > that he well-operated.

4. R. Carboni, *La Sinfonia*, which precedes *Il Sartore di Parigi* in S-o-T II.
5. Ibid.
6. Ibid.
7. Ibid.
8. A.M. Ghisalberti, *Rassegna storica del Risorgimento Italiano*, anno XX (33): 'G. Galetti e le cospirazioni del 1843/44'.
9. Ettore Montecchi, *Mattia Montecchi nel Risorgimento Italiano*, Società Nazionale per la Storia del Risorgimento Italiano, Rome, 1932.
10. Domenico Spadoni, in *I Cairoli delle Marche*, says that Giovanni Battista Cattabeni fought in Venice in 1848 but not for the Roman Republic where his brother Vincenzo was involved. In *Buffi e Buffoni*, Carboni had G.B. Cattabeni fighting for the Roman Republic and has Mameli at the Falcone trattoria at a time when, in fact, he was still in Genoa. Carboni published *Buffi e Buffoni* only after the deaths of Mameli, Montecchi and Cattabeni (Cattabeni died in 1868). This raises many queries about the historical truth Carboni claimed for certain sections of *Buffi e Buffoni*.

    Carboni may have represented Mameli as praising him for vanity's sake. The introduction of Cattabeni in *Buffi e Buffoni* when he was absent from Rome is odd. It might be thought Carboni invented the Montecchi-Cattabeni link after their deaths. But he mentioned his friendship with Cattabeni in the preface to *Misererio* and listed him as a subscriber to *La Ceciliana* while he was still alive. Moreover one character in *Buffi e Buffoni*, Pietro Stagnetti, was still alive in Rome to contest inaccuracies when the play was published. *Buffi e Buffoni* has not its claimed historical accuracy, but nevertheless it probably

reflects Carboni's experiences rather than being fantasy.
11. R. Carboni, 'Con Permesso' (Introduction), S-o-T II.
12. Stendhal, *Promenades dans Rome,* Gallimard, Paris, 1997.
13. Quoted in G. Andreotti, *Il Ministro deve Morire,* Milan, 1976.
14. Carboni, 'Con Permesso', S-o-T II.
15. Ibid.
16. Stendhal, *Promenades dans Rome.*
17. Quoted in Oliviero Jozzi, *Il Palazzo Torlonia,* Tipografia Forzani, Rome, 1902.
18. R. Carboni, 'Molto in Poco' (Preface), *Misererio,* S-o-T II.
19. Ibid. Records of Carboni's arrest and interrogations are not in the State Archives; Rome. They may have been removed at the request of those who obtained Carboni's release.

Rome 2
1. Carboni, *Buffi e Buffoni,* S-o-T II.
2. Nicholas Troyat, *Gogol,* London, 1974.
3. Filippo Zamboni, *Ricordo del Battiglione Universitario Romano,* Trieste, 1926.
4. Carboni to Brusco, from Palermo, 31 July 1860, Bertani papers, Museo del Risorgimento, Milan (MRM).
5. A deduction from Carboni, *Schiantapalmi,* S-o-T II.
6. Quoted in G.M. Trevalyn, *Garibaldi and the making of Italy,* Longman, London, 1911.
7. Montecchi, *Mattia Montecchi nel Risorgimento Italiano.*
8. Carboni described Forbes as an American but the only Forbes recorded among the Republicans was an Englishman, Hugh Forbes.
9. R. Carboni, 'Squillo di Tromba' (Trumpet Blast), *La Ceciliana.*
10. Carboni, *Buffi e Buffoni,* S-o-T II.

Go North, Young Man
1. Mazza 431, AMS-SAT.
2. S-o-T II.
3. A.C.–R.C., ANL.
4. Alfred von Seefeld's diaries and papers held by his grandson, Germany.
5. R. Carboni, Oggi *non si ama* (Nowadays there is no love), *La Ceciliana.*
6. Mazza 431, AMS-SAT.
7. Ibid.
8. Antonio Gallenga, cited in Aldo Garosci, *Antonio Gallenga,* Turin, 1979.
9. London Post Office Directory, 1852.
10. S-o-T II.
11. R. Carboni, *The Eureka Stockade,* Melbourne University Press, Melbourne, 1969.
12. R. Carboni, 'Preface', *Misererio,* S-o-T II.
13. Ibid.
14. W. M. Thackeray, 'May Day Ode'.

15. R. Carboni, 'Preface', *Spiantacore,* S-o-T II.
16. Yves Hersant, 'Alleluia', *Critique,* Feb./Mar. 1981, Paris.
17. Carboni, *The Eureka Stockade.*
18. Carboni, S-o-T II.

Australia: Great Works
1. Unless otherwise specified, quotes in this chapter are from Carboni, *The Eureka Stockade,* Melbourne University Press, Melbourne, 1969.
2. Margot Beaver, W.H. *Archer Civil Servant,* MA thesis, University of Melbourne, 1971, is the source of information on and quotes from Archer, except for Archer's diary entry cited in note 4.
3. Carboni to W.H. Archer, 28 August 1853, ANL.
4. W.H. Archer diary, 22 August 1851, University of Melbourne Archives.
5. *The Age,* 5 March 1853.
6. J.B. Humffray, diary, Ballarat Municipal Library.
7. S.D.S. Huyghue's manuscript, Mitchell Library, Sydney.
8. Deduction from Antonio Carboni's letter to Raffaello Carboni, 8 January 1856, ANL.
9. *Argus,* 22 September 1854.
10. *Argus,* 29 August 1854.
11. Captain Kay RN. Report of the Select Committee on Mr J.F.V. Fitzgerald's case. Votes and proceedings of the Legislative Assembly First Session 1867, vol. II, 22.
12. Bentley to Police Magistrate, Ballarat, 13 October 1854, Ballarat Public Library.
13. Carboni to Archer, 18 October 1854.
14. Weston *Bate, Lucky City,* Melbourne, 1978, 60.
15. S.D.S. Huyghue's manuscript.
16. Rede to Chief Commissioner, 22 October 1854.
17. Ibid.
18. Carboni to Archer, 20 September 1853.
19. Vern to Goldfields Commission of Enquiry.
20. Rede to Hotham, 7 November 1854, quoted in Bate, *Lucky City,* 279.
21. Meeting at Government Office, Melbourne, 27 November 1854, quoted in *Three Despatches from Sir Charles Hotham,* Public Records Office, Melbourne.
22. Rede to Chief Commissioner, 27 November 1854.
23. *Argus,* 24 October 1854.
24. Rede to Chief Commissioner, 2 December 1854.
25. Apparently in reference to the 18 October article on the Reform League as a germ of an Australian Congress.
26. P. Smyth, 27 November 1854.
27. Goold's diary, cited in Moran, *A History of the Catholic Church in Australia,* Oceanic Publishing Company, Sydney, 1896.
28. *The Age,* 10 April 1855.
29. The circumstances in which it was decided to build the Stockade suggest

it was to stave off the Camp forces. But in a statement published in *The Age* and the *Argus* on 10 April 1855, Lalor declared categorically that it was 'never erected with an eye to military defence'.

The Stockade, Lalor explained, was built for fear 'government spies would mix with the volunteers ...' and as a 'distinct place ... in which men could muster together and be drilled ... it was an enclosure to keep our men together'.

Not only did the Stockade concentrate the diggers in one point as a target for Camp forces, but there spies gathered all the information the Camp needed. Lalor saw the need for unity and discipline. He achieved the first but not the second-neither to screen out informers nor to prevent looting.

Lalor was a courageous amateur in a skirmish against professionals. The professionals made mistakes too. The slaughter by the Camp forces after they won the battle discredited the government.

30. As reported in Carboni, *The Eureka Stockade*. It is broken German.
31. C.C. Mullen, 'Brass Bands Prominent in the History of Victoria', *Victorian Historical Magazine,* February 1965.
32. Rede to Chief Commissioner, 25 November 1854.
33. Pasley to Colonial Secretary, 30 November 1854.
34. Captain H. Butler-Stoney, Victoria, London, 1856.
35. John Bullas's manuscript, Ballarat Municipal Library.
36. Evidence of William McCrae of the Star Hotel and Anne Diamond to the Commission of Enquiry.
37. Jebbie and Dennis Phillips, A *Black* American *at the Eureka Stockade,* Bowyang, 1982.
38. *The Age,* 5 December 1854.
39. Report of the Select Committee on J.F.W. Fitzgerald's case.
40. John Lynch, *The History of the Eureka Stockade,* Australian Catholic Truth Society, n.d.
41. Letter, 9 December, Lalor papers, Dixson Library, State Library of New South Wales (DL–SLNSW).
42. When Hotham asked the various consuls to issue a proclamation recommending that their citizens refrain from any subversive activities, Tarleton responded that 'there are not any Americans engaged in this affair'.

The same day (4 December) Hotham's secretary J.H. Kay responded for him that

> the leader of the rebellion is a young American, He [Hotham] has seen a person who is just arrived from Ballarat, who was in the insurgent's camp; he saw this person, and says he is their most active leader.

Presumably the American referred to was James McGill. Dressed in female clothes supplied by the actress Mrs Hamner, on the 5th he went to Melbourne by a coach which must have crossed Sir Robert Nickle and the reinforcements headed in the opposite direction. Next, in officers' uniform, McGill found refuge on the ship *Arabian*. Americans interceded with Hotham and presented McGill to him at Toorac House. McGill was told he could leave the colony. Instead, pretending to be an invalid, he stayed at the health officials' quarters at Port Phillip Heads until after the state prisoners' acquittal. Later in 1855 he returned to Ballarat where he met Carboni while he was writing *The Eureka Stockade*.

Hotham closing an eye on the man whom, at least at one moment, he considered the leader of the rebellion made nonsense of the implacable prosecution of the thirteen state prisoners and his harangues against foreigners.

Hotham also received Fergusson, the American who had been released in Ballarat, leaving his blue blankets to Carboni. Tarleton arranged for him to meet Hotham because of newspaper complaints that the American had bought his way out of prison. According to Fergusson's account, Hotham asked how he knew he would not be charged for treason. The American, who must have kissed the Blarney stone, responded that

> he had no fear of treachery or bad faith in one of whose heroic deeds at Aboukir and Trafalgar all England was proud to boast. Such an answer seemed to be unexpected to him [Hotham] and touched his heart. He laid his hand upon my shoulder and said, 'Go about your business, boy, you shall not be hurt'.

No wonder the praise was unexpected: Hotham was born the year after the battle of Trafalgar (1805). The battle of Aboukir had taken place six years earlier.

43. Smyth to Archer, Archer papers, ANL.
44. Lalor papers, DL–SLNSW. It is a loose, undated sheet but internal evidence suggests Rede is the writer.
45. J.H. Kay to Tarleton, 4 December 1856. McGill is not mentioned. See note 42.
46. Bright, 'Butler Cole Aspinall', *Cosmos Magazine,* 28 February 1895.
47. *The Age* and *Argus* trial reports.
48. Hypocrite-hunting was almost as popular on the diggings as licence-hunting: Carboni pointed out that Tom Kennedy did not burn his current licence at the 29 November meeting. But as Carboni's current licence was produced in the Melbourne court, he was not in a good position to criticise the Scot.

The friction between Carboni and Kennedy probably arose because the two vehement redheads were too much alike.

49. Carboni to Colonial Secretary, 31 March 1855. Compensation claim correspondence, Public Records Office, Laverton, M55/450 (PRO).
50. After his trial Carboni briefly enjoyed a heroic reputation, but the accusation by John (also called Jack) Lynch that Carboni was a coward stuck longer.

Lynch, an Irish stockader who was to become a government mining surveyor and mayor of Smythesdale, wrote:

> [Carboni's] hut was situated within the Stockade in the very vortex of the hurricane. It was neatly set off at one end with a thick-built turf chimney. Into this queer hiding-place the fiery son of Mars skulked, and there lay safety ensconced like a snail in its shell, until all danger was over.

Carboni is more vivid, detailed and convincing. He talks of his tent rather than a hut, claims it was the second outside the Stockade and that, awoken by firing, he observed the clash from his chimney, which presumably had an opening on one side.

Carboni campaigned for compensation for damage suffered because of the Stockade clash but made no mention of damage to his tent. Yet Lynch said the tent or hut was 'in the very vortex of the hurricane'. Troops set fire to tents within the Stockade and the government later compensated those damaged, but not Carboni, which suggests Carboni's tent was outside the Stockade.

Carboni published his account a year after the event and distributed it on the Stockade site. The location of his tent and its fate is important in *The Eureka Stockade* and Carboni could hardly relocate it in that account without provoking immediate comment. He challenged his readers to disprove any of his facts. Lynch's account appeared only thirty-nine years later in the Catholic monthly *Austral Light*. His accusation was part of a polemic against the 'physical force' party. Lynch wanted to show that, despite their belligerent words, the physical force advocates were craven when push came to shove. He claimed Thomas Kennedy 'prudently withdrew from the scene of danger to seek safety in the seclusion of a pipe-clay cross drive in a blind shaft', and that Frederick Vern showed 'past mastership in the art of desertion'. Carboni was his third scalp.

Carboni was as trenchant as Lynch in his criticism of Kennedy and Vern. He saw himself rather as of the party of Lalor (and, presumably, Lynch) who took up arms because they were pushed to it. Possibly he was carried away by his rhetoric at the 29 November meeting and went beyond the notes included in *The Eureka Stockade*. He agreed that the diggers had to 'demand' the release of McIntyre, Fletcher and Westerby, whereas moral force men wanted to 'request' it. However, he had a deep-rooted respect for law. This emerged in his disapproval of Tipperary rowdies and his report on the burning of Bentley's Hotel, in his letters to Archer and in his recoil, while in the Stockade, at the suggestion that he requisition a horse.

(The impatience of Lynch with Carboni adds credibility to Carboni's comment that there was discrimination against him – along with Hayes, Manning, Seekamp and Josephs – in the Ballarat lock-up.)

The Lynch accusation seems ill-founded. One reason it has stuck is that it confirms stereotypes. A historian wrote to me, 'wouldn't it be a typical reaction of an Italian in a moment of crisis?'

Finally it might be asked where was Lynch when Carboni was in danger of his life on the charge of fighting in the Stockade? The charge was well publicised, but Lynch kept quiet about Carboni's alleged skulking in his tent until years after his trial.

Perhaps Father Smyth imputed cowardice to Carboni: writing to Archer after the Stockade clash he reported, 'Raffaello is a prisoner; he is not wounded; I could say more but more I will not say'. Maybe he thought Carboni should have been wounded, or at least run the risk of being wounded, but it is impossible to be sure.

Was it cowardly of Carboni to remain in his tent once awoken, even if it was outside the Stockade? He chose discretion as the better part than valour, whereas someone like plucky Thonen might have run to the Stockade itself. Yet although hundreds of Stockaders who had left the enclosure must have been woken up by the firing, I have not heard of any who rushed into that death trap. Carboni's behaviour was not lion-hearted, but he did not claim it was.

51. Sherard to Colonial Secretary, 16 July 1855, PRO.
52. Daly to Hotham, PRO.
53. Carboni to Colonial Secretary, PRO.
54. Court members to Hotham, 4 October, PRO.
55. In this section I am indebted to an unpublished essay by Carolyn Hopping, 'Raffaello Carboni and The Eureka Stockade', University of Melbourne, 1968.
56. In 1857, the Local Courts' legislative powers were transferred to elected Mining Boards, while their judicial powers went to the Court of Mines. The Local Courts had introduced miners into the legal system, enabling quick clearance of many lingering disputes. But they were less successful with complex new issues partly because the diggers themselves were divided on questions such as the employment of machinery and cooperative companies with outside capital. Confidence in the Local Courts declined because of the haphazard elections and suspicion about the members' motives.
57. Daly to Hotham, PRO. For information on the Court I am indebted to Donald Just, *Victorian Mining Judicature under the Goldfields Act of 1855*, Honours dissertation, University of Melbourne, 1971.
58. Hemy Foster to Commission of Enquiry.
59. Australian Archives, Canberra (CRSA 712 j55/15444).
60. *Geelong Advertiser*, 7 December 1855.

Homeward Bound
1. Calcutta Directory, 1857.
2. R. Carboni, 'Una burla di Marzo', *La Ceciliana*. Carboni claimed to have spent All Saints' Day (1 November) in Canton. Ships which brought cotton fabrics from England to Calcutta took opium to Canton before returning home with tea by the Cape of Good Hope. Carboni passed through Egypt on his way back to Italy rather than sailing by the Cape of Good Hope.

Urbino Once More
1. Carboni's itinerary is from S-o-T II.
2. A. Carboni to R. Carboni, 8 January 1856, ANL. The abbess Veronica Fioravanti, Raffaello's aunt, was also attracted by the glint of Ballarat gold. Raffaello had asked Antonio to send her, on his behalf, a present of lemons and pastries. In a note transcribed in Antonio's letter to Raffaello, she told him her community of sisters prayed he would 'persevere in the good', adding that if she did not survive until his return they would meet in Paradise. She also thanked him for his gift but asked for … a little gold.

Milan
1. Carboni, S-o-T II.
2. Mazza 431, AMS–SAT.
3. Ibid.
4. Bertani papers, MRM.
5. Carboni to Sig. Antongina, Bertain papers, MRM.

Palermo
1. Carboni to A. Bertani, 17 July, Bertani papers, MRM.
2. Stato nominativo personale dell'Intendenza dell'Esercito Meridionale, Mazza 146, AMS–SAT.
3. Carboni to Avv. Brusco, 31 July 1860, Bertani papers, MRM.
4. Ibid.
5. 'Con Permesso', S-o-T. Born in Selkirk, Scotland, in 1819, Gideon S. Lang became a squatter near Buninyong. He was an explorer, *Sydney Morning Herald* correspondent on the NSW goldfields and wrote about the Aborigines, as well as being a member of the colony's parliament. Touring Europe in 1857, despite warnings from Austrians, he visited Garibaldi in Como. He decided that Garibaldi was not merely a warrior, but aimed at Italy's political regeneration and expressed his admiration in letters to the London *Times*. It has been claimed his representations to the English government led to its insisting on the Austrian government treating Garibaldians as belligerents, that is, regular soldiers rather than bandits. (*Sydney Mail*, July–December 1880, quoted in Nancy F. Sizer, 'Gideon Scott Lang', RAMS, July 1961.) Although Carboni calls Lang 'Russell's agent', the British Records Office has not been able to find correspondence between Crispi and Lord John Russell in either its Russell papers or the Foreign Office Records. But John Priest, in *Lord John Russell*

(London, 1972) notes the 'many conspicuous gaps' in the Russell papers deposited at the Public Records Office.
6. Fonda Depretis, Archivio Centrale dello Stato, Rome.
7. Carboni to Brusco, Bertani papers, MRM.
8. Quoted in Francesco Brancato, *La Dittatura Garibaldina nel Mezzogiorno e in Sicilia*, Trapani, 1965.
9. Crispi papers, State Archives, Rome.
10. Mazza 146, AMS–SAT.
11. Carboni to A. Bargoni, January 1861, Bargoni papers, Museo Centrale del Risorgimento, Roma (MCRR).
12. Ibid.
13. Ibid., 22 February 1861
14. Ibid., 14 March 1861.
15. Ibid., 19 April 1861.
16. Ibid., 7 March 1861.
17. Ibid., 19 April 1861.
18. Ibid., 7 May 1861.
19. Ibid., 7 March 1861.
20. Ibid., 19 April 1861. Presumably Carboni was contrasting himself with bespectacled (that is, myopic) Cavour.
21. Ibid., 7 May 1861.
22. Ibid., 19 April 1861.
23. Giuseppe Garibaldi, Le *Memorie,* Bologna, 1932. Landing at Marsala, Carboni's Garibaldi used the slogan *'Lo schiavo che vuol finir le sue pene / Deve schiantar le proprie catene'* ('The slave who wants to end his pains / Has first of all to break his chains'), which Carboni cited in the bull-game scene in *Buffi e Buffoni* and also used as a chapter heading when describing Timothy Hayes chairing the Ballarat licence-burning meeting.

Turin
1. Franco Molfese, Lo Scoglimento dell'Esercito Meridionale, *Nuova Rivista Storica,* Fasc. 1, 1960.
2. Army Records Office, Rome.
3. Esercito Italia Meridionale, Mazza SAT 306.
4. Carboni, S-o-T II.
5. Ibid.

Naples
1. Unless otherwise indicated, quotations in this chapter are from S-o-T II.
2. Carboni, S-o-T I.
3. Bargoni papers, MCRR.
4. Carboni to von Seefeld, 7 February 1867. Original held by von Seefeld's grandson.
5. SAT.
6. Henry d'Ideville, *I Piemontese a Roma 1867–70,* Milan, 1982.

7. Letter reproduced in S-o-T II. From 1865 there were various editions of *La Ceciliana*.
8. d'Ideville, *I Piemontese a Roma*.
9. Letter reproduced in S-o-T II.
10. Ibid.
11. SAT.
12. Ibid.

Rome 3
1. 'Il Congedo dei Volontari', *La Ceciliana*.
2. Unless otherwise indicated, quotations in this chapter are from S-o-T II.
3. M. Montecchi, *La Gianta Romana e il Comizio Popolare all'Amfiteatro Flavio*, Venezia, 1870.
4. The accounts of the funerals of Mameli and Mazzini are based on contemporary reports in the Florentine daily *La Riforma*.
5. S-o-T II.
6. Henry d'Ideville, *I Piemontese a* Roma *1867–70*, Milan, 1982.
7. For Richard Divall, Australian Opera conductor and associate professor of music at the University of Melbourne, the eclectic collection of songs, marches and dances for piano solo, as well as patriotic choruses and poetry printed in Carboni's volume *La Ceciliana*,

> at first sight seem to be somewhat slight. However, in performance Carboni's music comes alive with an especial spirit of Italianità Carboni's compositions are reminiscent of the 'slancio' of early Verdi, as well as the elongated lyricism of Vincenzo Bellini. While harmonically slender, they sometimes have an instinctive personal character. The song 'Sano Italiano' and the toast 'Casa di Bacco' are perhaps the finest. The patriotic choruses merit performance for both musical and historical reasons.

Some of the works have been performed. Richard Divall has orchestrated several pieces. The scores are held by the State Library of Victoria.

Two of Carboni's scores are included in *Spartiti Musicali dal Risorgimento alla Prima Guerra Mondiale 1846–1919,* Palombi, Rome, 1978. The words for the Carboni song 'Sono Italiano' are set somewhat like the Italian boot. His use of mimetic form, heavy type for emphasis and patterns of key words to summarise arguments, make some of his pages look similar to those produced by the Futurists forty years later. The defence of self-advertisements by the Futurist Fortunato Depero would have been underwritten by Carboni: 'Self publicity [by artists] is considered anomalous, the mania of social climbers and a brazen lack of modesty ... if we wait for recognition by others ... we would die 5,000 deaths from hunger.'

Both the Futurists and Carboni can give the impression of trying too hard. But if they were a group anxious to destroy the old and gallop towards the future, Carboni, in isolation, was celebrating the new which had aged precociously.

8. Carboni introduced his collection of music *La Ceciliana* with the words 'men with strong heads and sane livers are needed to take the place in Apollo's temple held by Rossini, Bellini, Donizetti, Pacini, Mercadante and Verdi'.
9. Luigi Huetter, *Strenna dei Romanisti* No. 18, 119–24 ('Un Romano Errante'). This pioneering essay noted Carboni's topographical inventions.
10. The English writer William Howitt, who had drawn a parallel between English officialdom's behaviour at Eureka and at Sebastopol, campaigned in Rome about this time for use of eucalyptus trees in the Pontine Marshes. Eventually they were planted.
11. Carboni would have been surprised to hear the story De Mérode recounted to Prince Franz Arenberg. In turn, Arenberg told it to his friend Bernhard von Bulow, the German chancellor at the beginning of the 20th century, who recorded it in his memoirs published only in 1930–31. De Mérode was present when Pius IX gave an audience to an ultra-Montanist German count. The count held forth indignantly against the Italians' treatment of the pope who, from time to time, nodded his agreement. But when the German left, Pius said, 'That great German beast understands nothing of the grandeur and beauty of the Italian national idea'.
12. Santa Cecilia Conservatorium Year Book, 1873.
13. Carboni's death certificate gives the via Nuova address and also his time of death: 8 a.m., 24 October 1875.

Bibliography

Primary sources are indicated in the *Notes and Sources*. Among the secondary sources used were:

Barnes, John, *La Trobe: Traveller, Writer, Governor*. Halstead Press, 2017.

Bate, Weston. *Lucky City: The First Generation at Ballarat, 1851–1901*. Melbourne University Press, 1978.

Blainey, Geoffrey. *The Rush that Never Ended: A history of Australian mining*. Melbourne University Press, 4th edn., 1993.

Blake, Les. *Peter Lalor: The Man from Eureka*. Neptune Press, 1979.

Clark, Manning. *A History of Australia*. Melbourne University Press, 1979.

Galbally, Ann. *Redmond Barry: An Anglo-Irish Australian*. Melbourne University Press, 1995.

Lorch, Jennifer. 'Details concerning the life of Raffaello Carboni.' *Quademi dell'Instituto Italiano di Cultura*, no. 4, Melbourne, 1971.

Molony, John. *Eureka*. Viking, 1984.

Rando, Gaetano. *Great Works and Yabber-Yabber*. Institute of Modern Languages, University of Queensland, 1998.

Ryan, Peter. *Redmond Bany: A Colonial Life 1813–1880*. Melbourne University Press, 1980.

Serle, Geoffrey. *The Golden Age: A History of the Colony of Victoria, 1851–1861*. Melbourne University Press, 1963.

Withers, W.B. *History of Ballarat: From the First Pastoral Settlement to the Present Time*. F.W. Niven & Co., 1887.

Essential for background on Rome were:
Balleydier, Alphonse. *Histoire de la Revolution de Rome.*
d'Ideville, Henry. *I Piemontesi a Roma.*
Falconi, Carlo. *Il Giovane Mastai.*
Gregorovius, Ferdinand. *Diari Romani (1852–74).*
Negro, Silvio. *Seconda Roma.*
Ravaiglioli, Armando. *Vecchia Roma.*
Roncalli, Nicola. *Cronaca di Roma.*

Christopher Hibbert's *The Great Mutiny* was the main source for the Calcutta chapter. For the London section I relied mainly on M.C. Wicks, *The Italian Exiles in London* and J.B. Priestley, *Victoria's Heyday.* The main Palermo sources were Lucio Zinna, *Come un sogno incredibile;* Stanislao Nievo, *Un prato in fondo al mare,* Fausta Samaritani, *Ippolito Nievo, I Giomi Sommersi;* and Francesco Brancato, *La Dittatura Garibaldina nel Mezzogiomo e in Silicia.*

La Storia di Torino; La Storia di Milano (vol. XV); and *La Storia di Napoli* (vols IX–X) were used for the Turin, Milan and Naples chapters. Alfredo Comandini's *L'Italianei nei Cento anni del secolio XIX* was useful for all the Italian chapters.

Index

à Beckett Boyd, Martin 146
à Beckett, William 57, 146
Acerbi, Giovanni 197
Aguyar, Andrea 42
Akehurst, Arthur Purcell 140, 154
Albani, Filippo (Prince) 13, 22–3
Albani, Giovanni Francesco (Cardinal) see Clement XI, Pope
Albani, Giuseppe (Cardinal) 6, 26–7, 31
Aloo, John 155
Allen, Thomas 119, 122, 126–8
Amos, Gilbert 91–2, 95, 103, 122, 126–7
Angela (friend of Carboni in Rome) 18, 22, 44, 172, 227
Anna (friend of Carboni in Hanover) 46, 172
Antaldi, Maria 246
Antaldi, Raimondo 10
Archer, Alfred 59–60
Archer, William 58–60, 64–5, 79–80, 83, 90, 93, 95, 112, 138–40, 150, 152–3, 158, 162, 165, 167–9
Ariosto, Ludovico 170
Armelline, Carlo 39
Armytage, William 194
Arrivabene, Carlo 50, 236
Aspinall, Butler Cole 148–9, 217
Asproni, Giorgio 213

Badcock, John 135
Bakhunin, Mikhail 226
Balleydier, Alphonse 36

Bargoni, Angelo 199–201, 204–7, 213–14, 216–18, 235
Bargoni, Emilia 213
Barry, Redmond 146, 148–50, 211–12
Bartolomei (Colonel) 200
Bassi, Ugo 43–4
Bastogi, Piero 238
Bath, Thomas 67, 70
Beattie, James 152
Bellazzi, Federigo 198, 217
Belli, Giuseppe Gioacchino 19
Bentley, James 87–8, 91–6, 98, 101, 106, 114, 130, 148, 161–2
Bentley, Mrs 88, 101
Bencivenga, Gaetano 236
Beretta, Antonio 188
Bertani, Agostino 41, 43, 188–91, 193, 195, 2043, 210–11, 217, 231
Bertoni (Urbinite priest) 4
Big Larry (goldminer) 82
Binney (acquaintance of Carboni) 130, 147
Bismarck, Otto 190
Bixio, Nino 43, 190, 194
Black, Alfred 113, 119, 123, 126
Black, George 96, 98–9, 102, 105, 108, 113, 115–19, 123, 149, 157
Bonaparte (Carboni's dog) 63
Bonaparte, Gerolamo 215
Bonaparte, Napoleon 7, 183
Borromini, Francesco 8
Boschetti, Amina 215–16, 218, 222, 225

Boyd, Arthur 146
Boyle, Felix 105, 128
Bramante, Donato 19
Brandt, John 124
Brentano, Paul 72, 149
Brown, Frank 174
Bruckner, Anton 7
Brunetti, Angelo *see* Ciceruacchio
Brunetti, Luigi 36, 38
Bueno, Ignacio 44
Bullas, John 127
Byron, George Lord 28

Cadorna, Raffaele 228, 231
Caesar, Julius 7, 15, 53
Cairoli, Adelaide 222
Cairoli, Benedetto 198–9, 202–3, 207, 213–14, 217–18, 222, 232, 236
Calasanz, Jose St 7
Campbell, John 163
Campbell, Joseph 135
Canning, Lord 173, 175
Canova, Antonio 29
Capodiferro, Girolamo (Cardinal) 20
Caracalla, Emperor 8
Carbonari Carbonis 30, 71
Carboni, Antonio 4, 6, 9, 11, 64, 79–80, 136, 153, 162, 177–80
Carboni, Biagio 4, 6, 11, 30, 79, 95, 179–80
Carey, Frank 87, 89, 102
Carlo, Alberto (King) 37, 217
Carlyle, Thomas Mrs 51
Carr, Alfred 66–7, 129–32, 135, 147
Carter (Goldfields Sub-Inspector) 128, 135, 147
Castiglione, Baldassare 9
Cattabeni, Andrea 32–3
Cattabeni, Giovanni Battista 24–6, 31–2, 37, 39, 44, 216–17, 226, 230, 233
Catullus 7
Cavioli (Urbinite) 180
Cavour (Benso Camillo, Count of Cavour) 183, 191–5, 198, 206, 208, 210, 212, 223
Cenni (Garibaldian in Palermo) 202
Cesi, Beniamino 225
Chisholm, Caroline 59
Cicero 7
Ciceruacchio (Brunetti, Angelo) 33, 35–6, 38, 41, 44, 232
Civinini, Giovanni 213
Clarke, Marcus 159
Clement XI, Pope (Albani, Francesco) 5, 7–8
Coen, Maurizio 21
Cola di Rienzo 232
Colonna, Teresa 234
Columbus, Christopher 232
Conaci, Francis Xavier 38
Concini (Urbinite) 180
Coppin, George Seith 146
Cordero di Montezemolo, Massimo 199, 227
Cordova, Filippo 192, 195
Cormann, Ferdinand 20, 44
Crippa, Francesco 188
Crispi, Francesco 183, 188–93, 195, 199–201, 204, 211, 217
Crispigni, Francesco 232
Curtain, Patrick 114, 119, 127

Dalhousie, Lord 173–4
d'Amore, Nicola 222
Dante, Alighieri 7, 25
Darwin, Charles 229
Davis, Mrs 129
d'Azeglio, Massimo 33
De Camillis, Ferdinando 224–5
de la Varenne, Charles 195
Della Porta, Giacomo 20
Della Rovere, Alessandro 205
de Lesseps, Ferdinand 43, 234
de Longville, Harry 127
De Mérode, Frédéric 219–20, 226, 243
Denison, William 141
Depretis, Agostino 193–5, 199, 217, 223, 236

de Rosa, Juan Manuel 80
de Sanctis, Francesco 13
Desmaris, Paul 29
D'Ewes, John 87–8, 101
Diamond, Anne 114–15, 128–9
d'Ideville Henry 220, 234
Dignam, Thomas 135
Dirimera, John 38
Dixon, Robert (also known as Nixon) 166–7
Donizetti, Gaetano 10, 17
Donnelly, John 135
Dougherty, John 135
Downing, Matthew 90, 107, 110, 139–40
Duke of Genoa 195
Duke of Norfolk 241
Dumas, Alexandre 189
du Val, Claude 70

Emerson, Ralph Waldo 38
Engels, Friedrich 55
Ernst Augustus, Elector 46–7
Esmond, James 122
Evans, Gordon 96, 122, 154, 167–8
Eyre, Vincent 21, 44, 49, 59

Farie, Claude 143
Farrell, John 88, 95, 101
Fawkner, John Pascoe 171
Federico, Duke of Montefeltro 5, 11, 47
Ferdinand and Isabel, King and Queen of Spain 19, 38
Ferdinand II King 143
Fergusson, Charles 136
Ferrari, Andrea 37
Ferretti, Gabriele (Cardinal) 34
Fioravanti, Girolama 4, 6, 233
Fioravanti, Girolamo 6
Fioravanti, Veronica 6
FitzRoy, Charles 84
Fletcher, Thomas 96, 101, 105, 108
Foglietta (Urbino tobacconist) 180
Forbes (Captain) 44, 122
Foster, Henry 131, 138, 152, 166–8

Foster, John Fitzgerald 102, 133
Fraser (lawyer on goldfields) 108
Fuller, Margaret 38

Galilei, Galileo 229
Garibaldi, Anita 44
Garibaldi, Giuseppe 2–3, 25, 34, 39–44, 51, 55, 80, 115, 119, 170, 183, 188–99, 201–4, 206, 209–11, 216–17, 223, 226–7, 231, 234–5, 240–1
Garibaldi, Menotti 240
Garibaldi, Ricciotti 231
Gavazzi, Alessandro 36–7
George I, King (previously Elector George Louis) 47
Ghislanzoni, Antonio 212
Gizzi, Pasquale (Cardinal) 34
Glendenning, Dr 130, 147
Goethe, Johann Wolfgang 18, 28, 46, 220
Gogol, Nikolai 35
Goodenough, Henry 130–1, 134–5, 144, 148–9, 160, 162, 192
Goold, James 60, 106–7, 140
Gordon (goldfields storekeeper) 129, 147
Gower, John 135
Goya, Francisco 7
Grandoni, Colonel 89
Grant, James 148, 171, 217
Green, John 91
Gregorius, Johann 88–9
Gregorovius, Ferdinand 237
Gregory XVI (Pope) 6, 16–17, 19, 22, 25–6, 33–4, 90
Guevara, Ernest 'Che' 241
Grey, Henry 83, 141

Hackett, Charles 116–17, 127, 149
Hackett (Turnkey) 143
Hafele, John 119, 129
Hagerty (Sergeant) 135, 149
Haines, W.C. 163, 168, 211
Hance (employee of Bentley) 88, 101

Hamner, Mrs 71, 156
Harris (Sergeant) 136
Harrison, James 141
Hasdrubal (Carthaginian General) 8
Haydn, Franz Joseph 7
Hayes, Anastasia 136–7
Hayes, Timothy 88, 96, 108, 110, 113–14, 134–7, 147–8, 151, 162, 217
Haynau, Jakob 39, 51, 92, 133, 138
He Sing 52
Holbech, Hugh 83
Holbech, Jane Sarah (Lady Hotham) 29, 81–2
Holyoake, Henry Thomas 96
Horace 7, 100, 154
Hotham, Charles 80–5, 87, 93–4, 96, 98–9, 101–3, 105–8, 112, 116–18, 128, 133–4, 140–3, 145–6, 152–3, 158, 160, 163, 166, 168–71, 173, 191, 194
Hotham, Francis 80
Hotham, Lady *see* Holbech, Jane Sarah
Howitt, William 171
Hugo, Victor 7
Humffray, John Basson 66, 96, 98–9, 102, 105, 108, 112–13, 120, 122, 131–3, 145, 163, 171, 217
Huyghue, Sam 77, 93, 101, 127, 155

Ireland, Richard Davis 148–50, 152, 217
Irving, Washington 58
Irwin, Samuel 96, 217

Jellačić (Jellachich) de Bužim, Josip 138
Joseph, John 132, 134–6, 138, 145–6
Johnstone (Goldfields Commissioner) 88–9, 97–8, 100, 112, 120

Kay, J.H. 84
Keats, John 28
Kelly, Ned 147
Kennedy, Tom 91, 96, 98–9, 102, 105, 108, 110, 119
Kenworthy, Dr 122, 131, 136

King, John 128, 131
Kossuth, Louis 51

La Farina, Giuseppe 182, 191, 198
Lalor, Peter 88, 91, 96, 108, 111, 113–15, 118–19, 121–4, 127, 129, 131, 134, 136, 140, 148, 156, 163, 170–1, 211, 217, 243
La Marmora, Alfonso 224
Lambruschini, Luigi (Cardinal) 38
Lang, Gideon S. 191
La Trobe, Charles 57–8, 65, 80, 84
Leo XII (Pope) 9, 14
Leopardi, Giacomo 18
Livy 7
Lodge, Clara Maria 70
Louis Napoleon 39, 43
Louis-Philippe 32, 35–6, 38
Loyola, Ignatius 28, 220, 230

Macarthur, Edward 125
McGill, James 122, 142, 161
McIntyre, Andrew 92, 96, 101, 105, 108
MacKay, George 141
MacMahon, Charles 84, 96, 168
Majolini, Achille 202
Mameli, Goffredo 39, 41, 43, 190, 231–3
Mamiani, Terenzio 37
Manara, Luciano 40–1, 232
Maniscalco, Salvatore 198
Manning, John 74, 96, 100, 114–15, 120–1, 134–6, 139, 144, 146, 162
Manzoni, Alessandro 184, 201
Marchetti Milzetti, Giacinta 33
Maria Clotilde (daughter of Vittorio Emanuele) 215
Mario (Giovanni Matteo di Candia) 215
Martin, James 88
Marx, Karl 55, 231
Mattei, Stanislao 10
Maximilian (Governor of Lombardy and the Veneta) 184
Mazzini, Giuseppe 24, 26–7, 37,

39–41, 43, 48, 51, 122, 163, 192–3, 197, 206, 210, 217, 226, 231–2, 234, 236, 243
Medici, Giacomo 189
Melbourne, Lord 56
Metheldina (Carboni?) 179
Metternich (Count Klemens von Metternich-Winneburg) 36, 183
Michelangelo (Buonarotti) 20, 229, 232, 239
Militades (Athenian General and statesman) 9
Milne, Robert 87, 101
Mini, Luigi 179
Modena, Gustavo 210
Montecchi, Elena 25
Montecchi, Mattia 24–6, 31, 35, 37, 39, 41–2, 44, 51, 163, 215, 226, 230–1
Montefiore (to whom Carboni entrusted his gold) 178
Montemajor, Captain 190
Mooney, Tom 88, 95
Moore, J. 165–6, 168
Moore, Teddy 129
Mordini, Antonio 50, 195, 197–9, 201, 204, 213, 217, 235
Mozart, Wolfgang 7

Napoleon III 183, 226
Nealson (American carpenter) 120
Nelson, Francis 59
Nelson, Horatio Lord 194
Neri, Filippo (Saint) 14, 238
Nicholas I, Czar 171
Nicholls, C.F. 145
Nicholls, Henry 119, 123, 157, 160
Nickle, Robert 125, 134
Nievo, Ippolito 190–1, 198, 201–4, 207, 210
Nixon, Robert *see* Dixon, Robert

O'Connell, Daniel 19, 110, 146, 148
Oddie, James 163
Oudinot, Nicholas 40–3
Ovid 7

Paganini, Niccolo 236
Palma, Giovanni Battista 38
Palmerston, Lord 191
Palotti, Vincenzo 18
Panizzi, Antonio 49
Panton, Joseph Anderson 65
Papadopoli, Antonio 226
Pappalardo, Salvatore 216
Pasley, Charles 121, 126, 128, 163
Pasley, Sir Charles William 121
Patti, Adelina 217
Paul III, Pope 20
Perry, Charles 60
Perry, Mrs 57
Petrarch, Francesco (Petrarca) 7, 229
Peters, Andrew 135–6, 144, 170, 191
Petronilla (cousin of Mattia Montecchi) 25, 35
Pilo, Rosolino 207
Pius IV, Pope 14
Pius VIII, Pope 31
Pius IX, Pope (Mastai Ferretti, Giovanni Maria) 32–9, 42, 51, 59, 89, 111, 162, 219, 227, 230, 241–2
Powell, James 140, 154
Price, Inspector 143
Prince of San Teodoro and Duke of Arpino 218, 225, 233
Priscilla (Roman friend of Carboni) 217–18

Quinn (digger neighbour of Carboni) 128

Radetzky, Johann 34
Raphael (Raffaello Sanzio) 4, 9, 11, 18–19, 30, 44, 133, 137, 221, 227, 231
Ratazzi, Urbano 210
Rede, Robert 72, 76–7, 86, 88, 91–3, 95, 98, 101, 103–5, 112, 114, 116–21, 126, 132–3, 140, 149, 157–8, 199
Reni, Guido 13
Renz, Ernst 224

Ricciotti (lawyer) 22
Richards, Lieutenant 136
Riso, Francesco 188, 197–8
Ristori, Adelaide 182, 212–14, 218, 222, 226, 230, 233, 239–40, 242
Robertson, Johnny 130
Romano, Liborio 194
Ross, Charles 114, 119–20, 122–3, 127, 129, 156, 158, 162
Rossini, Gioacchino 10, 17, 30, 144, 235
Rossi, Pellegrino 26, 37–8, 89
Rothschild (banker) 235
Russell, John 191
Russell, H. 174

Saffi, Aurelio 39
Saint Yves, Francois 175, 217
Salicetti, Aurelio 39
Sallust 7
Salvado, Rosendo 38
Salviati, Luigi 43, 201–2
Salvini, Tomasso 225
Sangallo (Antonio Cordini) 20
Scevola, Mucius 22, 26
Scobie, James 86, 88–9, 91, 94–6, 98, 130
Schubert, Franz 7
Scogli, Geltrude 11, 179–81, 243
Scott, Walter 28
Seekamp, Henry 70, 74, 106, 110, 132, 134–5, 145–6, 162
Seretta, Salvatore 202
Servadio, Giacomo 235, 238
Shakespeare, William 18, 25, 218, 233
Shanahan (Irish goldminer) 77, 128
Shanahan, Mrs 77, 128
Sherard, W.C. 157
Sibyl of Pietralata (Peterlato) 9, 175–6
Silvagni, Davide 224–5
Sirtori, Giuseppe 189
Smyth, Patrick 89–90, 95, 103, 106–7, 114–18, 120–1, 129, 133, 136, 139–40, 149, 152, 157, 217, 242, 244
Spada, Giuseppe 30–1, 44, 150, 227, 230, 234

Stawell, William 102, 141, 146–7, 149–50
Stendhal, Henri Beyle 26–9
Sturt, Evelyn 134–5
Synott, Patrick 135

Tacitus 7–9
Tamajo, Giorgio 195
Tarleton, James 104, 106, 145
Tasso, Torquato 8, 225
Taylor (Sub-Inspector) 116–17
Teyssedze, Auguste 224
Thackeray, W.M. 53
Thalberg, Sigismund 236
Thaon de Revel, Genova 210
Thomas, J. Wellesley 120
Thonen, Edward 114–15, 119, 124, 127, 129
Torlonia, Alessandro 27–9, 38, 222, 227, 234–5, 241
Torlonia, Giovanni 27–8, 30, 234
Torlonia, Marino 28
Torrearsa, Marchese 199–200
Tuohy, Michael 135, 139, 144, 152

Ugolini (Urbino contemporary of Carboni) 181
Ullathome, Thomas 107
Umberto, Prince of Savoy 217

Valeriani, Giacomo 225
Vecchiotti, Luigi 10–12, 176
Verdi, Giuseppe 204, 210, 212, 237
Vern, Frederick 96–7, 99, 110, 113–15, 118, 121, 123, 127, 131, 142, 156, 170
Vespasian, Emperor 8
Victoria, Queen 47–8, 51–2, 70, 81, 99
Vignola, Giacomo Barozzi 20
Virgil 7, 216
Vittorio Emanuele, King 183–4, 190, 192–5, 198, 204, 206, 209, 215, 226–7, 238
von Seefeld, Alfred 46–8, 224–5, 235

Watson (Magistrate's clerk) 161
Webster, Graham 108, 149
Webster (Goldfields Commissioner) 127, 152, 240
Wedekind, Edward 46
Westerby, Edmund 91
Westerby, Henry 96, 101, 105, 108
Wey, Francis 219
Wills, William 154
Winchelsea, Lord 60
Wintle, George 139, 143
Wise, Captain 104, 126–8, 133, 146
Wiseman, Thomas (Cardinal) 51, 59
Wiesenhavern, Carl 123–4, 154, 166
Withers, W.B. 62, 75
Wright, William Henry 103–5, 118, 120

About the Author

Desmond O'Grady was born in Melbourne and graduated from Melbourne University but worked in Sydney as foreign, then literary editor of the weekly *Bulletin*. He married a Roman in Rome and lives there as an author and by writing for many publications such as *Sydney Morning Herald*, *The Age*, *New York Times*, *Washington Post*, *Commonweal*, *Guardian*, *Sunday Times*, *Daily Telegraph*, *Spectator*, *Tablet*, *Corriere della Sera* and *Internazionale*. He has written film and play scripts about Raffaello Carboni.

Photo by Christopher Warde-Jones

www.ingramcontent.com/pod-product-compliance
Lightning Source LLC
Chambersburg PA
CBHW030851170426
43193CB00009BA/573